MW00638951

Praise for

DANGEROUS COMPANY

"Sam Patten is an American original, and the tales he tells in this superb memoir reflect our country at its best: adventurous, idealistic, results-oriented, and altruistic. He is also naive at times and excessively hopeful at others. As the reader follows Sam's travels and travails across the globe, what comes across most of all is a belief in the possibility of progress and the ability of individuals to help make it. Sam is transparent about his pitfalls, with a candor that used to be part of the classic American persona but increasingly seems like a quaint relic in our polarized, rhetoric-filled society. I was left with hope and a belief that Americans still can make a difference in the world, even after all the mistakes we have made over the decades."

ERIC RUBIN, former US ambassador to Bulgaria

"Sam Patten plays both devil and saint: an American who dared to get his hands dirty in the realities of the world, so very distant from the sterilities of the screen. And he writes well about it."

DUDLEY FISHBURN, former member of Parliament under Margaret Thatcher

"*Dangerous Company* is a fascinating tale of sex, romance, power, and brilliant success (the purple finger in the air) to sordid associations with the bad boys of American politics, followed by Patten lying in a pool of his own blood, wondering if some aggrieved potentate had ordered a hit. Across five continents Patten was not just 'present at the creation' but its midwife. It's a memoir that reads like a Ken Follett novel and a must-read for deep staters and denizens of the vast world beyond the Beltway alike!"

CHRISTOPHER BURNHAM, former assistant secretary for the US Department of State and under-secretary-general of the United Nations

"Long ago I told Sam he needed to write a book, and oh Lord, did he ever! His riveting behind-the-scenes tales of diplomacy and intrigue— how the sausage is made, where the bodies are buried, and a how-to (and occasionally how-not-to) survive and thrive in the heady world of high-stakes power battles in foreign capitals around the globe is on full display. Here Sam's life well lived explodes on the page in full color and makes for a fascinating read."

MARK PFEIFLE, former US deputy national security advisor for communications

"I strapped in and let Sam Patten take me on a swashbuckling, hair-raising, danger- and escapade-filled adventure through Russia, Iraq, Kazakhstan, Georgia, and Mexico. Did it seem crazy when we got to Congo? Yes, it did. But such is the invisible underworld of expert hired guns paid to bring American-style politics to places probably not ready for it. Given the journey, it is no surprise when Patten ultimately ends up in Ukraine and the maw of Donald Trump's Russiagate, at the wrong end of the spear of Robert Mueller's investigation. Read this book."

STEVE LEVINE, author of *Putin's Labyrinth: Spies, Murder, and the Dark Heart of the New Russia*

"Sam Patten set out to see the world and have an impact. He saw the world, traveling from one hot spot to the next, and he had an effect—but not always the one he planned for. In Russia, he worked on democracy promotion and was a close friend of the assassinated opposition leader, Boris Nemtsov. It was at home that he made a mistake that almost landed him behind bars. In this absorbing and honest memoir, he tells a story of political intrigue at the highest levels and the price he paid when success was at hand, but judgment failed him."

DAVID SATTER, Russian scholar and author of *The Less You Know, the Better You Sleep: Russia's Road to Terror and Dictatorship under Yeltsin and Putin*

"The quiet American abroad, Sam is an original. His on-the-ground impressions of key moments around the world in recent history give the reader the look and feel of the times. Sam was a man in the arena and he has written a vivid and useful tale."

ED ROGERS, founding partner, BGR Group

www.amplifypublishing.com

Dangerous Company: The Misadventures of a "Foreign Agent"

For more information, please contact Amplify Publishing
620 Herndon Parkway #220
Herndon, VA 20170
info@amplifypublishing.com

Library of Congress Control Number: 2023906299

CPSIA Code: PRV0523A
ISBN-13: 978-1-63755-775-4

Printed in the United States

TO MY BELOVED SON, MAX.

SAM PATTEN

DANGEROUS

THE **MISADVENTURES**
OF A "FOREIGN AGENT"

COMPANY

amplify

The Old Rectory
Englefield
Reading
Berkshire RG7 5EP

20 October 2018

Dear Judge Jackson,

I am Sam's Godfather. He worked for me as an assistant when I was a Member of Parliament. For many years when I was on the Board of Overseers of Harvard University and executive editor of *The Economist*, I would also see him. So ours was a friendship that developed in his adulthood despite the separation of an ocean, our ages, and perhaps of politics.

I admire this capacity for friendship that he has. He has never asked me for favors nor been disingenuous towards me. He is fun and straightforward and un-dogmatic. Even though I am now in my 70s, he makes the effort to see me when he comes through London.

I have known him to be a dolt on occasion (none more so than the one that occasions this letter). But after some 40 meals together over 25 years, he has never been anything but kind and compassionate without—for all his adventurous life—being callow or cavalier.

Sam is an international guy, at ease in the Congo or Russia, London or Kyiv. That is rare these days when most Americans of his age and background are safely ensconced behind domestic bonds-trading desks. He deserves credit for that.

How many Americans these days (unlike the past!) are prepared to go to central Africa to engage in the bustle and dangers of uncertain democracies? How many are capable of the modesty of manners, the susceptibility to foreign mores to make this leap?

Educated and openhearted, he is an appealing American abroad. A dolt not to have registered, but not a criminal in intent, nor a man requiring further punishment.

Do a Godfather's duties include prison visiting? That is a question I hope not to need to answer, not for my sake but for his.

With my thanks to you for reading this letter, and all respects,

    Dudley Fishburn
    Member of Parliament under Margaret
    Thatcher's government

PART
ONE

CHAPTER 1

THE OTHER SIDE OF THE EARTH

This unhappy dichotomy was in some ways the story of his life,
which brought on feelings of both elation and remorse—the
elation of having a special, privileged knowledge of East and
West, the remorse of finally fitting into neither.

GARY SHTEYNGART, *The Russian Debutante's Handbook*

ALMATY, KAZAKHSTAN, APRIL 1997

A friend had given me the gas pistol when she saw my frightened look
at the prospect of walking home from her apartment late at night.
Almaty did not light its streets in the early days of independence, and
bandits and wild dogs own the darkened streets here.

It was only about ten to fifteen minutes on foot between her place
and mine, but thinking back to that night in Washington just before
I arrived here, I was on edge, not knowing what or who might come
out of the shadows.

Kazakhstan is the Wild East, quite literally on the other side of the globe from the East Coast of the United States. Until now, the massive country stretching from China's western border to the Caspian Sea had been shrouded by the Soviet Union. I'd come here to discover something. Not so much the oil or gold or other minerals that drew the others. The chance for adventure is what I followed here.

In one way or another, every day is an adventure here, near the heart of Central Asia. There is Russia to the north, China to the east, Iran to the west, and Afghanistan and India to the south. With the dust still settling from the Soviet Union's collapse a mere five years ago, it feels like this is the place from which a new world will rise among the descendants of the khans.

I'd tucked my friend's gas pistol away in my underwear drawer and had never fired it nor frankly even knew how. But now I'm scrambling for it. There it is!

Right now I'm trapped in my apartment on the ninth floor of a huge, crumbling colossus of an apartment complex that had always reminded me of the set of *Blade Runner*. Two men outside my door are trying to get in and even flashed what I guessed is a fake police badge in an effort to get me to open the steel door myself. I can only imagine their intention is to rob and, if need be, kill me, so I'm not going to make it any easier for them.

Short on options, I call the police.

"Rosiika district precinct, I'm listening," the dispatcher answers.

In the best Russian I can manage under the stress, I tell him my problem. "There are two guys trying to open my door. They said they are with you, but I doubt that's true. Could it be? Please come quickly."

Bam, bam, bam. Their fists pound on the door, as if insistence will make me change my mind. I try to tune out the noise so I can think clearly. Just when I think I've succeeded, I notice they've stopped banging. But that's not necessarily a good thing. Have they really given up?

When I look through the peephole of the steel exterior door, the two men who said they were with the police start rooting around for tools in a gym bag they'd brought with them. One pulls out what looks like a crowbar, and that's when I go looking for the gun.

Then I sit down on the floor of the eleven-story apartment's hallway with the Walther PPK–looking gas pistol in my sweaty palm and wait. It occurs to me that his thing doesn't fire bullets, but rather tear gas cartridges, so if I fire toward the door, I will also be making the only exit near impassable. They'll probably come straight at me once they get the door open. Fuck. I'm dripping sheets of sweat now.

Suddenly, there's a very powerful series of knocks on the door. They sound different than before. Like *Magnum P.I.*, I creep alongside the wall and peer again through the hole. There's a new set of characters out there. Four guys in full battle regalia, kitted out with Kalashnikovs and bandoliers of extra 7.62 rounds crisscrossing their chests. One way or the other, these guys are coming in, so I put the pistol in my pocket and open the door.

"Which way did they go?" the largest of the paramilitary cops asks.

I shrug, and they pair off—two running up the stairwell and two down. Outside, on the street below, I see two UAZ jeeps with more similarly attired militiamen pouring out. The elevator door opens, and a man in an officer's cap steps out. I invite him in and nervously offer him a drink, which he refuses.

He takes my statement as his *Spetsnaz* crew cases the building. It took them less than ten minutes to arrive. *I'm going to write a letter to the editor of the local paper thanking them*, I think as he wraps up, salutes, and sees himself out.

This must be one of the perks of an authoritarian state, I tell myself darkly as I pour a generous drink. That was scary, sure, but I survived, and I feel a little light-headed about the whole thing. While I got knifed on the streets of Georgetown six months ago, here in Kazakhstan, the cops just saved me from what could have been an even worse outcome.

A few weeks before I arrived in Kazakhstan, I'd been mugged together with my grandmother walking to a dinner party in Georgetown. Fresh off working for a successful US Senate campaign, I spent several weeks with her in Washington to prepare for setting out to the Wild East by talking to the limited number of experts who can place Kazakhstan on a map. My grandmother and I have always been close, and my four years at Georgetown strengthened that bond.

Ambling down O Street, we encountered a surly-looking fellow walking toward us with his hood pulled over his head. In her genteel fashion and slightly European accent, my grandmother wished him a good evening, but he just grunted in return. Suddenly, I was overcome by a bad feeling.

That's when we learned the hooded one wasn't alone. One of his cohorts grabbed my featherweight grandmother from behind, and when I went for his arm, another stabbed me in the side. My pelvic bone blocked the knife from hitting any organs, and I was left with a hilt-width wound that soon healed.

But the memory of this brush with violence didn't quickly fade.

Then I was less concerned for my own welfare than that of the nearly octogenarian Susan Mary Alsop, my grandmother, whom the State Department categorizes as a national treasure. She told the *Washington Post* after the incident that I'd behaved "like a Secret Service agent," which made it sound more heroic than it was.

And that's why I feel cagey walking down these dark streets, where I stick out like a sore thumb. Whether here or there, I need to be on my guard.

With danger just offstage, the days seem more alive here than at home. I am the aide-de-camp of the American head of a Canadian oil and gas company that did the first privatization of an existing oil field in the hydrocarbon-rich country. My boss, Bruce, came here with Chevron and has a Teddy Roosevelt–eque swagger to him—and mustache to boot. Everything seems new and exciting.

It is at the oil company's makeshift office on the mezzanine above the lobby of the old Dostyk Hotel where I first meet Aizhan Kulakhmetova, a new translator. On our first field trip together, scouting out locations to build gas stations with a Chechen business partner, I pull her out of the path of a Kamaz truck, perhaps saving her life.

She will return the favor when she tips me off to a plot hatched between the Canadians and some shady Russian partners to set Bruce up for taking a fake bribe. By giving him the heads-up, he's able to foil the plan and negotiate a golden parachute out of the company, and I will follow him to the new advisory services firm he starts up.

Wise beyond her years, and very beautiful, Aizhan captures my heart. First she goes back to Maine to finish her college education while I stay behind in Kazakhstan and work, but then we learn we will be three. We marry and have a son, Max.

Aizhan's father is Nurlan Ablyazov, whom I'd met even before her because he publishes a bilingual newspaper. Our friendship began when he recruited me to write restaurant reviews. He would engineer the where and when and then accompany me, keeping me company while I tasted the given dining spot's specials.

Neither of us know it yet, but he will later be beaten and nearly killed for reporting on the government's corruption. But he will survive and tough it out in Kazakhstan a bit longer, although eventually he'll have to live in exile.

Later still, Nurlan's second cousin Mukhtar, an "oligarch," will be thrown in prison for trying to overthrow the government. When they let him out, he will allegedly funnel away billions of dollars and flee.

But before anything bad happens to Nurlan or his cousin, Aizhan and I make a go of living in Almaty with our baby boy. Her family is a big help, and we both have networks of friends we've built here.

After all, it was late 1994 when I first set foot in this faraway land. I'd arrived that first time on the heels of Susan Collins's unsuccessful campaign for governor in Maine. Then the notion of Kazakhstan being on the exact opposite side of the earth was appealing. Collins called me back a year later, when she decided to run for the US Senate seat being vacated by Bill Cohen, for whom we'd both worked. After she won, I came back to Kazakhstan.

My friend John Mann joins me in the business with Bruce. Between that and his Sunday-night program reading the news on Kazakh state television, John becomes something of a rock star in the country. We provide public relations for foreign investors and some Kazakh companies. Life becomes less wild and more urbane.

Kazakhstan has grown up a little, and so have I.

Though John and our old set of friends still live the lives of young Americans abroad in our twenties, I start missing home. They don't have kids yet, and Aizhan still needs to finish college. Now Senator Collins hires me to run her office in Portland, Maine, which some call one of America's most livable cities.

Bruce will throw us a party, and I will title the invitations "Farewell to Shangri-la." An advisor to a government minister I've invited will call me and ask me what I meant by that expression.

I will tell her it is something like paradise.

PORTLAND, MAINE, 2000

In the early spring of 2000, Collins recommends me to the Bush-Cheney campaign to be their staffer in Maine for what will be my third statewide election campaign.

For all the adventure of Kazakhstan, there are not yet real political campaigns there. I throw myself into the Bush campaign with the passion I'd put into Collins's campaigns and the hope to use it as a pivot to wider horizons still. This could be my ticket to being a part of America's foreign policy.

Massachusetts's Republican governor rightly reasoned there was no chance Bush could take the Bay State, so he sends his political crew up to Maine to help out. Having Kennebunkport in Maine helps, but notwithstanding, George W. Bush visits at least three times, which is a lot for a small state.

When Ralph Nader comes to Maine, I dress up like a bear and attend his rally with Max—stuffed into a tiger suit—strapped to my back to dance around and wave a sign calling Al Gore the "Occidental Tourist."

But fun and games aside, it's an all-consuming grind for six months, intensifying the closer we get to November. On the Thursday before the election, we have New Jersey governor Christine Todd Whitman doing events in the southern part of Maine, Massachusetts governor Paul Cellucci up north, and we're hustling to prepare for former defense secretary Dick Cheney and his entire family to arrive for a rally. To drum up a crowd, the campaign even hires a country-western singer to open for them. That does the trick.

Thursday night, I invite the local TV stations to our Old Port headquarters to cover the grandmothers and kids hand-painting signs to welcome the Cheneys to Maine. In all the chaos, I forget to invite the Fox affiliate.

Yet they're the first to arrive, which is strange because seeing their reporter reminds me of my oversight. Stranger still, she has a cameraman with her—usually Fox affiliate journalists carry their own camera. Something is off; I'm just not sure what. We prepare to do a stand-up interview, and I can tell she's nervous.

Once the light goes on, it becomes clear she's not here for the signs or the kids or the grandmothers. She reaches into a folder and takes out a piece of paper. I can see her hand is trembling.

"You'll see here," she announces with a slight quiver, "an arrest report from 1976 for a George W. Bush for operating under the influence in Kennebunkport."

Sweet Mary, mother of Jesus, I think. I look at the cameraman and try to motion for him to cut, but he just smiles and keeps rolling. The room full of families with paint and cardboard signs has heard this

DANGEROUS COMPANY — 13

and falls deathly quiet. Desperately scrambling for a way out, I stare at the document and notice it has been printed on the old thermal fax paper. The ticker is blank. Some "anonymous" tipster faxed this to her station, and here we are. I mean, isn't Fox supposed to be on our side?

The blank ticker is a clue. I can't prove it, but we've both been set up.

"Right now we're days out from what may be the most competitive presidential election of our lifetime," I tell her. "And the fact that you and I are standing here talking about this," I dismissively wave the fax, "it just seems fishy, that's all."

She lets me make a photocopy, which I fax to Austin while I call my direct report to let him know to go stand by the machine on his end.

Within forty-five minutes, Bush; his wife, Laura; and their two daughters are live on CNN. Bush owns his mistake and says he hadn't disclosed the DWI before—he was twenty-six years old at the time—because he didn't want his daughters to think drinking and driving is okay. Weak excuse, maybe, but he took responsibility. After eight years of Bill Clinton, this was eye-opening.

I find the arresting officer, now long retired. He's distraught at the notion he is to blame for throwing the election, and I assure him it's not his fault and ask him to just tell me what happened.

The young Bush was driving slowly on a road that curved along the coastline, sometimes veering slightly into the breakdown lane. His sister Dorothy was in the front seat and a couple of their friends were in the back. The first thing out of Bush's mouth, the cop said, was, "Officer, I made a mistake."

I'm pretty impressed by the humility and the accountability, as if the campaign scrub paycheck isn't enough. I'm sold on this guy.

———

As a reward for my efforts, Collins promotes me to her DC office and gives me the portfolio I cherish: foreign policy and defense.

Coming to Washington, I have stars in my eyes and long to be in the thick of international affairs and, as I had been in Kazakhstan, actually operating things on the ground. Yet because of my youth and inexperience, I do not yet fully realize these are two separate things. As her partner and later husband, Tom Daffron, told me early on, I'm not really a Capitol Hill kind of guy. He may well be right.

I'm sitting in the Senate barbershop waiting to get my shoes shined. We all need our occasional escapes from the office, and a shoeshine or a haircut is mine.

Two serious-looking men are ahead of me in line. One is talking to the other about democracy-building in Mongolia, next door to Kazakhstan.

It's close enough to intrigue me. Ever since I left it, I've day-dreamed about what change in this faraway but geostrategic country could look like. Might it be a country where my father-in-law, Nurlan, could publish his newspaper without getting smashed the head? Or might it even be a place where Max could want and have a future?

But these guys aren't dreaming, or at least the US taxpayer funds involved in the enterprise they're talking about are real. Usually I'm pretty shy, but this is too unusual, too interesting, and in a way too close to home. So I interject and ask, "Is this democracy-building you're talking about really a thing?"

"Not only is it a thing; the International Republican Institute is looking for a Russia program officer to manage their technical assistance to political parties in the newly independent states of the former Soviet empire," he tells me.

Something clicks. Within weeks, I'm IRI's new Russia guy.

Before long, I get my first invite to a reception at the Russian embassy. It sits on a hill above Georgetown. One has to wonder what our authorities at the time were thinking when letting the then Soviets build there because the spot has line of sight—and unobstructed audio surveillance range—all over Washington, DC. I want to bring my wife, Aizhan, as it would be a fun cultural excursion for her, so I call ahead to ask permission for a plus-one.

Perhaps that's what put me on the radar screen.

The gate to the embassy's compound stands on Wisconsin Avenue. As Aizhan and I cross into now-Russian soil, a cheerful young man with a mustache named Sergei checks us off the list and escorts us across the plaza that led to the chancellery. It seems like he'd been waiting for us.

Each of the large reception rooms is packed with people, and in one of them I can see the new Kazakh ambassador.

He would be a good contact, I figure. So I wait patiently among the semicircle of people surrounding him for my turn to introduce myself and establish a point of contact for, at the very least, help with future visas.

Just as my turn is about to come, Sergei pops out of the crowd and buttonholes me. "Let's get to know one another," he says, handing me his business card, which reads "First Secretary."

Awfully young for such an important-sounding job, I think. In exchange, I hand him mine, and we chat aimlessly, just long enough for the Kazakh plenipotentiary to escape my grasp.

A couple of weeks later, I am sitting at my desk in IRI's head-quarters staring out the window at H Street on a languid Thursday afternoon. As I turn back to the funder's report I'd been editing, my eye catches Sergei's card. IRI has already decided to send me to Moscow as the in-country office director. Perhaps it would be useful to get one of their diplomat's take on the political scene there, if only to use as a contrast or control for everything else. As everyone does in parting in DC, we'd talked vaguely about lunch.

I pick up the phone and call Sergei's number. It rings and rings and rings. Just as I am about to hang up, he answers. We agree to meet at the Daily Grill, a spot that is equidistant between us, just below Dupont Circle.

About thirty minutes later, it's my phone that's ringing. I forget his name, but let's call him Special Agent Jeff McGillicuddy (pseud-onym). He and Special Agent Mutt Summerville (also a pseudonym) would like to speak with me, and while they won't say what about, I assume it has to do with one of my various friends being vetted for an administration job. "How about tomorrow morning?" he suggests with a not-so-subtle hint of urgency.

When—punctually—they arrive the next morning, I usher the two FBI agents into IRI's conference room, with the world maps on the wall, which I assume will convey to them what serious people we are. They start to listen politely while I start to explain to them what democracy promotion is all about. Then SA Jeff cuts me off as SA Mutt—the good cop—makes a hurt face, as if he really cares to hear me finish.

"We're interested in someone you might know," he says as the faces of various acquaintances from the Bush-Cheney campaign run through my head. "His name is Sergei."

This catches me off guard, and I feel a sudden chill. US-Russian relations at the beginning of the Bush administration were not all love and kisses, and a week or two before this morning, Washington had expelled fifty Russian diplomats following a spy scandal. Humor always calms my nerves.

"Missed him on the first fifty?" I ask like a smart aleck, which neither agent finds funny. "Coincidentally enough, I'm having lunch with him this afternoon," I tell them, and they look at each other and smile with what I suppose they consider subtlety. I'm under no obligation, they tell me, but if I feel like being patriotic, they invite me to give them a summary of my lunchtime conversation.

As it turns out, there is no need.

When I arrive at the Daily Grill, there is a line of people waiting for tables stretching out to the hot sidewalk. There is Sergei, sweating uncomfortably in the blaring sun. I go to the hostess to ask how long the wait is, and she replies, "Mr. Patten, your table is right this way." I hadn't made a reservation.

She leads Sergei and me to a window seat facing M Street. As we sit down, the rattan blind meant to filter the summer sun rises three feet, just enough to make us visible from the street. Sergei and I look at each other, and I shrug.

Our conversation is less interesting than I'd hoped. Predictably, he seems to think pro-Vladimir Putin parties are the only games in town, and I'd be wasting my time with anyone else. Suddenly, he looks animated and leans forward in a conspiratorial crouch to ask, "Do you have a program in Belarus?"

"Why, yes," I tell him. "It's on our website." I'm there to learn about Russia, not talk about a tiny country between it and Europe. But he won't let go.

"Can you send me a fax with information about your Belarus program?"

"No. Again, you can look on the website." I ask him for restaurant recommendations in Moscow.

When I get back to the office, I call Mutt and Jeff and give them a summary of my otherwise useless lunch. When you're reporting to your own government, you don't feel like a snitch. Or even if you do, you tell yourself it's okay. At the end of the day, we're all on the same team, I firmly believe.

Like it is for America, it is my goal to push the boundaries of human freedom. If I really were a Patten, then I'd also be a Winthrop, and it was the onetime governor of the Massachusetts Bay Colony John Winthrop who, in 1630, dreamt of our national purpose being a "city on a hill."

By some factor, founding father John Jay is my great-grandfather on both sides—that's right, my parents are second cousins. A Huguenot, Jay fled religious persecution in France before coming to America. Later, he brokered the peace treaty between the United States and England in Paris. My great-grandfather Peter Jay had been a diplomat in Europe just before the Great War.

My father's biological father, he learned in his middle age, was not Bill Patten, as he'd thought, but an older Englishman named Duff Cooper. As a young MP, Cooper helped propel Winston Churchill's coup within the Conservative Party. At the time of the Munich appeasement, Cooper had been First Lord of the Admiralty, a post he resigned in protest.

Another borrowed backstory of mine when it comes to Russia in particular is the career-long hawkish crusade my late step-grandfather Joe Alsop led against communists abroad. In 1957 Joe had been caught in a honey trap in Moscow with a young man who was a KGB ruse. They tried to blackmail him twice—once during the Eisenhower administration and again during Vietnam—and both times he told them to go fuck themselves.

If Sergei is the best the Russians have got, then I can do this. Though their first decade of independence has been tough, Russians can get back on the track of democracy, and I will help make that happen.

As another pilgrim, my cousin Jonathan Phillips, who is studying theater at Moscow's Stanislavsky school (MXAT), will wryly smile when I arrive on his doorstep a month later: "Thank goodness—the cavalry has arrived."

CHAPTER 2
PUTIN'S WINK

SEPTEMBER 2001

Boris Yefimovich Nemtsov stands out from the field of Russian politicians. I see him as Russia's Alcibiades. I'm not alone. When Margaret Thatcher visited Russia in 1993, she insisted on traveling 250 miles southeast of Moscow to see him in Nizhny Novgorod, where, as a bright young governor, he was throwing himself wholeheartedly into the transition then underway.

With men like Boris in charge, Thatcher suggested in her memoir, Russia could have a bright future. But after being called to Moscow to serve as first deputy prime minister, Nemtsov went on to fall out with Russia's first president, Boris Yeltsin, for his tendency to call things as he saw them. Instead, Yeltsin's entourage chose the little-known Federal Security Bureau agent Vladimir Vladimirovich Putin as the ailing president's successor.

While think tanks in Washington were hosting roundtables on the theme "Who is Putin?" the former spy was busy consolidating power. Though at first he had to hold on to some Yeltsin "family" loyalists, like Kremlin chief of staff Alexander Voloshin, he brought a new team of figures who owed their loyalty to him. A few "oligarchs"—a term Nemtsov actually coined to describe the robber barons of free-market Russia who enjoyed great power under Yeltsin—balked at first but then considered it safer to flee Russia for the United States or London.

Nemtsov joined forces with three other reform-oriented politicians from the 1990s: Anatoly Chubais, a member of the "family" who oversaw the privatization of state assets; Irina Khakamada, a striking Japanese Russian woman who'd been an advocate for small business; and Yegor Gaidar, an economist and former prime minister who, with Chubais, directed the "shock therapy" mass privatization program of the early 1990s, creating a new class of billionaires and thrusting millions into grinding poverty.

While neither Gaidar nor Chubais were very popular, they were smart, pro-market, and friendly to the West. Putin's first economic measures—like a 13 percent flat tax, pension reforms, and a determined campaign to get Russia into the World Trade Organization—were well received in the West. Ironically, Gaidar had drafted most of these policies. Putin held Chubais over from the previous administration to run the state power grid that covers eleven time zones. They may not have been popular, but they were smart.

Even though I know some of this background from my time in neighboring Kazakhstan, I still have to catch up with a lot of recent Russian history very fast. As another opposition leader tells me early on, "Everything that happens today flows from our history, which itself is very controversial."

The attacks of September 11 strike New York and Virginia during my first trip to Moscow. Putin is the first world leader to call US president George W. Bush to express his sympathy and support. This changes much of the dynamic of the Russia-US relationship. At the time, I'm too overcome with worry about Aizhan and Max. The home we are leaving is only a few miles from the Pentagon, and I'm shocked by the scale of the attack we've just witnessed.

On the twelfth, I decide to go ahead with all the planned meetings rather than sitting around the hotel room or office just hand-wringing.

One of these meetings is with Viktor Tyutin, chief of staff to the People's Deputies faction in the Duma, Russia's lower house of parliament. An older man, Tyutin's résumé was blank prior to 1995, but I was told he held the rank of colonel in special services, and he'd been attached to the Soviet embassy in Washington around the time I was born. He could have even been the one who spray-painted the word *faggot* on the side of Joe Alsop's Georgetown home.

Tyutin begins with a long, avuncular monologue on how sorry he is about the terrorist attacks on America the day before. It feels canned, and I'm tired of pity from Russians. You can't get over the sense they are secretly gloating. So I try to change the subject. I ask what he thinks of Nemtsov's peace overtures in Chechnya?

At this, Tyutin's demeanor darkens, and his hands begin to shake.

"Why don't you tell your friend Nemtsov to go to New York City and explain to your people what it is like to deal with these fucking animals!" he thunders as his clenched fist slams the table. Though the democratically minded Nemtsov is not yet my friend, I suddenly want him to be.

One of my first orders of business, it seems, is to get on Boris Nemtsov's radar screen. I will go on to spend more than a year following him from the Arctic to the North Caucasus to a city in Siberia most famous for hosting a penal colony in the bad old days. I would combine these trips with a poll briefing or media training to make the best use of his time. What this affords is an unvarnished look at the campaign trail in Russia in an exercise that is soon to become extinct.

The following spring, we are at a country fair in the northwestern city of Vologda, and Nemtsov is posing for a photo with three pregnant women, each of whose face beams with rural beauty and wholesomeness and no trace of makeup. One is even wearing a kerchief over her braided brown hair, evoking in my mind the model citizen collective farmworker lionized in the old propaganda posters.

Throughout Russia, Vologda is known for the purity of its butter, and something about the place makes you long to pick up a scythe and start threshing wheat.

"You don't think I should take this picture, do you?" he grins at me as the photographer snaps away.

No, I think quietly to myself, *it is definitely off message and will likely reinforce his reputation as a ladies' man. But you can't deny that the guy has magnetic charm.*

When I'm not advising on photos, under my arm I carry a thick binder filled with the cross-tabs, which break down every poll-question response against a range of criteria, like age, profession, voting history, and the like. Each cross-tab is a "slice" of what, say, women in their forties who are not particularly religious think about things versus everyone else. There are literally thousands of slices one can explore, though only some of them actually matter. Roughly speaking, one-fifth of Russians fall into the liberal camp, so it's not a huge universe.

The binder is a useful prop for a political advisor, too, and it lends authority when I sagely tell Boris things like, "All voters are motivated by one of three things: fear, greed, or guilt."

At this, he looks at me mischievously and asks, "What's guilt?" He's being polite, and funny, but what he means is that won't work in Russia—the guilt part, that is. Then he thinks for a few seconds and replaces guilt with pride. It's really the flip side anyway, he explains, and he's right. They will respond to appeals to pride, though this, of course, opens the door to nationalism.

Thankfully, it is early summer, though still brisk, when we're visiting the near-Arctic port city of Arkhangelsk. Nemtsov asks me why I'm not joining him for a visit to the nuclear submarine base near there. "It's probably better for you if I don't go," I tell him, while secretly I'm touched at his devil-may-care thinking of including me despite the obvious risk. I could imagine the headline: "Nemtsov brings American spy to strategic facility . . ."

Wherever we go, I try my best to be inconspicuous. Usually, it's for the best. Once, in Tula, he pointed me out in the audience when someone asked a question about Americans. "Ask him," he said. Otherwise, I'm invisible.

Now we're at a concert in Stavropol, in the Russian Caucasus and the general vicinity of Chechnya. Diana Gurtskaya, a blind Georgian Russian synth-pop star, is the main act and is singing a melancholy tune to her dead mother about her first love, who is not like the others, because he is reliable, affectionate, and kind. It makes me think of a hit song on the radio about wanting a man like Putin, who doesn't drink, doesn't beat me, and won't leave me. Are Russian men really that awful?

Not a bad turnout—thousands of young people are attending the free concert. It's August, and everyone is wearing T-shirts. I wonder if anyone's collecting contact information on all the people— potential voters—who got a free ticket, and then I remember it's not really my event nor my job to micromanage. When it's over, we board a private jet someone has loaned the party for the flight back to Moscow. Gurtskaya is from a land near Chechnya, Boris tells me, as if being a blind pop singer wasn't interesting enough.

When we meet for coffee at the Baltchug Kempinski on the bank of the Moscow River, Nemtsov introduces me to Alla Pugacheva, whom he calls "Russia's Madonna." He offers to introduce me to tennis star Anna Kournikova, but I know she's dating hockey star Pavel Bure, and moreover I am myself married.

In early fall, we go to the western Siberian city of Tyumen, landing at night, against which you can see gas flares from the nearby oil fields, like the Bedouin fires in the U2 song "Beautiful Day." The air above the frozen tarmac smells like bitumen. The next day is packed with campaign events, like a chemical factory tour, a meeting with students at the local university, and finally, a stop by the local TV station for a live appearance on the evening news.

Boris is more animated than on an average day in the Duma. His stump speeches to students mainly are more heated, and now on local TV, he is speaking plainly now about the Kremlin's growing authoritarianism. He calls out Putin by name, which crosses a line. I notice one of the cameramen look at the nervous host and shrug, and the interviewer looks back toward the control room and says something to Nemtsov. The studio goes quiet.

Getting up from his chair and pulling the microphone off his shirt, Boris walks over to me with his face visibly contorted in rage. I've never seen that on him before and am alarmed. A tiny droplet or two of spittle hit me in the face when he speaks.

"You wanted to know what media censorship looks like." Noting my surprise, he dials back his anger slightly. "You can tell your friends in Washington this is how it goes—someone in Moscow picks up a phone and tells these guys to cut the signal immediately."

I look at the monitors, and they've gone to black. My knee-jerk reaction to anger is often to pivot to humor, even when it might be considered inappropriate.

"At least it means they're watching," I respond. After all, we're in Siberia and two hours ahead of Moscow. He glares at me, not in the slightest amused, and starts barking at his press secretary. Of course, he's right. This is very serious. The rules are changing right in front of our faces. Up until now, they'd only restricted us on the national channels, but the noose is tightening even on regional TV.

I'm no longer just an NGO guy trying to build capacity in a transitional country, which is the job for which I was hired. No, I've become a partisan.

———

One of Moscow's distractions, especially for a young man in his early thirties, is the strip club. It is its own kind of museum, really, not only for the beauty that is just skin deep—for me, anyway—but also a reminder of how we can be creative when we are forced to innovate.

I'd learned this back in Maine, on my first political campaign, when the chips were down and I was working late in a now-empty head-quarters in a strip mall, where such an establishment was the only place to find a drink.

It is in that other cold land, my own, that I first discovered the trans-formative power of the strip club—not to ogle flesh but to drown my sorrows. It is 1994, and I am the spokesman for one of the only Repub-lican campaigns that cycle not poised to win.

The cavernous hall of Mark's Showplace is filled with poles off which comely young ladies are swinging, and then in a well about half a floor below is a platform as big as a dozen foosball tables put together, with fewer people and only intermittent dancers. That's where I go to order a double scotch.

This dark oasis populated by mostly nude women is the perfect place to lick my wounds. But because of what's just happened, I'm mired in the depths of depression. For months I've poured my heart and soul into what is now clearly going to be a losing campaign. We'd been outraised, outmaneuvered, and outfoxed.

My thoughts grow darker still as I stare into the peaty gold concoc-tion that lends me a little lift—not enough. Every other guy in the place is giddy or leering or in some zone of contentment, but I must be visibly down in the dumps. A dancer is doing a floor routine in front of me, and despite the fact I'm the only one at the huge table, I scarcely notice. She slithers in my direction.

"I'm Crystal, honey," she informs me. "Can I ask you a favor?"

I nod affirmatively, both shy yet also honored to be in her confidence.

"Could you just smile a little? It would make my job a lot easier."

Crystal's just flipped a switch in my brain, and I oblige her with the awkward pleasure of a kid who just figured out how to break into the candy store. We become friends. In the days and weeks that follow, we chat in the parking lot when we're both smoking—she between shifts and me when I just need to clear my head a little. We're just two cogs in our respective machines who share a bad habit, an occasional wink, and a smile.

The night before the election arrives, and again I'm alone in the office. Channel 8 News calls and wants to come by and get some footage of our Get-Out-the-Vote activity. Fuck! I can't tell them we don't have one. That would sound too pathetic. They say they'll be by in forty minutes, and my head spins. I look out the window and see Crystal smoking and tell them, "Okay."

November in Maine is already pretty cold. I put on my coat and cross the parking lot. By now, Crystal's no longer alone. Tammy and Pam, who just got off their shifts, are now smoking with her. There's some commotion behind the back door suggesting some others are on their way out or taking a break. I'm too desperate for small talk and just blurt it out: "Ladies, can you help me out of a jam?"

Now I've got Crystal and five of her friends in the otherwise empty Collins for Governor office, and I set up a brown folding table and scatter chairs around it before they have time to talk among themselves and realize what a harebrained plan this is. Then I unplug all the office phones and put them at stations on the table in front of phone books and toss all the cords underneath.

"It's make-believe, ladies," I tell them. "Act as if you're calling names in the book, asking if they support Collins and reminding them to vote tomorrow." They're totally brilliant, and thankfully they've all still got their coats on because I told them this would only be a few minutes. On

cue, the camera truck arrives.

A reporter and a cameraman with a handheld come in for the quick shot they wanted. Luckily for me, none zoomed in on the phones themselves because there are no lights flashing. They interview me improvising and get some nice B-roll of Crystal and her colleagues playacting GOTV calls.

First the camera crew and then a few minutes later Crystal and her coworkers leave the office in the strip mall, and once again it's just me. I pick up the phone and let people know not to be surprised by the eleven o'clock news.

———————

Konstantin Kilimnik, or Kostya, is the senior-most member of the IRI Russia team and the closest of the half dozen of us to me in age. He's been with IRI for seven years by the time I arrive. He's maybe a head shorter than me, with a tousled mop of brown hair crowning his own. The only one who has served in the military, he spent some time translating for Russian arms merchants in Sweden before hitching his wagon to the little American NGO that does democracy work.

Max knows Kostya as the guy with the car. Whenever he sees a Fiat Punto on the traffic-choked streets of Moscow, he blurts out happily, "Kostya's car!" Married to Katya, a dermatologist, he has two young daughters bracketing Max in age. The fact we both have families gives us something in common—the rest of the Russian staff are younger and have yet to expand their respective franchises.

By the time I get to Moscow, there hasn't been an expatriate director in the office for nearly a year. Kostya has been running the administration by keeping the books, arranging travel, and managing our subgrant program to a handful of small Russian NGOs, like the League of Women's Voters in Saint Petersburg or the Institute of Political Technologies in the Ural city of Perm, the site of an infamous prison camp from the not-so-long-ago Soviet days.

Because he's a family man, Kostya travels less than the others and is almost always in the office. He likes concrete, tangible projects, like printing books. When I arrive in the fall of 2001, we're just getting back from the printers a handbook for legislative staff, offering tips for being more interactive with constituents. We deliver several of these to each of the 450 offices in the Russian State Duma, with a letter from me announcing how eager we are to help implement any of the practices the book suggests. Only one Duma deputy sends me a thank-you.

"How nice of you generous Americans to help us simple Russians. Were it not for you, we'd still be in the dark when it comes to this whole democracy business," nationalist Vladimir Zhirinovsky writes in a letter dripping with sarcasm. Kostya and I are the only ones who find Zhirinovsky's note funny, which speaks to our shared sense of gallows humor. Because he tends to see things more darkly—and even act a little bit like Winnie-the-Pooh's sidekick Eeyore, the depressive and stubborn donkey—previous directors sidelined him and even jokingly called him "Carry-on" because of his short stature.

There are two sides to Kostya, whose parents came from different Soviet republics: the Russian side and the Ukrainian one. The Russian is mired in the barriers of the present and what just can't be done. In contrast, the Ukrainian persona can be quite accommodating and creative when it comes to working around the constant limitations this place seems to throw up just when you feel you are actually making progress. Sometimes I sense they are fighting inside him.

"You're probably not going to want to do it, but IFES [the International Foundation for Electoral System, another US-based democracy group] is asking us to cosponsor this conference the Central Election Commission seems to be holding just for show," Kostya tells me one morning.

He's right. The whole thing seems pretty precooked. It's agenda focuses on the third reading of the draft law, which means it's already essentially a done deal. But they're only asking a few thousand dollars, and we have a budget for parliamentary training programs, which, as the Zhirinovsky letter indicates, have been pretty moribund. So why not, I figure, and say, "Let's do it."

When the appointed day comes, true enough, the conference has a Potemkin feel to it, in reference to a Russian nobleman who was a lover and advisor to Catherine the Great. When she insisted on touring the provinces by train, Potemkin had two-dimensional cutouts of happy, prosperous villages erected along the route to disguise the peasants' miserable existence.

By the same token, the Central Elections Committee seems to be increasing just for show. Headquartered in Chinatown in a tall, dark gray building nestled among other forbidding organs of the Russian state stacked side by side, as if they were suspended in jars of formaldehyde on the shelf. On entering, we're told to take our seats and stay in them until the event begins. There's going to be a special guest, we're told in hushed and excited tones by the organizers.

The special guest, I quickly come to learn, is Putin himself.

I'm sitting still long enough that I start twitching when my cell phone lights up. It's a Kazakh opposition politician I'd invited because his country is facing similar election-law changes. He's downstairs at the door, but they won't let him in. Can I help?

Surely this is a misunderstanding, I think as Putin slides through a back door and into his seat at the dais. He seems younger in person, and his hair looks blond as opposed to the gray I'd expected. As discretely as I can, I get up and look for an organizer to help me sort out the Kazakh visitor's problem and get him inside.

"No," the first competent-looking functionary I find tells me. "It's not possible."

Just sit down and be quiet, she gestures.

Now I get angry. My organization is a cosponsor of this dog-and-pony show. We gave them thousands of dollars, and for what? For this price, the very least I could expect is that our guest is respected. I find another election commission staffer and insist.

"Do you really want an international incident here?" I stammer in the most menacing tone I can manage in Russian.

"It's not my problem," a doughty woman tells me matter-of-factly. "Take your seat, and your friend can come in only after the president has left."

I could escalate, I think, but I can also get thrown out of the country that afternoon, and that would probably be the end of my democracy-promoting career. Sullenly, I trudge back to my seat and fall into it with a thud, no longer as concerned about being discrete. It's a small matter, really, but I've just been steamrolled.

When I look up, I can't help but notice that Putin is staring straight at me. My expression is a bewildered pout. He smiles and winks before looking away. The wink seems to say, "Nice try, asshole."

Back at the office, I'm scanning through the calendar of seminars across the great expanse of the Russian Federation, and the dark metaphor of this conference seems to capture the futility of my mission here.

———

During our second fall in Moscow, a band of several dozen heavily armed Chechens manages to get to a theater on a street called Dubrovka and take 850 members of the audience hostage in a bold and terrifying act. Playing there is an elaborate production of a musical called *Nord-Ost* that, having cost $4 million to develop, is the most expensive show on the Russian stage and one that critics called a "theatrical version of McDonald's," which is another way of saying lowbrow in an extremely culturally focused country.

The hostage-takers allow a few opposition politicians in to negotiate at the outset of the siege. I am unable to get Irina Khakamada, who the Chechens requested as an intermediary, to go into detail about what it was like. She tells me she just doesn't want to go through it again. But Grigory Yavlinsky, founder of the other liberal opposition party, Yabloko, and the one who told me that Russian history is controversial, is more willing to describe it: "They had no real plan," he explains to me and a small group of foreign businessmen after the fact. "They were like kids, high on the thrill of having succeeded beyond their wildest dreams. When I asked them what their demands were, they told me Russia must get out of Chechnya, full stop."

A gifted storyteller, Yavlinsky pauses here for effect before continuing. "I told them that's not how it works; it's not a practical goal. What you need is a staggered withdrawal, with so many soldiers gone by such and such a date and so on. It was pretty clear they hadn't thought it through, so we sat down and sketched out a plan. Once they agreed on it, I left the theater and took their demands to the Kremlin and showed it to [then chief of staff] Sasha Voloshin and Putin himself. When I was done explaining it, Putin asked me if I could guarantee it would work. 'Well, of course, I can't guarantee,' I told him, and at this they looked at each other, smiled, and thanked me for my effort."

What follows is a preventable tragedy. Russian security forces pump an unknown gas that is probably a fentanyl derivative into the theater's ventilation system, wait for it to take effect, and then storm the place and kill all the Chechens. But they haven't prepared to resuscitate the hostages, and 170 people die while rescue workers struggle to get the antidote out of the government.

Usually, in Russia, people come last.

Aizhan and I are regular theatergoers. She sees this as one of the real benefits of our posting and is frequently arranging for us to see both classics as well as some avant-garde productions. Fortunately for us, *Nord-Ost* did not meet her discriminating tastes, so, like other Muscovites, we just watched the unfolding horror from the relative comfort of the other side of town.

In the wake of 9/11, I come to believe the best "revenge" is to democratize the Muslim world and increase our programs in places like Tatarstan and Bashkortistan. I nearly get arrested going to Dagestan with a young member of our team who has family there. The infamous Imam Shamil, a Daghestani warlord, successfully led the resistance to the Russian army in the North Caucasus for the first half of the nineteenth century and inspired the likes of Tolstoy.

By the time we get to Moscow, an estimated 40 percent of Russian women are marrying Muslim men because of the high value their culture places on family and the lower incidences of alcoholism and physical abuse compared with Russian men. In popularizing Putin at his public launch, promoters concocted a pop song that declared, "I want a man like Putin, one who won't get drunk, one who won't beat me, one who won't leave me." Stereotypically speaking, these attributes apply more toward Muslim men than Putin, but one can suppose it was a kind of cultural appropriation for branding purposes.

Officially, 10 percent of Russians are Muslim, but given shifting demographic trends, the real number is likely higher. Historically, Tatars have had enormous influence in the country. Saint Basil's Cathedral in Red Square was built in the sixteenth century to celebrate Russia's capture of the Tatar capital of Kazan, so the schism is old and deep. In the case of Chechnya, it is searing.

Eventually, Putin will co-opt the Chechens, but for now the specter of terrorism hangs over Moscow like a dark cloud. The extent to which this is simply a pretext for bolstering the security state is unclear. Many, including my friend and mentor in Russian affairs David Satter, have written that the FSB orchestrated the 1999 apartment bombings in Ryazan, a suburb of Moscow, that killed almost two hundred residents in their sleep as a *provokatzia* (intentional provocation) for renewing the military conflict in Chechnya.

And Chechens are fighting back. Once I was on the Moscow metro when a Chechen widow blew herself up in a subway car on a different line. The trains kept rolling in a defiant signal of Russian toughness.

Fear opens a gateway for authoritarianism. Civil libertarians back at home are decrying the Patriot Act and the power it gives the American government to snoop on citizens. In a country that has been run by its security services for the better part of eight centuries, this dynamic is obviously much more intense. One evening, Aizhan, Max, and I are sitting at home watching a television program when it is interrupted by the news. Putin is holding a cabinet meeting, and the ministers all bow their heads submissively as he speaks from the head of a long table.

"That is pretty creepy, don't you think?" Aizhan observes. It never ceases to amaze me how someone who grew up under the Soviet system is quicker to catch the erosion of freedom than one who grew up surrounded by it.

———————

One of the reasons I hired Marina is that she wrote a book on marriages in Russia. The other, more important reason is we need someone competent to manage the portfolio of women's programs, and she certainly fits that bill. But I know my marriage is in trouble, and for some irrational reason I believe having a Russian feminist on staff will change that. I bring her book home and put it on the shelf in our dining room, as if its presence might improve things.

"Do you really need to work all the time?" a cousin of Aizhan's who is visiting while passing through Moscow asks me earnestly.

Internally, I bristle at the question: *Why am I the only one who seems so committed to this work, and who is he to lecture me anyways?* But the real reason the question makes me so defensive is that this young man is probably right. I really should be trying harder, and not only because we share a child, which seems to be the glue holding us together.

Ever since I invented a translating assignment back in Kazakhstan to spend some time with her, when I pulled her back from the path of a speeding truck, we have always been on the move. First she went to college back in Maine, then we moved back to Kazakhstan, then back to Maine, and then Washington, and now here. Sometimes it seems we are tag-teaming one another in a mad rush through young adulthood without skimping on adventure.

I am also impatient, full of myself, and even brash. I'm fearful about pushing the line at work, as meddling foreigners are beginning to get expelled, and worried about where all this leads professionally. None of this bodes well for nurturing a still-young marriage. I can be short with Aizhan, and she's not one to suffer fools gladly. Max is picking up on all this and seems more nervous than he should be, even in Russia.

Other than Kostya, who is technically an employee, I'm the only one of my friends here who is married and with child. My friend John Mann is married to a Kazakh Russian DJ, which puts no cramp on his clubbing life, and my cousin Jonathan is a single, good-looking actor. Any advice I get on domestic relations is from Kostya, and this is generally pretty useful. Usually, it just involves listening to my wife.

And my drinking is getting worse.

There were times back in Kazakhstan when Aizhan would have to help me walk out of bars, but compared with Russia, those are the junior leagues. Washington sends me back to Kazakhstan from Moscow in 2002 to reopen IRI's office there. It had been shuttered because our last country director had been beaten up at gunpoint in the late 1990s, in a sign of how well democracy was doing there. After hiring a human rights lawyer named Evgeniy Zhovtis to register us legally, I find a great new trilingual and nonthreatening country director.

To celebrate these accomplishments, I go out on the town in Almaty with old friends. It's one of those nights you don't bother sleeping, because your flight is so early the next morning.

By the time I head to the airport to fly back to Russia, I am so loaded a policeman takes me aside and says I can't board the plane. I push back, tell him I don't believe there is such a rule, because I am not the pilot, so why should it matter. He takes me into a small room, where I am quickly surrounded by a half dozen cops and then read the relevant regulation. I am wrong, but I sobered enough from the closed-door episode they let me proceed.

The next fight is with a customs official when he says I can't take Kazakh cash out of the country. After telling him he is almost as much of a crook as his president, the next thing I know, I'm waking up on the tarmac in Moscow's Domodedovo Airport with an empty wallet, a fat lip, and a hell of a hangover.

In Russia, I fit right in. Going through passport control, I see a familiar sight: the man in front of me is so drunk he has to be held up by a friend. His friend tells the border guard, "He's one of ours," and she just waves them ahead.

JULY 2003

Spaso House sits on a little green oasis of a plot of land between the flashy steel buildings of the Novy Arbat, the towering spire of the Ministry of Foreign Affairs (one of Moscow's "seven sisters," or "Stalin skyscrapers"), and the Smolenskaya Passazh business center, shopping mall, and metro station as if it were a country house dropped from the sky on to one of Moscow busiest areas. It is the residence of the US ambassador and is surrounded on three sides by gardens. The house itself is built in the Palladian style, with tall windows topped by semicircles that let in cascades of light—and probably plenty of sonic microphone beams too.

On the third of July, a glorious summer day, I am standing outside, waiting in line under a warm sun, with roses blooming in front of the stately mansion. I'm not used to there being such a process for getting inside though. There are tables set up out front, where visitors are screened before being let inside, and from the looks of it extra security as well.

Yes, this is the closest thing the ambassador has to an open house each year—Independence Day on the workday side of the actual holiday—and that in itself breeds some excitement. But still, there is a peculiar energy in the air today, and there's a media stakeout and a cluster of rabbis.

One never knows who is going to show up at these things. Last year I ran into Senate minority leader Trent Lott and teased him about how the navy destroyers built at Bath Iron Works in Maine are of superior quality to those of our rival yard in Pascagoula, Mississippi, Lott's home state. I asked him what his plans were to take back the Senate. Who will it be this time?

"Did you hear what happened?" my National Democratic Institute (NDI) counterpart Dan Kunin asks me when I run into him and his Georgian wife. I hadn't. In fact, I'd stumbled out of bed without reading the news and came straight here without stopping by the office, as Spaso House is only a few blocks from my apartment.

Aizhan and Max are in Kazakhstan visiting relatives, so I

predictably had too much to drink last night and was out late. "They popped MBK's moneyman," he tells me with bulging eyes, referring to Platon Lebedev, the chief financial officer of Mikhail Borisovich Khodorkovsky's oil company.

Khodorkovsky, or MBK, is Russia's richest man, first among the oligarchs. He has modernized YUKOS, a major Russian oil company, and set up one of the country's biggest banks, Menatep. He is also behind a series of strategic donations that win him affection in the West—he even funded a program for young leaders that took Dan to Oxford for a week. More to the point, he is the only one of the crew of billionaires still in Russia who is standing up to Putin.

In February, Khodorkovsky had challenged Putin during a televised meeting between the president and the oligarchs—a forum Nemtsov had initiated a couple of years prior—when he accused a state-run oil company, a competitor of his, of endemic corruption. Now he is said to be quietly funding opposition parties, including the Union of Right Forces.

Dan's telling me about the arrest puts everything in a new context. The hubbub outside the front door and the nervous-looking embassy staff suddenly makes sense. If Khodorkovsky is now in open war with Putin, to whom would he turn for help? The obvious option is the Americans. Now I can see him in the garden. He's darting away from the crowd of anointed gawkers and well-wishers, heading away from the party and deeper into the garden.

This is the second time I've seen MBK in the flesh. The first was a talk at the Moscow School of Political Studies, a high-minded liberal gabfest that IRI has supported over the years. There he showed up with a half dozen handlers in flashy suits and crocodile shoes who seemed immensely proud of themselves but utterly useless to him as he sat by himself, ignoring them, reviewing his PowerPoint presentation, and then, by himself, setting and adjusting the HDMI cables into the projector.

When he spoke, his voice was quiet and a little high-pitched. As one who is naturally shy myself, I felt a strange affinity with him then.

So I follow MBK, catching up to him just before he disappears into the bushes. Maybe he's exploring the garden, looking for a private place to make a call or perhaps to take a leak. It's just the two of us now, and it's clear I've chased him down, so I confront my own shyness and address him.

"Mikhail Borisovich," I say, extending my right hand to shake his, which he has not yet offered. I introduce myself and explain what IRI is, and I tell him I like some of the things he's said about Russia's urgent need for reform. Then, with my other hand, I pass him my business card and tell him when he decides to run for president I hope he'll consider giving me a call.

I don't think there's anything absurd about what I just said, but judging by the look on his face, Khodorkovsky does. His expression is one of mild bewilderment; then he smiles, puts my card in his pocket, and says thank you. I leave him to go about whatever he was up to in the bushes.

Nearly four months from now, Khodorkovsky's plane will land in Novosibirsk to refuel. He will be traveling throughout Russia giving speeches to young audiences about civic life and modernizing their country. He's been warned to leave Russia, as other outspoken oligarchs like Vladimir Gusinsky and Boris Berezovsky have, but he refuses. On the tarmac in Novosibirsk, masked, heavily armed policemen in black jumpsuits will storm his plane and take him into custody.

Then, at yet another reception at Spaso House, I will accompany one of our former subgrantees, Elena Nemirovskaya, head of the Moscow School of Political Studies, who has since graduated to Khodorkovsky funding. Sandy Vershbow, the ambassador, is greeting his guests at the door, and Elena won't let go of his arm.

"Has 'he' made the call?" she asks insistently. The call she's asking about is President Bush calling Putin to urge MBK's release. The ambassador mumbles something indistinctly to the effect that something is in process. If so, it is a process that will go nowhere. The tens, if not hundreds, of millions of dollars Khodorkovsky's spent wooing the West now seem like a tremendous waste.

By imprisoning MBK, Putin shows himself to be his own man and not another Yeltsin, who depended on the oligarchs for his reelection. There are no sacred cows in Putin's Russia, and he may milk or carve up whichever one he pleases. He also demonstrates what happens to those who break the new deal and try to play politics. Khodorkovsky will spend ten years in prison, much of it in Siberia.

DECEMBER 2003

"Your friends aren't going to make it," the head of First Channel tells me as we stand watching the DAK boards set up on the walls of Russia's Central Election Commission.

Marat Guelman claims to have opened Russia's first private gallery and is ostensibly a liberal, though he is also behind the soft-focus version of Putin's image. His people at First Channel accepted the Get-Out-the-Vote ads I produced for airing as public service announcements on his station, even though one of the guys in his control room correctly identified them as stealth Union of Right Forces (SPS) spots, so I don't say anything rude back to him.

One year from now, Ukraine will erupt into its Orange Revolution, spurred by Russians falsifying the results feeding electronically into their own national election committee, but tonight we are meant to pretend that this is a great technological breakthrough. It strikes me as fishy.

In order to get into Russia's parliament, a party must get at least 5 percent of the total vote. SPS is mired in the low threes, according to the board over our heads. The same goes for Yabloko, another liberal, pro-Western party that refused to run jointly with SPS after its leader cited concerns about ideological purity. With such small numbers, it is easy to play with fractions and have a big impact.

"Our country is a giant crematorium," Khakamada once quipped. "Only here the dead are spared."

Looking around the election watch party in the election committee, I finally realize what she meant.

I call Tatiana to find out where Boris is, and she directs me to a wine bar across town. There the mood is funereal. He sees me and waves me over to a low table, where he is sitting in front of a goblet of merlot.

"Men are like fine wine," he tells me. "We get better with time." His philosophical mood cheers me up a little. This election was his second act, and now it is unceremoniously over.

His phone lights up, and he answers it. His voice is gentle and consoling, and after a short conversation he asks me if I know who that was, which, of course, I don't. "It was Khodorkovsky's wife, Inna," he tells me. "She thanked me," he says, "for being the only person in Russia who stood up for her husband." For a moment he just stares at me, looking to see if what he'd just told me sunk in—that he is loyal to his friends, even when they are in trouble. Now his mood begins to darken, and I decide it's time to leave. It feels like tonight is the night democracy died in Russia.

My last Christmas in Russia is a gloomy one. It brings with it the realization that everything I'd worked for these last couple of years had essentially been for naught. When I arrived here, there were at least two pro-Western, liberal parties in the Duma, and soon there will be none. The only real opposition party now is the Communists, and should they come to power again, that would arguably be even worse for the West. I hadn't made anything better. In fact, one could argue I did the opposite, though that would overstate my actual agency.

Before the dust has yet settled, Khakamada announces she's running for president. Taken at face value, it seems absurd. How is a country with dominant strains of chauvinism going to respond to a half-Japanese female presidential candidate? But if we've learned anything, it's that this is not a contest to be taken at face value. Running against Putin in a system without independent media of consequence, with potential funders threatened with prison, and the entire apparatus of the state against you, it is, well, absurd. Why shouldn't it be Khakamada?

Her strategist asks me to look at the storyboards of an ad they are planning to produce to promote Khakamada's campaign. It features two Asiatic Chukchi walking across the frozen steppe and finding a patch of clear ice. Peering through their hoods, they see the top of

Saint Basil's Cathedral from above. One looks at the other and says, "I hear the round eye used to live here." Then it fades to black.

I beg them not to make the ad. It would lead to violence, I fear. But it certainly is powerful.

"The goal is to shock people to their senses," the Moscow-based strategist explains to me.

"Well, it will certainly shock them," I tell her, "but whether it leads to a better result is another story." My Asiatic wife, our mixed-race son, and I narrowly avoided getting killed by an angry mob of skinheads just the year before when we were bicycling near the Duma after Russia lost a soccer match to Japan. The crowd then wanted to burn Khakamada's office.

The presidential election of 2004 comes and goes as a nonevent. Putin is overwhelmingly reelected, and Khakamada gets almost exactly the same score as SPS did in the parliamentary election three months prior: four point something.

"We wanted better, but got the same as always," former prime minister Viktor Chernomyrdin once said of an earlier political debacle. But it's a good line, and it fits. Though I am disappointed, I'd have to be blind not to see it coming. Between the end of liberal parties in parliament and this most recent flash of exoticism, I volunteer for IRI's program in Iraq.

The morning after Khakamada's "victory" party, I walk the three miles from our apartment to the office. The Garden Ring is not as bucolic as it sounds. Alongside a road with four lanes of usually congested traffic in either direction, there is plenty of carbon monoxide to complement the moist, gray cold that holds it in the air a moment longer on a late winter morning in Slavic Rome.

As I near Bolshaya Sukharevskaya Square, I make a diagonal cut through a little park to save time. There I nearly trip over the corpse of a bum who died underneath a park bench the night before. His feet are sticking out into the path, and a porcine militiaman is disinterestedly writing up an incident report. The cheapness of life here hits me. The dead man was not alone in his misery, but for him it was now over. The oyster-colored pallor of his skin now matched the sky above.

It takes only a few minutes to pack my things. Leaving this place should be a cause for celebration, but instead I feel very hollow and sad.

MARCH 2003

Sergei Karaganov is a well-dressed man with a cleanly shaven head that shines when the light hits it the right way. We are nine months before the tragically disappointing December election, and a year before I nearly tripped over that corpse on my last trip to the Moscow office. I've heard Congressman Tom Lantos is coming to town and talked my way into a Spaso House breakfast with him.

The embassy produced Karaganov as a Kremlin-affiliated foreign policy thought leader with whom the iconic congressman, a San Francisco Democrat who had in his youth been rescued from the Holocaust by the brave Swedish diplomat Raoul Wallenberg, could discuss the state of the world.

With Lantos, Deputy Chief of Mission (and later ambassador in his own right) John Beyrle, and me surrounding him at a little round table in a sunny breakfast nook, Karaganov appears nervous. After all, he's outnumbered. And he's also unable to understand—so he says—why America is about to invade Iraq. Like any good Russian intellectual, he expresses his consternation snidely and tells Lantos we are about to make a mistake of epic proportions.

At this, the old man lowers his brow and glares fiercely at the shiny-headed Russian. He speaks calmly and quietly, but with an unmistakably steely tone that defies rebuke. "The Fifth Fleet is in position, Mr. Karaganov," Lantos explains. "By now, you should understand that we're not fucking around."

For what feels like a full minute, you could hear a pin drop on the parquet floor of this high-ceilinged, elegant room. Brought up with an unnatural phobia of awkward silences, I leap into the void to restore the veneer of civility. "Like Chekhov once said of his plays, if a revolver appears in the first act it will most definitely be fired by the third. I think that is, in essence, what Congressman Lantos is telling you," I diplomatically try to explain.

Lantos gives me an appreciative look as Beyrle shoots me one that is closer to an eye roll that says, "I can't believe you just said something that cheesy, but it seems to have worked."

Karaganov looks a little relieved, but still uncomfortable. I have just earned the cost of my breakfast.

It's less than a year later, and I've already decided I am going to Iraq, so I throw myself a going-away party at the Hard Rock Café on the old Arbat. Boris Nemtsov makes an appearance and takes me aside. "I don't get it," he said. Not so long ago, I caught him laughing about the fact that American proconsul in Iraq Paul Bremer invited Yegor Gaidar, an SPS party leader and former Russian prime minister during the disastrous "shock therapy" conversion to a market economy and mass privatization in the mid-1990s, to Iraq to brief the interim government there on how to do it. "Here we are, a Christian country—well, sort of—and we can't get democracy right. How do you expect the Iraqis to?"

Frankly, I have no idea what to say, so I try on another popular Russian phrase: "Hope dies last."

CHAPTER 3

RETREAT IS NOT AN OPTION

WASHINGTON, MARCH 2001

It's tough to tell which is shinier: his face or his suit. My boss told me I have to attend this briefing, and looking around the high-ceilinged room in the US Capitol at dozens of other fidgety foreign policy staffers, I'm not the only one who got pressed into this. Someone called in some favors. Whoever is promoting Iraqi dissident Ahmed Chalabi, they sure do have juice.

Chalabi is smooth—greasy, in fact. The US taxpayer has just given him $20 million for a government-in-exile to take over Iraq once Saddam Hussein is gone. I was an intern on the Hill during the first Gulf War, and that was ten years ago. Saddam is still there, and it's hard to believe he's going anywhere. But according to this Chalabi guy, the Iraqi people are yearning for the chance to rise up and overthrow him and replace his tyranny with the first Muslim democracy in the Middle East—after we teach turtles to fly, that is.

To hear Chalabi tell it, all Iraq needs is a little push, and he and his merry band at the Iraqi National Congress would do the rest. We'd be welcomed as liberators, Iraq would make peace with Israel,

Iraqis would choose wise leaders like him, and all would be well in that restive region. Like the other staffers there, I am playing with my BlackBerry to let everyone else know how in demand I am, but occasionally I pretend to listen. The knowing look you give to appear like you're paying attention is a Washington specialty, even if you know nothing at all.

But credit where credit is due. This is the second time in my life I've ever wondered about Iraqi politics. Once before, during Desert Storm, when I was a student and taking a contemporaneous course on security and defense issues in the Gulf, and in a campus newspaper I cofounded I argued for war. But then there wasn't much talk about what would come next, assuming Baghdad was toppled, which it wasn't. At least Chalabi is talking about an Iraq without Saddam. The realists surrounding Bush the father did not think it would be prudent to decapitate the snake.

September 11 is still almost seven months in the future. Beyond another flare-up in the West Bank, no one is thinking much about the Middle East.

But the Chalabi show gets me thinking about something that will become a recurring theme in my career: regime change. I remember hearing the stories in my grandmother's living room from people who ought to know about Kermit Roosevelt as CIA station chief in Tehran in the 1950s, holding back a communist revolution. And "the Very Best Men," like Frank Wisner, Des Fitzgerald, Richard Bissell, and Tracey Barnes, had tried with varying degrees of success and failure in Eastern Europe, Southeast Asia, Cuba, and Central America, respectively, through the second half of the now over twentieth century.

I should probably know better because my late stepgrandfather, Joe Alsop, never lived down his hawkishness on Vietnam. He even had to go to my father's college graduation in disguise so as not to spur unrest on a celebratory day. Angry protestors used to cut his columns out of newspapers and carry them around for when they stepped in dog shit. They'd wipe their feet with them and then mail the feces-covered clippings back to him. After his death, we discovered he actually kept a drawer full of these.

But Joe was partially vindicated after his death. A hard line on the Soviets worked, and it was Ronald Reagan's toughness that brought the Soviets to their knees. Given this, we simply have to learn from the mistakes of the past and stay the course. We need to stand up to our enemies and, when necessary, replace them. That will take both will and some technical know-how. *Maybe*, I think for a second, *this is my purpose.*

BAGHDAD, APRIL 2004

I am on one of Air Serv's small twin-prop planes, which cater to the NGO community, flying from the military airfield near downtown Amman into Baghdad. We fly east across the desert for about an hour until we near the territory of Baghdad International Airport.

Coalition forces have secured the immediate territory but not the kilometers beyond it, so pilots have to make corkscrew landings to avoid the threat of rocket fire. That means a succession of sharp ninety-degree banks that descend to the earth. The first time you do it, your stomach feels like it got left behind one or two turns above. It's a relief to touch down, even if it is Iraq.

The airport seems empty. Commercial flights have not yet resumed since the invasion. An unmarked jet landed around the same time, and a self-important young man about my age, in a blue blazer, khakis, and Ray-Bans, greets his Blackwater team of mercenaries at what would otherwise be baggage claim. He is hustled into one of a convoy of Chevy SUVs that speed off, leaving a cloud of dust behind it.

I squint into the sunlight and see in the parking lot a Western-looking guy hunched over, smoking a cigarette. As I approach, dragging my luggage behind me, the even younger man who comes into view bears a striking resemblance to Ashton Kutcher, though he's more ragged around the edges.

His name is Lazar, and he's from Belgrade. IRI recruited him from the OTPOR movement that brought Serbs to the streets to demand Slobodan Milošević's ouster two years ago. Serbs like Lazar earned a lot of street cred for that, and attracting Americans for this assignment proved challenging.

Lazar gives me a friendly handshake and leads me to an orange-and-white Opel Vectra taxi idling nearby. No convoy, no bodyguards. The guys back at the hotel look forward to meeting me, he says.

We pass a statue of what looks like Icarus where the airport territory ends and what the US military calls Route Irish, the road into the city, begins. Though it didn't yet seem it in April 2004, this relatively short stretch of road would soon become one of the deadliest on earth. Lazar sits in the front seat with the driver as I take in the surroundings from the back seat, with windows unrolled for the welcome breeze.

The first exit from Route Irish is for a neighborhood called Jihad.

I ask Lazar if that is where the rocket fire directed at incoming planes is coming from, and he just shrugs. "Probably."

———

Iraqi women like what J. Paul Bremer is doing with his hair. That is one of many findings from Steven's constant focus groups. T. E. Lawrence was once sheriff of Baghdad, and now Bremer is proconsul of Iraq—a superambassador, if you will. Steven Moore, who is running IRI's program when I arrive, is no stranger to the game of embedding oneself in another country's political world.

In 1996 Steven's father—a California-based political consultant who infiltrated student groups for Richard Nixon and more recently helped action hero Arnold Schwarzenegger get elected governor of the Golden State—sent him to Moscow to help him advise Boris Yeltsin's troubled reelection campaign. In this sense, he is my forerunner, just as he is in Iraq.

He takes me around the Green Zone, the gated enclave where the Iraqi government used to operate and from which the Coalition Provisional Authority (CPA) now occupies Iraq. To reach this Emerald City within a city, we cross the Fourteenth of July Bridge. Steven leads me down long marble corridors in the Republican Palace, with big wooden doors on which there are makeshift signs that read: "Ambassador Jones," "Ambassador Neumann," "Ambassador Blackwill," and so on.

"Why so many ambassadors?" I ask him.

"Because this is where they send old ambassadors to die," he flatly retorts.

Behind an unmarked door, there is a stairwell, and we climb up to the roof. The air is refreshingly cool, perhaps because it is wafting up from the swimming pool below, where young CPA staffers splash and work on their tans between shifts. Careful not to trip over any of the cables that lead to hastily erected satellite dishes, we walk over to the edge and look across the river toward the city at night. There are fewer lights than one might expect of a city of seven million, thanks to rolling electricity shortages, but the ones that do burn at this hour look like stars.

"There's a lot of good we can do here," Steven relays, "but you have to get out of this zone to do it." The CPA just sit down below and write reports to Washington; they only know what their translators and the military tell them, he explains. He is omitting his obvious point of pride. His focus group also reports pipe information from actual Iraqis into this cloistered microcosm. Up until now, the news has largely been good. Iraqis have been hopeful about something better coming in Saddam's wake, even if their former overlord is still at large.

But all is not well in the land of a Thousand and One Nights.

A couple of weeks ago, *al Hawza*, the newspaper belonging to the radical Shi'ite cleric Moqtada al-Sadr, ran an article blaming coalition forces of indiscriminately killing Iraqi civilians. In response, Bremer closed the newspaper in what is not a good look for an occupier who claims to bring democracy. Al Sadr's followers have begun protests in another ironic twist. Saddam executed Moqtada's father, and the Shi'a, broadly speaking, have had the most to gain from his toppling. Yet the Sadrists are the first to start demanding that, having done our job, we pack up and leave.

The next morning I get my first assignment. Her name is Salama al-Khafaji, and she arrives with a bang.

The newest member of Bremer's handpicked governing council, Dr. Salama replaces a member who had just been assassinated. She is a dentist, and by all accounts very down-to-earth. She has the potential to speak to the people of the Shi'a street in places like Sadr City, our CPA bosses believe. She can help blunt the damage Moqtada is doing if she communicates effectively. I am to be her coach.

Since our meeting here at the Al Hamra Hotel isn't until 10:00 a.m., I hit snooze when my alarm first sounds around seven. Eight minutes later, I hit it again. *Just a few more minutes, please.* I am anticipating its third bout of bleeping when there's a much bigger noise. *Boom!* My unlatched window above the bed blows open, and the ground nine stories below us shakes. I wait a moment before cautiously getting up to look out the open window. Outside on the street, a black funnel of smoke rises, and after a moment of silence, an older woman begins wailing somewhere.

Steven, Lazar, Ron (the country director), and my deputy Chris Hobbes and I gather in the hallway and then convene in Ron's room. Our security contractor reports to Ron, who also holds the satellite phone with a New York area code. It was close, but we're all okay. Insurgents were trying to target a coalition convoy but only ended up killing a young Iraqi boy who was passing on a bicycle.

"I hope you're still up for media training," Ron says.

"Sure," I tell him, not wanting to sound yellow. But my stomach is filled with butterflies.

Neither the bomb blast nor the security perimeter that's been set up around the wreckage deters Dr. Salama, who arrives with her escort and advisor, the green turban–wearing Sheik Fateh. He and

Ron shuffle off somewhere, and I sit down with Dr. Salama—the first dentist I've ever met wearing a full black abaya, with gloves. Out of this getup, her face appears moonlike.

After the introductions, I begin going through my slide deck on the basics of political communication. She notices my hands are involuntarily trembling as if in part of some aftershock from the bomb. Now I see the maternal side of her.

"Don't worry," she assures me. "Everything will be all right."

For me, maybe it would. Other than the portly Sheik Fateh, Dr. Salama has little in terms of security. A month after our first meeting, she travels to Najaf to try and negotiate with Sadrists who had occupied the holy city. On the road from Baghdad, her convoy is attacked, and her son, who had come along to help protect her, is killed. Despite this devastating loss, I don't notice a big change in her, except perhaps that she is now a little less gentle and a lot more determined.

Months later, when I take a break to go home for a very brief late-summer leave for my grandmother Susan Mary's funeral, she asks me to "say hello to your mother from me." Her meaning, I suppose, lies in the bond between mothers both of the living and the dead.

———————

For reasons that don't seem fair, IRI fires Steven. The official story is that he was moonlighting as a blogger, and this created a security threat for the whole operation. Given that NBC is headquartered one floor below us in the hotel, this doesn't really hold water.

Good colleagues are hard to find in these parts, so to speak, and I was counting on Steven's knowledge of polling and past experience with foreign campaigns. He'd been here nearly a year, during which he'd learned more than the accumulated knowledge of the rest of us. I'm certain our paths will cross again in the future.

We'll have to leave the hotel for the election, our security company insists. Statistically speaking, we're safer in a random house somewhere in the neighborhood. Having grown fond of the al Hamra's pool, its so-so but reliable restaurant, adjacent bakery, and the bar, I protested at first. Then Ron said we could have a pool at the new house.

Money starts pouring in as the election nears. We get a new colleague of comparable age and experience to me named Patrick to run our civil society program. An American, Patrick is based in Budapest, where he runs the European office for Freedom House, another pro-democracy group. He has a wry sense of humor and is a welcome addition to our little band, which Chris often likens to that in Henry V's Saint Crispin's Day speech.

Meanwhile, the CPA picks up stakes and leaves Baghdad—a couple of days early even to psych-out the insurgency, which is already yearning for a helicopter over the US embassy in Saigon-like fashion. Unlike the CPA yahoos, the State Department is going to run things right, they let us know.

It's summer in Iraq, which means hellish heat. The three gates of hell, a Baghdadi saying goes, are June, July, and August. All sides here seem to be pulling back and recalibrating, adjusting to the changes. Now there is something ominous in the air, and even when it's still light out, it feels as though the skies have darkened.

A red flag like this can't be ignored. So I call the relatively recent ambassador John Negroponte's office and tell his secretary I've got something he'll want to be briefed about, and the sooner the better. She gives me an hour later that day.

The benefit of an unlimited research budget is that it allows you to pinpoint the moment in time when things start going wrong. That is what we saw—in a poll—in early September 2004.

Strategists don't take August polling results seriously, because the assumption is that's a month when pretty much everyone tunes out. So when my deputy Chris and I see movement in the numbers during what the Iraqis call the "third of gate of hell," we make note of it but want to confirm with a follow-up. The national data set for the next month does just that: for the first time since the invasion sixteen months ago, more Iraqis think things are going poorly than well.

In other words, they're losing patience with us.

Like a tall, skinny owl, the bald-crested Negroponte welcomes Ron and me to his domed lair in the heart of the Republican Palace, where two political assistants sit with notebooks and inscrutable, though less friendly, faces. The sight of him brings to mind his nephew and takes me back twenty years to the first time I went away to school at age twelve.

Dexter School stands on a hilltop overlooking the countryside that unfolds to the west, away from Boston. Built in Spanish-mission style, with red terra-cotta roof tiles, this oasis could be in the hill country of Texas, were it not for the seasonal foliage and the prim New England sensibilities of the boys and masters who arrive in coats and ties every morning and then change into gray or maroon jerseys in the afternoon to play football on the surrounding fields.

I don't love football, but at Dexter everyone has to play. When John Fitzgerald Kennedy was around my age, he was also a Massasoit, which means he also wore the maroon uniform, as depicted on a postage stamp. Coach Dalrymple calls my friends and me the daisy pickers because we prefer sitting on the sidelines and talking about history and currents events to the hurly-burly of the pitch, where I just get knocked on my ass the moment after the quarterback says, "Hut three."

Finally, the scrimmage is over—thank God! I run up the hill with everyone else to shower, dress in the same coat and tie we wore in that morning, and board the Chestnut Hill bus.

Pinned to the lapel of my tweed coat is a Mondale-Ferraro campaign button. I'm walking down the aisle toward my seat, in front of the one belonging to John Huston Finley IV, who will lecture me on why I need to become a conservative. Finley's grandfather taught my father classics at Harvard in the sixties, and he's taken an avuncular interest in my political awakening.

As I'm settling in my seat, a big lug of a guy named Barry reaches out from his and snatches the pin off my chest.

"She should be at home taking care of her cokehead son," he snorts in reference to former congresswoman Geraldine Ferraro, "not running for vice president. What do you think? We should all have broken homes?" Brad demands in a not-so-subtle dig at the oddball kid from Maine.

Barry throws my pin on the ground and is about to stomp on it when the equally big but more disheveled Dmitri Negroponte pushes him back, picks my campaign paraphernalia off the floor, and hands it back to me. Dmitri's uncle John is the US ambassador to El Salvador, *out of which the not-so-secret campaign to train and equip the Nicaraguan contras is based.*

Dmitri doesn't care much about politics; he's more into computers. But apparently he's got an ingrained sense of fair play, which I've suddenly come to appreciate. I thank him, put the pin back on, and slink to my seat, wishing I could just disappear. Finley is smirking, of course.

I begin by thanking the storied ambassador for his nephew Dmitri's sticking up for me on that Dexter bus so many years ago. He smiles warmly. A little sugar helps the medicine go down.

"The hope that we're going to make life better for people is fading fast," I explain as he listens carefully. Then I point to a handful of indicators from the latest poll as to why this is so and why it suggests darker days ahead. One of the aides asks for an electronic copy of the presentation, and I pause for a moment, thinking how the desk riders in DC would react if this got out. Self-preservation is an instinct, even when it's bureaucrats rather than terrorists one is worrying about.

Reluctantly, I agree. America has 130,000 pairs of boots on the ground here, and these are the folks representing our government. If IRI hiccups, surely they'll understand the bigger picture. "Please keep it close hold though," I plead.

The first thing I learn the next day is that in the State Department there appears to be no such thing as "close hold"—at least where there lies an opportunity to embarrass the president, that is. The front page of today's *Washington Post* reads: "Republican poll contradicts Bush on Iraq." Fuck.

And the second thing is that, when faced with an embarrassment, the home team's first instinct was to dispose of me. Until, that is, they completed the thought. Not to blow my own horn, but right now I'm the driving force behind their highest-profile program worldwide. If they axe me, getting someone of equal or greater caliber in place before Iraq's landmark election would be pretty near impossible.

Notice of my firing doesn't get delivered to Baghdad; the honchos back in Washington decide to walk that back and instead collectively punish our entire field team with new levels of micromanagement. They send an angry, little, beady-eyed man out to scream at us on a regular basis and report back to them like a junkyard dog. In addition to that, they send us all up to Kurdistan for several weeks to think about what "we" had done.

Ordinarily, this would make me an unpopular guy on our team. But these are not ordinary times. It's only four months until the election—in other words, the moment at which things start getting real. During this period, I also learn the desk riders in DC have invented a new nickname for me among themselves: Kurtz (in reference to the subject of Joseph Conrad's *Heart of Darkness*). I take it not as a putdown but as a compliment.

Still, I vow to quit once the election is done. How can I continue to loyally serve an outfit that was so ready to throw me under the bus? Until then, though, I resolve that success is the best revenge. That is why for the next few months I will work harder than I have on anything so far in my life.

The good news is, there is plenty of work to be done. After all, this may be the single-most robust example in America's history of our pouring resources and energy into another country's election.

If the Iraqis are turning against us, then the democracy lessons are working.

———————

They complained? I'm dumbfounded, but Ron says they really did, and I'd better come back to Baghdad. I'd been down here in Basra for a few days making arrangements to open an office and paid a courtesy call to the US embassy outpost to get their read on the local political scene. They were surprised by my unannounced visit, sure, but not only did someone gripe to Ron about it; they also reserved a couple of seats on a helicopter headed north the next morning.

Mohammed calls himself Iraqi Sam, which I take as a compliment, but to avoid the appearance I'm building a cult, I call him Dabdoob, which means "bear" in Arabic. He always dresses in brown and looks like a bear cub. Dabdoob has become my right hand and has orchestrated all our meetings down here. I give him and two other Iraqi team members who joined us on this trip the seats on the chopper and elect to drive back with the security guys.

I've got a three-man detail, all Brits. There is good-natured jostling within the security company's contractors between the Royal Marines and the Airborne guys, or ex-paratroopers. To hear it from the Marines, the paratroopers are likely to have damaged their heads from too many jumps. As if to bear this out, one of them helped himself to a glass of water from a stagnant tank while we're visiting a downtown internet café yesterday.

Now he's doubled over with stomach cramps and bouts of dry heaving while the two close-protection officers are caring for him. Our six-hour road trip is not getting off to a good start.

Together with the Brits, we have four Iraqi gunners. It's a big consort, but the security situation has gotten a lot worse since the spring. So we bundle into two "soft-skin"—that is, not armored—cars and make for Iraq's Route 1, which the military has dubbed Route Tampa, most likely in honor of the Florida city that hosts the Special Operations Command headquarters.

The open desert is wide and empty. After about an hour, we pass an old Bedouin astride a camel, and later a shepherd with a very large flock of sheep. As we approach Nasiriyah, our car overheats. Damn! Since the Iraqis are all Shi'a, and this is friendly territory for them, we leave them with the broken-down car and continue on, past Najaf and Hilla, where an offshoot of the Tigris River feeds a little oasis of fertile greenery. But that welcome sign of life fades quickly back to drab sand as we near the "Triangle of Death."

Since my meeting with Negroponte, the Sunni insurgency has gathered steam. Fallujah was an early flash point ever since April, when a convoy of Blackwater security guards were captured, killed, and hung from a bridge. The so-called triangle is where there's been a particularly high frequency of attacks on coalition forces. Here we're stuck behind a beat-up old Suburban at a US military check-point manned by a couple of tired and dusty-looking soldiers whose patience is wearing thin.

"Let's see some ID," the first soldier demands of the wild and googly-eyed driver, who indicates he doesn't have any. Neither do any of the passengers, and they all seem to think it's pretty funny. The second soldier, behind sandbags with his hands on an M2 atop a tripod, doesn't think it's funny and starts yelling at the Suburban crew. I have a bad feeling this isn't going to end well. But after a tense couple of minutes, they are waved through.

When we near Baghdad, the security team leader decides it makes more sense to approach the city from the west. What he doesn't seem to take into account—or consider a real concern—is Operation Phantom Fury, the coalition's effort to clear Fallujah and Ramadi, both of which are west of Baghdad, of insurgents.

This circumstance best explains why the next checkpoint fires a warning burst from their heavy gun just inches over the top of our sedan, causing us to screech to a stop, leaving rubber tracks on the scorching road behind us. The Brits are all screaming inside the car, and with reason. They'd followed protocol, and the driver had lowered his visor to reveal the Union Jack to the checkpoint before they opened fire. Originally from Fiji, the guard in the front passenger seat steps out of the car with his hands in the air and slowly walks toward the American soldiers.

After checking him out, they wave us forward. Behind the sandbags are a couple of young reservists from Tennessee, and they are very apologetic. There exists a decent chance they didn't recognize the UK flag and perhaps thought we were Reebok terrorists. My guys are not assuaged and tell the contrite soldiers I'm a congressman, which makes them now visibly worried. We press on.

At the next checkpoint, we get yet another, albeit smaller caliber, warning shot. When the Fijian guard steps out of the car again, hands raised, someone behind the sandbags yells, "Iraqi, go home! Go away!"

No chance to show we're not Iraqi but plenty of opportunity to understand how many Iraqis must feel. We pull back out of sight and wait, stumped as to what to do. That is when a military convoy rolls past and stops. We explain to the cigar-chomping major why we're sitting there, and he thinks it's the funniest thing in the world.

Perhaps he and the googly-eyed Iraqi back in the Triangle of Death know something we don't. The convoy escorts us to a safe house near the airport, where we collect our wits before heading into the city.

The Brits want to file a complaint about the two friendly fire incidents, but I suppress it. "We're talking about less experienced soldiers far from home," I explain. "Let it rest. Only dweebs file complaints."

———————

Whatever danger my expatriate colleagues and I face, it is nothing compared to the terrifying realities our Iraqi national staff have to navigate every day. We have protection. Washington fires the Brits and replaces them with Blackwater. When I object, my status with the IRI brass falls from golden boy to troublemaker. But quibbling aside, we have men with combat experience and guns protecting us.

Every day, when one of our Iraqi team comes to work and then goes home in the evening, he or she is at grave risk. Al-Qaeda's Iraqi franchise has issued a death threat against "collaborators."

First it is the cook who receives a death-threat letter. Then there are others. The recipients are rightly terrified but bravely refuse to quit. After all, they aren't really working for us. They're working for their own futures and that of their country. Each and every one is an Iraqi patriot. One supposes the resistance believe they're the real patriots. We all have opinions—it's hard to say who is right. At the same time, it's easy to say terrorism against your compatriots is wrong.

One night, when I was on leave, US forces arrested our office manager's father for being a Sunni male. There might have been some pretext, but I was visiting my family in Kazakhstan for the holidays, and it was my Ukrainian roommate, Volodya, who sorted it out somehow. That was one of many episodes that helped me understand why a good number of Iraqis hate us.

It wasn't just Arab Sunnis "resisting." The first time I went to Sadr City in April, a cheerful man named Ryad translated for us as we visited the local offices of the major Shi'a parties. For him, we were a side gig; his day job was interpreting for the US Army's First Armored Division, which was occupying that part of Baghdad as the war with the Sadrists began. To punish him for this, thugs from the al-Mahdi army (Sadr's) killed Ryad and strung his corpse up from a lamppost on a heavily trafficked street as a warning to other "collaborators."

I chided Khalid, one of our senior managers, one morning when he was an hour late, and I'd been waiting on him to get something done. He was stuck in traffic caused by a burning Humvee, in which sat the charred remains of US soldiers. "How will I ever be able to forget that?" he asked with troubled eyes.

Yet in spite of all these real and present dangers, no one on our national team ever complained. A few had to stop working for us for their or their families' safety, but several dozen women and men of all ages, ethnicities, and sects decided it was worth the risk. Being in the company of such courage is inspiring.

———————

"When I grow up, I want to be a terrorist and drive a car bomb into a building filled with people," the little boy says.

"When I grow up, I want to be killed by a terrorist," the little girl rejoins.

We're shooting an ad on a playground next to Baghdad State University, at the tip of Jadriya, where it juts out into the Tigris River. Lance and Tony have flown in from the States to help create a media center with which we'll flood the airwaves with content encouraging Iraqis to vote.

The turnout that matters most, to my mind anyway, is the Arab Sunnis. Repressed under Saddam, the Shi'a and Kurds will come out in droves. No goosing required. But the Sunnis are demoralized, marginalized, and pissed. The guilt of the disgraced Ba'ath Party is tossed over the collective lot of them, including legions of army officers whom Paul Bremer—in his great wisdom—fired and put out on the streets.

Getting Arab Sunnis to vote when they're outnumbered and suspicious of the whole enterprise is a tall order. So we test a raft of pop-culture figures and find one who is standout popular with Sunni males: Khalil al Rifai.

When David Lean shot *Lawrence of Arabia* in the early 1960s, he originally cast the Iraqi actor Rifai to play the role Omar Sharif eventually filled. The military coup that overthrew the Hashemite Dynasty in Iraq shut down all travel abroad, trapping the rising star. Though he missed that chance to become big in the West, Rifai went on to be a sort of Arab Laurence Olivier. And he is still alive.

Dabdoob finds Rifai, now in his eighties. Old men of the desert seem to have a stamina we lack. Courageously, he agrees to film an ad with us. It is another Tony script titled "Act like a Man!" In it, a young man tells Rifai how he's afraid to vote, and the old man slaps him gently upside the head and delivers the key line.

We fail to consider it's not fear but grievance that threatens Sunni turnout. They're being screwed by the coalition and are about to get it even worse by a Shi'a-led government. Still, it's a powerful ad.

Getting these ads on TV is less simple than it is at home.

Sa'ad Bazazz, Saddam's former propaganda chief, owns Sharkiya, which is the most popular channel among Sunnis. His channel refuses the ad with the kids but accepts "Act like a Man!" Another channel won't accept wire transfers, which the new Patriot Act regulations tie up in knots for weeks. Only cash.

One typically blistering hot day, I step out of the armored Volvo sedan we now have to travel in and walk with purpose toward the office building on Haifa Street. Now we have Blackwater bodyguards, and one carries a duffel bag that held a little over $1 million in cash as four others make a human square around us as we enter the television station's office.

"If anything gets squirrely, don't lose that bag," I tell the one who held it with one hand and a MAC-9 machine pistol with the other.

Behind the general manager's desk sits a bald, young, and spry Lebanese with a cigar clenched between his teeth. In front of him, on the desk, rest two Glocks, which he brushes aside so I can lay down the bag, open it, and start unpacking the loot.

"You're short," he says after a cursory scan.

When I ask him if he'd take a check for the difference, he shoots me a bemused look, shrugs, and says why not. No sooner do I safely return to our compound across town than the Lebanese calls.

"Your check bounced," he says, sounding less amused.

I'm glad I'm no longer in his office. The only real enforcement mechanism you have to make sure your ads actually run is the denial of future business. We have a big enough budget that allows us to buy larger amounts of airtime than I've ever seen on a campaign back home, and even this tough Lebanese guy has incentive to cut us some slack.

We're running nearly a dozen different pieces on national TV all driving the same message: get out and vote. It is a bigger ask than it is in other countries, like Lithuania or the United States, where citizens queue politely in short lines in order to perform a fairly ordinary civic routine. No, by the end of January next year, Iraqis will be risking their lives to vote.

Then there are the talk shows. We are about to produce one of these when a truck bomber hits the residence next to ours.

————————

Almost half the work I do every day happens before we go to the office, which is only a block away. Often I rise when it's still dark, clean up whatever email traffic bubbled up when I was asleep, and start charting out the day. The first call to prayer is a good time to get coffee because none of the drivers or guards will be in the kitchen. Then I take a shower and shave, and I'm running a razor up my neck when it hits.

First it's just a big crack, popping in the bathroom's little window of sandblasted glass. You feel the force in a big wave, fortunately blocked in the main by the concrete walls, which hold. Then there is the tinkling of glass falling everywhere on stone floors. And then Ali, the house servant whom Ron brought with us from the Al Hamra hotel, starts to wail. Ali lives in the wall, or rather a small structure that is attached to it, and absorbs more of the blast than the main house.

But for a towel, I'm naked. Careful in where I place my feet, I look into Patrick's room next door to see if he's okay, but he's not there. Then next door to my own. Water is everywhere. The force of the bomb pushed the contents of the swimming pool through the french doors and across my room. I pick my laptop out of a puddle in the closet and place it on higher ground to dry out while I find my boots, a pair of shorts, and a shirt.

Amazingly, no one—not even Ali—is seriously hurt. After we all check each other out—and wait out a potential second strike, as one would have in a compound attack—we pack our things. The blast changes how we live the next couple of weeks, but not what we do. The president of IRI calls on Ron's phone to say how worried they all were and how much cleaning up we must have to do. I hang up. Lazar and I sweep the kernels of broken glass off the pool table and play one last round before decamping to the media center. The office becomes our new home, where we'll now sleep under our desks.

The aftermath of this bomb changes everything. By this point, our expatriate staff has grown to over a dozen non-Iraqis, but most are sent to Amman until the questions about how this happened can be answered. The one I'm sad to see go is Sarah, a beautiful young Iraqi American whom I've been trying for the sake of my long-distance marriage not to notice.

It also shatters the strange sense of normalcy into which we'd settled. Together with me and the remaining handful of pale skins, a monkey I'd bought as a gift for our office manager, whose father made her return it, also lives in the media center.

We pull off the talk show the next day, filming it in the convention center within the Green Zone. Because I have a badge with escort privileges, one of my duties becomes fetching our guests at the Assassin's Gate checkpoint and walking them to the set. One of these is a nuclear scientist who fled Iraq rather than help Saddam leapfrog the arms race. His name is Hussain al-Shahristani.

As I'm walking Dr. Shahristani past the same sentry whose now seen me come back and forth a number of times, the curious infantryman asks me what on earth I'm up to. "Making a talk show," I tell him, "for the election."

"Election?" he scoffs. "Why don't they just choose their king so we can all go home?"

Dr. Shahristani gives me a sidewise look and cocks an eyebrow.

"I know," I tell him. "I know."

———

Blackwater gives everyone a nickname so they can refer to us over the radio without compromising our identities, or so they say. I am "Yosemite" for reasons that are both obvious and implied. Perhaps I'm thought to have a short fuse. Sarah, who is the toughest on them, is dubbed "Princess." Never underestimate a mercenary's ability to get to the heart of the matter quickly.

If the first Gulf War had gone according to plan, we would have toppled Saddam in 1991 and replaced him with Sarah's dad. This was the endgame of the vision people at the CIA anyway. But it didn't, and Saddam was left in place. Sarah's dad was murdered, and her family became vulnerable.

Saddam's monstrous son Uday caught sight of a sixteen-year-old Sarah playing tennis in her white skirt at the elite Baghdad school she attended. He sent his goons to collect her, but Sarah's coach was brave enough to whisk her off the premises. Sarah's mother managed to ship her out of the country, and she completed high school in San Diego, California.

Her big brown eyes and the beautiful alignment of her face, framed in flaxen hair she'd sometimes wear up in a bun, belie a fierce and indomitable spirit. Unlike the rest of us, there is little of Baghdad that is unknown or frightening to her, so she is the first to tell the newly hired security company what they could do with their instructions. This earns my quiet admiration.

I get the impression my deputy Chris is dating Sarah, which is just one of the reasons I try not to notice her. When she offers to arrange a meeting between me and interim prime minister Ayad Allawi's young Egyptian political advisor, I play coy. While I'm in Kazakhstan for a brief holiday visit with my wife and son, she and Chris spray my bedsheets with her perfume.

They are teasing me, and I try to ignore it. Once the mission is accomplished, my disciplined restraint slips.

The election—Iraqi's first free election in 150 years—happens as planned. Because of the Sunni boycott, turnout is only 58 percent. In new elections in December, when Sunnis do participate, it will surge to nearly three-quarters. These numbers may sound normal to us, but bear in mind the fact that active insurgent groups have threatened to kill anyone who votes. This makes them extraordinary.

While I consider the Sunni boycott a personal defeat, the overall effect of this first election is still intoxicating. There is the famous image of a woman in a black abaya holding up her blue ink–stained finger to show she's voted that captures the moment for the world media. For me, there is just abundant relief. My resignation goes into effect, and now it's all over.

I have no idea what I'm going to do with the rest of my life, or how I'm going to feed my wife and son. But there is this euphoric sense it will all work out.

When I get to Amman, there is a brief reunion with the crew who were evacuated from Baghdad after the bombing. Sarah seems to be glowing. We have a big, celebratory, and boozy dinner at a hangout called the Library, and I go back to my room at the Four Seasons to freshen up and get ready for my flight home that evening. I am as bullish and full of myself as a young American abroad can be.

The elevator reaches the lobby, and there is a short man standing there. I lift my bags to hand to him, and halfway through the gesture realize this is no porter but rather King Abdullah of Jordan, my ultimate host here. Thankfully, I'm able to stop handing him my suitcase just before it's obvious and bow courteously instead. He's going upstairs to see Tony Blair.

By the time I get to the van that is going to take me to the airport, I'm walking on air. Gliding into the van, I see that Sarah is in the front seat. As we drive to the airport under the clear night sky and across a stretch of hills and desert, the windows are cracked slightly to let in the cool breeze.

I can't remember what we are talking about, but it is light and funny and probably flirtatious on both ends. When two people share something as big as we just have, it breeds intimacy. I'm wearing a pair of gold wire-rimmed eyeglasses with a slight Benjamin Franklin effect that I found at an optician's in Moscow. She asks me to take them off. Without thinking twice, I stop playing coy and comply.

Because it is throwing so much light off her face, I have to assume the moon is full. I don't stop to consider that this is one of life's moments. I simply feel it. And we kiss. We kiss until we both realize we are in a Muslim country and in the presence of a driver. After having been joined across seats by the lips, we pull back slightly and just look at one another until we arrive at her gate.

It's been nearly a year of living apart from my family. On my last visit with them, in Kazakhstan, where Aizhan and Max have been living while I've been in Iraq, relations with Aizhan felt strained. Under the circumstances, this might seem par for the course, but it was also difficult in Russia, and in Washington before we left. Before I am even conscious of what I am doing, I am surrendering to what others have told me is inevitable.

During the years in Russia, we did try to make it work. Max was our shared focus, and we acted like the kind of team young couples with a baby become. But our relations were also fraying, even then. The fact that I chose a war zone as my next assignment shows where my head was. Also, there was the question of Aizhan's career. She'd finished college at American University before we left for Russia, and now she wants to go to law school—the same goal I had let fall by the wayside.

Now I am leaving the land of Lawrence of Arabia for an uncertain return home. I've dramatically quit the job I once believed allowed me to live out my destiny, as it blended politics with international affairs. Sure, it may have been constraining at times, but at least it was steady. Our fate as a family depends on my ability to find some paying work quickly, which, in the best-case scenario, does not involve prolonged travel. The gap of a year away from one another will take some time to bridge. That requires a safe harbor.

We rent a house on a street called Tally Ho Lane. The neighborhood is kind of a cross between the *Stepford Wives* and *Leave It to Beaver*. Everyone is driving an SUV, which after Iraq strikes me as crass and unnecessary. In some ways, it seems to me that I have not really quite come home. Rather, it is like a stay of execution.

As my job search results in few promising leads, it is becoming clearer I will probably go back to Iraq in one form or another. And maybe it won't just be Iraq. Sure, I played a role in midwifing democracy there, but meanwhile "color revolutions" are breaking out in places like Georgia, Ukraine, and even Kyrgyzstan.

My value add to a potential employer right now is probably greatest in the field, even if I resist long deployments. I'll take what I can get while keeping an eye out for that steady job behind a desk at home.

But I wonder if I will ever really settle in.

CHAPTER 4
IF YOU DON'T GET IT, YOU DON'T GET IT

Nice wood-paneled walls, I think to myself. The room exudes old-fashioned power. On the coffee table is a book of photos from the Deep South. On the mahogany bar at the end of the room is a bottle of Maker's Mark bourbon, the sight of which causes me to salivate a little, so I quietly clear my mouth.

"Maybe you'd like to have a look from the governor's balcony while you wait?" a strikingly attractive and friendly receptionist asks. Lance shrugs cheerfully, so we follow her to the currently unused office of legendary Republican National Committee chairman and now Mississippi governor Haley Barbour. Sure enough, the balcony offers a commanding view. To the left is Congress atop Capitol Hill, and to the right is the South Lawn of the White House.

While Barbour is running Mississippi—about to be hammered by Hurricane Katrina—his longtime friend and fellow politico Ed Rogers is running the firm.

Barbour, Griffith, and Rogers, or BGR, is the top Republican lobbying shop in town. Tony and Lance know I'm looking for work, so they include me in a pitch to Rogers, who represents the Kurds— or half of them.

The Kurdistan Democratic Party, one of the two major players in the quasi-autonomous region, wants to be dominant.

Ed has that way southern gentlemen do of listening to you with a sphinxlike expression and saying little. After Lance and I finish laying out our capacities, Ed invites me—Lance has a conflict with his daughter's softball schedule—along on a trade delegation he is leading there so I can make the case for our campaign and party-building services. It's only been a couple of months at home, and already Iraq is beckoning again—even if the call is coming from a region that wants very much to break away from Iraq.

Days later, I meet his delegation in Istanbul, much like the beginning of an Agatha Christie story. From there, we fly to Diyarbakir in the east and spend the night in an old castle before waking at dawn to meet our Peshmerga escort who will drive us across the border to Saladin. Like Johnny Cash, Ed is dressed all in black. I'm one of a half dozen possibilities he is presenting to the Barzani family—one of the region's ruling clans—to see which will take root.

Because he is a man of relatively few words, the easiest way to evaluate Ed is by observing how others do. To the Kurdish prime minister, Ed is a man of magical abilities. Nechirvan, whose father was killed in the Kurdish struggle, is a nephew of Masoud, who is the regional president and basically regent. He is tall, good-looking, charming, and every bit the prince.

My pitch enjoys a soft and gentle landing in part because it was Ed who presented me and in part because the Barzanis like the role I played in recent Iraqi elections. When I'm done talking, Nechirvan lights up with a thousand-watt smile.

"We will work with you not just for one or two years," he says prophetically, "but for many, many years."

Over breakfast the next morning, I compliment our hosts on the sweetness of Kurdish honey, which one drizzles into fresh yogurt. By the time I get back to my room in the guesthouse, there is a giant Tupperware vat containing a full honeycomb sitting on my bed. I scratch my head and wonder how I'll ever get it through US customs.

But before that, we have to get through Turkish customs. As we're waiting alongside mile-long backups of fuel trucks carrying crude out and refined products into Iraq, Ed, still glowing from our last meeting, looks at me and says, "Kid, you're a damn rock star. Do you realize that?"

It's one of the nicest things anyone has ever said to me. I try to play cool about it, especially on this arid patch of scorching earth, which a single match could turn into a fireball visible from outer space. But Ed's affirmation of my value burns itself into my memory to be recalled when needed to bolster my fragile sense of self-worth.

To celebrate a successful trip, I lay over in Istanbul on the way home and have a tryst with Sarah, who slips out of Baghdad to see me. Barzani's honey goes to good use as the two of us continue what started in that van in Amman.

The trip to Iraq gets me thinking about unfinished business. Sure, this is "the other Iraq," but it's close enough to the actual one to take me back. Two more elections are coming this year, and while helping the Kurds, whose case for independence is as clear as day, helping secularists and Sunnis more broadly is essential to the country having real balance.

First, at my request this time, Sarah gets me a London audience with Ayad Allawi, the man Paul Bremer made interim prime minister but whose national alliance came in a distant third in the late January election. I fly there on Lance's and Tony's dime to urge him to hire us. Allawi needs to appeal to disaffected army officers and spurned ex-Ba'athists without blood on their hands.

Allawi is a disarming man of medium build who is seemingly young for his age. In 1978 he'd fought off a hit man with an axe Saddam sent to his London apartment to kill him. He listens politely and then asks me if I am Arab, which I interpret as "thanks but no thanks." He makes it clear he's seeing me because of his high regard for Sarah. I leave him with the outline of a plan anyway.

Second, Ed arranges a meeting for me at the White House to make my case for helping parties in Iraq that might maintain balance. The red-haired and fair-skinned Meghan O'Sullivan was an aide to Bremer, who became the president's deputy national security advisor for Iraq. My pitch to her is a little grandiose, but to my mind sensible and necessary. If you can get me $10 million, I will deploy teams to support centrists in the upcoming Iraqi elections.

Like Allawi, she hears me out before telling me, "America doesn't put our thumb on the scales."

We don't? Suddenly, I'm confused: It would seem to the casual observer that invading a country, toppling its government, and declaring what the future constitution and political road map will look like amounts to putting more than one's thumb on the scales. But since Ed made the introduction, I am well mannered.

Maybe I could go to the Gulf and pass a cup around the royal courts there to get my funding, she helpfully suggests.

Yeah, I think, *maybe I could do your job too*.

After a few more trips to Kurdistan, including one to observe

Iraq's second election, I return my focus to finding something I can do back here at home, in Washington, and preferably in government, where I could make policy and fix all those broken things I had witnessed in the field.

One of the hundreds of jobs to which I blindly apply over the internet is as speechwriter to a Republican senator—that's all the solicitation said. I get a callback, and it turns out to be Olympia Snowe, Maine's senior senator. Maybe this is what I need for a fresh start.

———————

Max calls my English basement on Capitol Hill "the rathole." Late one night, when we were returning from a family wedding in New England, he'd caught sight of cat-sized rats feeding off the garbage across the street, behind the Hawk 'n' Dove, a well-known local watering hole. I think he finds it more amusing than frightening.

According to Freud, at age five, a child is able to first see his parents as distinct personalities as opposed to interchangeable units in a support team. That makes me feel a little better about leaving his mother, even if it is self-serving. Now his mother brings him to me on the weekends, and we spend the days at the various museums that border the Mall.

Working for Snowe loops me back into my adopted home state, and she has always intrigued me. A daughter of Sparta—by means of Augusta and Auburn, Maine—Olympia Jean Bouchles was orphaned at age eight. Not long after marrying Peter Snowe, who becomes a Republican state legislator from Auburn, she is widowed when he is killed in a car crash.

Like the iconic Maine senator Margaret Chase Smith before her, Snowe first filled her husband's seat in the state house. In 1978, the same year my family moved to Maine, she went on to win the Second District congressional seat. In 1994 she won the Senate seat vacated by Democrat majority leader George Mitchell. In thirty-five years of elected office, she never lost an election, which is something few in politics can say.

Because she represents the aging state of Maine, because she was orphaned and widowed, and because she is a daughter of Sparta, Snowe is no stranger to death. For me, this means the day begins with the obituary pages, which are all included in the morning press clips. Having run for office so many times in a state with just over a million residents, there is usually a good chance she has met the deceased. So I draft a lot of condolence letters.

Sometimes the letters go through several drafts before she signs them. If I got something wrong, or rather not quite right, she'll call me in to fix it. While it drives me a little crazy, there is something about the respect she shows to the bereaved that is quite touching. Returning from a war in which Americans, including our own Mainers, are still dying, it is a fitting exercise for me. Having spent a year skirting death, I am reminded that while not everyone is lucky we also all die eventually.

Temptations of international work arise periodically, though I know I need to be Washington-based now for Max, especially as the separation solidifies. Yet I still entertain them. While daydreaming in my cubicle one afternoon, I get an unexpected call from Konstantin Kilimnik, my old deputy in Moscow.

Kostya's fortunes have improved considerably since hitching his wagon to Paul Manafort, the Darth Vader–esque Republican fixer who has set up shop in Ukraine. Would I be interested in running a pro-independence referendum campaign in Montenegro? I decline, with some regret.

Lance is a frequent drinking buddy these days, and he connects me with the recent past. We meet at the Monocle, a watering hole halfway between the Senate office buildings and Union Station. Wrapped in deep red wallpaper, interspersed with photos of various distinguished senators who have quaffed their thirst or broken bread there, it has a clubby feel. He's still going back and forth to Iraq, both on a continued contract with the media center and some new business up north for one of the Kurdish parties I helped him land.

We're deep in some whiskey-fueled debate when I feel a tap on my shoulder and turn around. It's Sarah, wrapped in white like a moonbeam. Maybe Lance orchestrated this, or maybe it's just a coincidence, but in an instant all my moping about having to write about the dead and Washington's inability to grasp my brilliance fades to dust in an instant. At first we both play it cool, but soon a magnetic energy between us takes over, and we tune out Lance and whichever former Baghdad colleague she came here with. I follow her upstairs to the ladies' powder room, where we fall into each other's arms.

Her breath is at once sweet and smoky, and her long dirty-blond hair is tied up in a bun atop her head, which I hold with one hand as I kiss her the way I wanted to on that minibus in Amman. We've both been drinking, but it's a long-denied desire that is responsible for our dropping all inhibitions as we begin tearing at bits of each other's clothing. I pick her up and place her on the vanity table, which plays host to our carnal embrace. The world could end right now, and

I would be happy. In fact, there is nowhere on earth I would rather be than inside her.

But our lovemaking comes to a rigid halt when the swinging door behind us bursts open. Like raccoons caught in the act, we both look and see an astonished Elaine Chao, the US secretary of labor. Chao's lips purse into an *O*, and she hurriedly backs out of the powder room.

The sense of utter bliss I'd just experienced is darkened by a passing cloud of guilt. I am a Senate staffer, albeit not a particularly important one. This is a place of work, and that was the minister of work. Sarah and I pull ourselves together, and she glances in the mirror before we slink downstairs. Our escape is not so easy, because seated at a table at the bottom of the stairs are Chao and her husband, Kentucky senator Mitch McConnell. She had just enough time to relay to him the indignity she suffered moments ago, and in unison their heads turn toward us dressed with matching expressions of being utterly mind-blown.

Sarah giggles. I grab my blazer from its hook beneath the bar and tell Lance and the video editor we'd better scram. Either we just offended a very powerful couple, or I'd just demonstrated in dramatic fashion why I don't fit well in staid Washington generally, and specifically the Senate, whose pieties I have failed to observe.

With a nod to Nick, who greets customers at the door, Sarah and I abscond into the sticky Washington night. I still have that vat of honey back in the rathole.

Toward the tail end of Bush's second term, I get my shot to serve the administration. A speechwriting job for an undersecretary of State opens up, and I begin a short stint at Foggy Bottom.

_____

She gives me a withering look, as if I've asked a question that is tiresomely inappropriate from someone of my station. Taken out of context, she's probably right. I'd just asked Secretary of State Condoleezza Rice what she thought of Astana, Kazakhstan, from where she'd just returned. My job is to walk her from one end of the building to another and brief her on the outputs of her advisory commission on democracy promotion—something altogether unrelated to her recent trip during the ten-minute walk.

"Let me put it differently," I say, pleading for a mulligan. "Did you ever see that movie with Jim Carrey called *The Truman Show*?" I ask her, referring to an offbeat 1998 comedy in which the protagonist, an insurance salesman, doesn't realize the world around him is all a giant TV set. "Was it like that?"

She smiles tightly in recognition, and a moment later, once she's taken the comparison in, begins laughing lightheartedly. "Yes," she admits, "exactly!"

I've had a crush on Rice ever since that time on the George W. Bush campaign when I was told I'd get to spend a whole day driving her around Maine, but then the higher-ups decided it made more sense to keep her in Texas to prepare the governor on foreign policy for an upcoming debate. Arguably, that was a better use of her time then.

Back in 2000, it was just before the beginning, and this is the end. We are weeks away from the end of the second Bush administration, and the task at hand is a bit of housekeeping: the final meeting of the secretary's advisory commission on democracy promotion. It is late 2008, and the administration is over. For the sake of formality, anyway, this commission has to be wrapped up.

My boss, Undersecretary Paula Dobriansky, has line responsibility for the commission, and as I'm her senior advisor for democracy promotion, the actual closure is my job, and that's what I briefed Rice on before wandering off on a tangent about Kazakhstan.

There is Lorne Craner, IRI's president, who tried to fire me when I was in Iraq but now acts as if that were all water under the bridge. And so do I.

Then there's Paula's former advisor and now assistant secretary for democracy, rights, and labor, David Kramer. Henrietta Fore, the head of USAID, sits next to Rice and the various other implementers: the National Endowment for Democracy; National Democratic Institute; IFES, with whom I cosponsored that useless event with Putin; and one that has long intrigued me and where my friend Patrick from Baghdad once worked, Freedom House.

Everyone agrees lessons were learned, important progress was made, but much remains to be done. This collegial ceremony is certainly not a victory lap. Indeed, it felt a little more like a wake. People seem tired and a little spent. It's been more than a half century since NSC 68, the 1950 national security memorandum that laid out America's strategy for the Cold War: "As we ourselves demonstrate power, confidence, and a sense of moral and political direction, so those same qualities will be evoked in Western Europe. In such a situation, we may also anticipate a general improvement in the political tone in Latin America, Asia, and Africa and the real beginnings of awakening among the Soviet totalitariat."

Paul Nitze, who wrote that memo, which I later studied at Georgetown, was a friend of my grandparents who appeared as a senior statesman in my childhood and was always kind to me, even telling me that my nominal grandfather Bill Patten was the smartest man on French politics he'd ever met. Nitze also once stumped me when I was in my teens by asking me who my heroes were.

Democracy promotion evolved out of the Cold War effort to "demonstrate . . . a sense of . . . moral and political direction." In the 1980s, Ronald Reagan formalized what had previously been covert efforts to evangelize democracy abroad and created the various entities around the table—except for Freedom House, which Eleanor Roosevelt and Wendell Willkie founded after World War II.

Two costly, faraway wars have grinded everyone down though. Among Americans at large, the enthusiasm for promoting democracy abroad couldn't be lower right now. Six months from now, the new secretary of state, Hillary Clinton, will announce her own strategy based on what she'll call the three Ds: diplomacy, defense, and development. While the unspoken D—democracy—may be implied within development, the word is intentionally absent as a pillar in itself.

Today the deacons of democracy sense what lies around the corner ahead. I've tightly scripted the event because roundtables invite quack-quack, and the secretary's time is limited. She doesn't like bullshit. Everyone plays their part and says their piece before we adjourn, concluding that even if we didn't set the world on fire, at least we left the torch still burning.

Flickering, at least.

In a few weeks, I'll walk Paula out of the building. It's a quiet and quotidian departure as I escort her to the parking garage before going back up to my small, windowless office to collect my few things. I'm tempted to linger, perhaps to go up to the eighth floor, where the diplomatic reception rooms project nineteenth-century grandeur onto the concrete brutalism of the rest of the building and pay a visit to the John Jay room, where my ancestor's portrait hangs.

Or if I could con my way into the line, the wood-paneled stretch that leads to the secretary's office, I could have a peek at Robert Bacon, my mother's grandfather, whose portrait hangs with those of other past secretaries.

But there is no time for sightseeing when one administration is clearing out and the incoming one is measuring the drapes. A friend rescues a large White House photo of George W. Bush about to speak to a crowd in Tbilisi from a trash cart rolling around the appointees' offices and saves it for me. It was an honor and a privilege to serve—I just wish it had been longer.

———————

The revolving door is what Washington lifers go through between ticket punches, like serving in an administration. I suspect even a swamp has its seasons, requiring the occupants to make transitions. As the Bushes leave and the Obamas move in, I transition back to a nonprofit—Freedom House.

My new day job involves pleading for money from USAID, George Soros's Open Society Foundation, and even the office I used to supervise at the State Department. One afternoon I run into a former State colleague on the street, and she asks me, "How does it feel to have to beg the people you used to supervise?"

I tell her I'm learning that is how life sometimes works, and she smiles sympathetically.

But at night, I wear a disguise and become a vandal.

Freedom House, a democracy and human rights watchdog group, hires me to manage their Eurasia programs, which mostly focus on Kazakhstan. My old stomping ground somehow managed to win the revolving chairmanship of the Organization for Security and Cooperation in Europe (OSCE), and in their application process promised to clean up their own act.

For us, this creates a role in monitoring and writing reports about whether the Kazakhs are or aren't complying with their commitments. Bottom line: they continue to clamp down on the media and civil society. IRI just withdrew the office I'd set up there in 2002–2003 in protest over government interference in their work.

Now, to put a fine point on it, they've convicted a well-known human rights lawyer to a four-year prison sentence on a trumped-up manslaughter charge. Yevgeniy Zhovtis may have struck and killed an intoxicated man who wandered onto an unlit highway at night, but he is no killer. He's being taken hostage.

I'd hired Evgeniy to do the Kazakh registration paperwork for IRI's office, so I take his imprisonment personally. I'm chatting with a clever colleague on the eve of a visit to Washington by Kazakh president Nursultan Nazarbayev, and we're complaining to one another about the Central Asian autocrat's nerve in renting light boxes at dozens of DC bus stops with his picture and a statement about how much he agrees with Barack Obama's vision of a nuclear-free world.

In doing so, Nazarbayev seems to be saying our human rights concerns are just silly window dressings beneath his consideration because he plays on a way bigger field. He was telling us to go fuck ourselves.

What if Zhovtis's face were stuck next to Nazarbayev's on each of these display ads around town, with the plea: When will you let this man go free? Paying my own cash, I have fifty such life-size posters printed with adhesive backs. The problem comes in the fact that the light-box campaigns end a day before I get the posters, so now I'm stuck with a $500 personal expenditure on a stunt whose backdrop literally disappeared overnight. How can I accomplish a similar objective?

I identify maybe a dozen strategic placements around town. One is the back of a construction sign that faces the exit to the Twenty-Third Street garage beneath the State Department, from which folks on the sixth and seventh floors leave every day and often get stuck at a light. The White House is tougher because of perimeter security, but I find places to stick them near the offices of other top-level foreign policy influencers. My coup de grace placement is in front of the Kazakh embassy itself.

As with the other guerilla postings, I've assumed there exists some form of CCTV, so I wear a disguise. This consists of a leather paratrooper's cap with deep ridges to absorb any impact when hitting the ground, a stick-on mustache and beard, and goggles. I suppose I look sort of like a modern-day Rasputin—only slightly more deranged. To avoid capture, or the recording of my license plate, I travel by bike. A stop sign on the corner of Sixteenth Street NW and O Street provides the perfect backing, so my sticker with Zhovtis's face will stare straight into the ambassador's office. I do this at dusk and am unnoticed. So proud am I of my work here, I snap a photo.

The next morning at work, when I'm in that post-breakfast daze, I draft a short article about a massive grassroots campaign in the United

States to pressure Kazakhstan to free the human rights lawyer. Then I post it together with the photo on an independent Central Asian news site and wait. After about an hour, I call my friend Rinat, who lives near the embassy, and ask him to walk by and tell me what he sees.

"Your poster is gone," he reports breathlessly, "and there are a few guys in suits standing around the front lawn smoking cigarettes and looking nervous."

It's fun to think about what probably transpired in that hour. Someone in Astana saw the article and flipped out. They likely called their embassy in Washington apoplectic with rage and screamed both for the embarrassment and the fact the embassy staff hadn't noticed it themselves.

Even after all this, I still have about a dozen posters on my hands. As luck would have it, my new boss, for whose hiring I had actively lobbied—former State Department colleague David Kramer—decides I need to go to Astana to observe the OSCE summit meeting that Kazakhs have insisted on hosting the week after Thanksgiving.

Astana in early December is arguably one of the least hospitable places on earth. Sure, Ulan Bator may be a slightly colder capital, but not by much. The diplomats and heads of state have motorcades to whisk them about, but we poor civil society folk have to hoof it between otherworldly structures in eye-watering, face-cracking temperatures. Two things about this trip stand out.

There I get to watch Secretary of State Hillary Clinton field the first question she's had from a journalist on Wikileaks, which had just released a quarter-million confidential US diplomatic cables. The first question she takes in a town-hall–style meeting at Nazarbayev University is from the wife of a Chechen newspaper editor the Kazakhs have jailed for allegedly revealing state secrets. Given Aizhan's father's history there, I'm naturally sympathetic.

But depressingly—and perhaps predictably—Clinton does not commit to raise the journalist's case with the Kazakh president. I sink in my seat. The next question is from a Kazakh government–sponsored "journalist," a striking young woman speaking in near-perfect English: "Madame Secretary, given your own recent experience with unauthorized personnel leaking state secrets, would you not agree Kazakhstan has acted responsibly in the manner that woman just raised?"

This would be a perfect moment for America's top diplomat to stand up for the principles we enshrine at home and promote abroad. *Knock that question out of the park, Madame Secretary. Tell them what a free press is!*

But Clinton disappoints again, with a mealy-mouthed response. It even sounds like she agrees with the fake journalist, though she may, for whatever reason, just be concerned about upsetting her host. I slink further in my seat and wish I were on Mars.

When I get an invite to the summit hall the next day, I make sure the posters are in my briefcase. Surely I can slap a few of these up in bathrooms, at least without being detected. Security is tighter—and more vigilant—than I expected though. The guard on the x-ray machine notices the roll and opens my bag. This is the moment when my colleague from Human Rights Watch, with whom I'd walked over to the summit hall, has the good sense to disappear.

Once they unroll them and get a gist of the message, more and more security men arrive. Finally, a well-spoken young man in a suit tries to level with me. I tell him I'm a political researcher and have discovered these posters in the course of my research. With his thumb, the young secret policeman fiddles with the edge of the stickers and asks me what my intentions are. I mumble something I intend to sound innocuous, and he smiles.

"I count twelve 'posters' here," he points, "and you will leave with twelve 'posters.' Do you understand?" If I didn't, he intimates, he'll create problems for my local office. I'm surprised at how civilized he is about it, but then again this is Kazakhstan and not North Korea.

Before flying home, I give the posters to a friend and don't know where they ultimately made it, but at least they are in the motherland. Fourteen months later, the Kazakhs will grant Zhovtis amnesty, shaving eighteen months off his sentence.

———————

The orange bike parked outside DC's swankier restaurants is a signal that Rinat Akhmetshin has already arrived. Whether he's wearing a tailored European suit or a T-shirt, shorts, and purple velvet loafers, the Russian-born guerrilla lobbyist doesn't try very hard to blend into the bland and imagination-free style of the ordinary swamp dweller. Aside from the fact he is hustling for his client like anyone else in his trade, there is little that is ordinary about Rinat, a Tatar by origin.

Steve LeVine, a *Wall Street Journal* reporter and close friend since my Kazakhstan days, introduced me to Rinat, one of his sources when I told him of my interest in helping the Kazakhstani opposition, and we became fast friends. At the time, Rinat was leading a crusade against the Central Asian regime in Washington on behalf of a former Kazakh prime minister whom I had grown to respect. He did an amazing job, perhaps best measured by the tens of millions of dollars the Kazakh government spent hiring lobbyists and publicists to counter him.

I think the former Kazakh prime minister, who I watched save the life of my old boss's son, asked him to be nice to me.

When I get to the table, a bottle of rosé champagne is being delivered. "It's too hot out there," he explains when my look begs the question: Isn't it still early? After all, it's not even noon. Not one to play holier-than-thou, I don't protest. Rinat's abundant thirst makes for entertaining lunches, financed by his generous expense account.

More often than not, Rinat's projects—real and conceived alike—are far out. Right now, he is squiring General Victor Ivanov, head of Russia's counternarcotics agency, around Washington in the hope of partnering with the Americans to wipe out Afghanistan's heroin exports. It was during the Soviet occupation of that graveyard of empires where Rinat met the man who went on to serve in Leningrad's and later Saint Petersburg's KGB directorate at the same time Vladimir Putin was deputy mayor there. I went to listen to Ivanov's pitch at the Carnegie Endowment because they have good coffee and pastries, and it was an excuse to get out of the office.

Ivanov is not particularly animated, and the event was basically a bore. The only time he cracked a smile was when he referred to Hillary Clinton's "Reset" policy with Russia, which some rocket scientist at the State Department mistranslated as "Overload." That was actually kind of funny.

"The burrata was flown in from Italy this morning. You should really try it," Rinat counsels. He takes a call while I enjoy Fiola's menu. It is probably the best Italian food in town, and certainly the most expensive.

Almost every time we meet for lunch, Rinat has a plan he wants to run by me, and unlike Ivanov's speech, it is rarely boring. He is eager to break into the Ukrainian market and has a plan to pitch the oligarchs there on a country-branding scheme he calls "bitches in Bentleys."

Basically, his plan involves hiring a bunch of eye-catching Ukrainian women to drive around Washington in luxury cars, selling the notion that Ukraine is independent, rich, and won't take shit from anyone. I express skepticism about the message and whether or not the project would just highlight rampant corruption in the former Soviet state. He shrugs. In addition to being a friend, I think he considers me a sounding board.

I counter with another idea: How about hiring a few dozen midgets to dress in traditional Kazakh garb and follow Nazarbayev around during his next visit to Washington to protest his autocratic regime and accuse him of forgetting about the little people? This intrigues Rinat, until I make a call to an agency in Los Angeles that specializes in Lilliputian actors and give him a rough quote.

"Too much," he scoffs.

It fascinates me to see an outsider like Rinat first diagnose—he holds a doctorate in biochemistry, and I sometimes address him by the honorific "Doctor"—and then play our system like an instrument. He has deep contacts in mainstream media outlets and is on friendly terms with a range of well-known political figures. It is more or less what I would like to do in other countries, and listening to his war stories gives me new insights into how my own works.

Lobbying is not rocket science—or biochemistry, for that matter. But Rinat's description of how to make a congressional hearing matter—which witnesses are real and which are there for effect, the role of a book or a magazine article or an op-ed in a broader campaign, what motivates staffers and journalists alike, and how to tell what shadowy role unseen forces play on just about anything Washington does— is a kind of master class.

Most professional lobbyists I know try to cast an aura of mysticism around their work, while Rinat is candid about the brass tacks. Also, he has hired enough of the nameplate firms to discern the few who deliver and the many who don't.

"In my world, it pays to be honorable," he tells me. "If I fail to accomplish the job for someone, I will give them their money back."

Of course, like most people in his trade, Rinat isn't here for the ideology. Mother Teresa needs neither a lobbyist nor a publicist, and some of his clients have plenty of sketchiness to go around. General Ivanov, for instance, is no saint. Rinat has probably dealt with folks who, if he failed to deliver and didn't give them their money back, might resort to unpleasant means. But at the same time, there is an authenticity to him that is refreshing.

"Never forsake prison or poverty," he tells me in a philosophical moment, elaborating that this is the most important Russian proverb. I commit it to memory.

Every now and then, at the end of these lunches, comes the "ask," which could be either a favor or a proposed collaboration. Today he asks me to draft a letter of recommendation for his daughter, who is applying to kindergarten. It's the sort of thing I'm happy to do because I'm fond of the girl. "Sure," I tell him, "but I don't I have much swing at any of the high-end private schools to which she's applying."

"That's okay," he said. "Just write the draft, please. Someone very important is going to sign it, so make it good."

It's been six years since I first visited BGR's conference room. I had some unfinished business promoting democracy to do before coming back here. The air in the halls of Freedom House is getting stale, and I need a mission that is tangible rather than conceptual. I need to put my thumb on the scales.

Now I'm sitting across the table from a Georgian named Irakli Alasania, who had been his country's ambassador to the UN during the Russian invasion three years ago. David Kramer recently told me he'd be the best next president Georgia could hope for—so surely he'll understand my leaving "da Haus" to go work for him.

Ed has set up a European office, headed by an Italian Croat named Ivo Gabara, who's reeled in Alasania this far. Always impeccably dressed and speaking in an elegant but clipped English, Ivo makes the life of an international man of mystery more appealing even than it is on its own merits.

Because I've done a parliamentary campaign in Georgia—for President Mikheil Saakashvili's party just before the war—Ivo and Ed think I can seal this deal. They're right. Whether through that 2008 campaign, the war while I was at State, or our focus on the country as a pretty positive example in a tough neighborhood while at Freedom House, Georgia has been on my mind for several years now.

This is a choice, though, in the clearest sense of the word. Going back to Georgia on a different side than the one on which I last waged a campaign there makes me a mercenary, albeit a political one. Leaving my perch at Freedom House to dive back into foreign politics as a combatant rather than an observer means I have to shed neutrality. I've played with this line before, but now I'm crossing it.

Ever since Iraq, I have tried to "go legit" and settle down. But between the speechwriting job for Olympia Snowe, a seven-month stint at the State Department, and a stab at think-tank life at Freedom House, I keep letting myself get pulled into intrigues beyond our shores: Kurdistan, Kazakhstan, Ukraine, and now Georgia.

I don't want to be the guy talking about faraway problems on a panel discussion somewhere or in a media sound bite. No, I want to be a man in the thick of it. Even if it's not for the government or some lofty ideals, like spreading human freedom, I can still do good by being a paid advisor if, that is, I get the right clients. I think back to an informational interview I had with Kissinger-McLarty Associates when I was so eager to get to Washington: "What we do," their managing director told me, "is private-sector diplomacy." That sounded pretty cool.

Such a profession involves working directly with those who end up moving the arrow on history's dial, not just "being in the room" when a decision is made by top-level bureaucrats. If clients are willing to pay me for my advice, that's a win-win. One thing I learned from the nonprofit world is that people tend to heed your counsel more when they have to reach into their pockets for it.

This is how, through a half dozen years of trial and error and feeling like a stranger in the city of my birth, I become a mercenary, or a gun for hire.

PART
TWO

CHAPTER 5
THE COUNT OF MONTE CRISTO

SHIDA KARTLI REGION, AUGUST 2011

We stop by a nondescript little ravine beneath a green hillock. Irakli tells me to take off my hat as I join the small crew of army veterans showing respect to the fallen heroes of Shindisi. There is little here but the remains of a small nearby stone church and a waist-high concrete wall to mark the spot. All of this and the helmets Tazo just brought.

Three years ago today, a detachment of just over twenty Georgian infantrymen held off a Russian tank brigade here for over an hour, Irakli recounts. Seventeen men were killed, and four survived. Amazingly, both sides in this David-versus-Goliath encounter suffered proportionally equivalent losses. But ultimately, the Russians, with their greater numbers and armor, prevailed. We cluster in a semicircle around a makeshift memorial of helmets and observe a moment of silence.

Tazo, one of our party representatives in the Shida Kartli region, is a giant of a man and stands at nearly seven feet tall. He knew some of the defenders. At the time of the invasion, Irakli was Georgia's ambassador to the UN. From New York, he played a key role in rallying international support to the aid of his homeland and abbreviating the length of the war to just over two weeks.

I breathe deeply and take in our surroundings.

It seems strange that the current Georgian government has done nothing to commemorate the fallen at this spot. It is hardly fitting there is no memorial for the heroism and sacrifice that this place hosted not so long ago.

From here, we drive into Gori—birthplace of Josef Jughashvili, a.k.a. Stalin. "Look at that," Irakli says, pointing at a series of buildings in the style of Red Roof Inns. "Those are military barracks, right here, next to the road," he explains in dismay. "Saakashvili's guy did that," he scoffs. "They were supposed to be so smart, but would you look at that. From here on the road, you can fire mortar rounds right into the barracks. What a genius!"

In Gori's downtown, we park outside a shabby-looking five-story government building, and a skinny man in fraying but well-kept clothes meets us at the door and leads us up into a dank stairwell.

On the third floor, we walk into a cavernous dark room, where bedsheets hang from lines strung between the walls to demarcate makeshift spaces where families are living. A little boy is kicking a soccer ball against one of the brick walls when we enter, but his mother tells him to stop. He looks at us with guarded curiosity.

These are just some of the tens of thousands of Georgians still displaced by the latest war. And these new internally displaced people join the ranks of the more than a quarter million still uprooted from Abkhazia and South Ossetia following the war of 1992–1993. They don't vote in any real bloc, so they are invisible—to the folks in charge today anyhow.

Nearly one thousand IDPs used to squat in the eighteen-story Iveria Hotel in the geographic center of Tbilisi, but they've been cleared out so the virtual skyscraper could be transformed into a Radisson Blu hotel, with an indoor swimming pool and "oxygen" bar on the roof, allowing the well-heeled a lofty hangout.

"Misha [President Mikheil Saakashvili, whose party we are trying to defeat] never cared about the IDPs because he considered them to be his predecessors' problem, not his," Irakli laments. "But this new wave—well, they are here because of a problem of his own making."

To Irakli, both wars are personal. In late September 1993, his father, a general, sent his sixteen-year-old son to lead a contingent of civilians fleeing the Abkhaz capital of Sokhumi and stayed behind to fight, which he did until the end, when he was one of the last two men standing. The episode has been likened to the Alamo. The elder Alasania was martyred there and died a national hero.

The more recent war was preventable, Irakli believes, as does the cadre of ex-ambassadors who make up the leadership ranks of his party. Before his UN post, Irakli had been Georgia's special envoy to peace talks with the breakaway Abkhazians—responsible with their Russian sponsors for his father's death.

When I ask why no progress has been made on this front, he tells me that he had all breakaway Abkhaz leaders at the table, ready to make a deal, and President Saakashvili didn't just refuse to see them. He went on TV while they were sitting in the restaurant waiting for them and blasted them on camera, and in the process scuttled any diplomatic solution.

I am beginning to see more clearly that Misha, whom I used to consider charmingly rakish, is actually a human wrecking ball.

Sometime later we take another trip with foreign journalists to a village near Akhalgori, north, beyond the demarcation line. I'd been squiring them around Chorvila, birthplace of Georgian billionaire Bidzina Ivanishvili that morning. Irakli and I figure they could use a little contrast to better understand the reality of Georgia right now. We're in two vehicles, and he's in the front with a couple of his veteran friends, who help us talk our way past the only checkpoint we encounter.

In the first village, a large man—taller even than Tazo—who vaguely resembles Jaws in *Moonraker* approaches our SUV and starts pounding on the hood with both meaty arms. Irakli smiles and tells me not to worry. "That's good," he says. "It means he likes us and is excited we've come!"

No one here has had cooking or heating gas in over a year, and those who have gathered in the mud-rutted main street have come out to see who we are and if we bring news of anything changing anytime soon. Here is both the best and the worst part of being a politician. When you experience the lives of others, if only for a moment, a sense of connection is born. But then comes a letdown as soon as you consider what little good you can really do for them—in that moment anyhow.

An older couple shows us the wall-sized hole a mortar left in their living room. A collapsed bed in the middle of the room has begun to rust, since the elements had been blowing in and out of here for a few years, and it, like the peeling wallpaper, reminds us that this aging husband and wife once slept peacefully here. Through the hole, in the distance, we can see the apple trees that this family can no longer harvest, because the field in between is mined.

"You still think your friend Misha did anything useful in this country?" Irakli snarls in a rare flash of anger from a normally agreeable man.

"Take my SUV," Irakli tells me with a wink, reminding me that I need to make a good impression. His sidekick Buka—no fan of mine—gives a rare, approving up-and-down look. I look like a billionaire's PR flak, Buka says with a smile. Maybe he's hoping that Ivanishvili, whom they're sending me to woo, will just keep me, and I'll be out of his hair forever. Buka likes to be the wise one and doesn't like competition.

We're now climbing a hill that overlooks Tbilisi, approaching the glass-and-steel palace built into the summit. This is where Bidzina Ivanishvili, Georgia's richest man, lives in what until now has been total mystery. Whoever serves him here says nothing about what happens behind the gates, as if bound by some kind of omertà.

Georgian President Mikheil "Misha" Saakashvili has jokingly—and perhaps with some implicit guilt—called Ivanishvili "the Count of Monte Cristo." Common Georgians know the inhabitant of this palace only through his many acts of charity, but few have seen his face. He made his billions, the story goes, in Russia back in the wild 1990s. This makes him politically incorrect to Saakashvili's world, even as Misha is happy to cut the ribbon on projects Ivanishvili has financed.

Right now, I am the Georgian Free Democrats' human offering to the count. *Well, I'd better not disappoint them*, I think as I look up toward my destination.

Designed by Japanese futuristic architect Shin Takamatsu, Ivanishvili's $50 million palace has been a source of speculation because
it contrasts so sharply with the fourth-century Narikala fortress on
a neighboring hilltop—and just about everything else in this ancient
city. It's the sort of place where you'd imagine finding a villain from
a James Bond movie.

State security officers sit in a nondescript sedan with tinted
windows, watching the comings and goings from this modern fortress and taking notes. Now the gate is opening. This time, private
security men in black suits scan the Toyota Landcruiser's undercar-
riage before waving my translator and me through.

We drive up to a plaza and park beneath a copy of Robert Indiana's
Love sculpture, perched on the cliff facing the giant steel cylinder
that is the entrance to the main building. Indiana rents my mother's
sail loft building in Vinalhaven, Maine, as his studio, so this seems
like a token from home.

Sliding doors magically open, and Irakli Garibashvili, the count's
personal assistant, greets us with practiced politeness.

"I was just a clerk in his bank when he selected me to work up
here," Garibashvili tells me with a mixture of modesty and amazement at his own rise. "He is always watching, and he rewards good,
loyal people," he adds as though he's offering a tip that may prove
useful at some later date.

One week ago, the famously reticent Ivanishvili released an open
letter condemning what he called the increasing authoritarianism of
Saakashvili's government. It landed like a boulder in a farm pond. Until
recently, Misha had been the golden child of the West, who never
missed an opportunity to herald his own victories over corruption and

modern reforms to the former Soviet state. Ivanishvili's claim that there was no business in Georgia that was free of government pressure and interference powerfully countered the Misha narrative.

Until now, the Free Democrats were just one of a handful of small opposition parties in Georgia fighting an uphill battle. In his letter, Ivanishvili stated his intent to unify and fund the opposition under a common umbrella and to defeat Misha's party at elections one year from now. Apparently, he agreed with what we've been saying and wrote that he had "no questions" about our leader, Irakli.

It was Alasania who hired me away from Freedom House, with David Kramer's blessing. Now we were in effect being purchased. A former diplomat, Alasania knew the value of effective communication. He resigned in protest from Misha's government but failed to win the Tbilisi mayor's seat a year before. To him, bringing me on would be a force multiplier because I had also worked for Misha during elections in 2008 and helped his government win a supermajority in parliament.

That is why he is dangling me in front of Ivanishvili now. But I have to wait my turn.

Assembled in the conference room and sitting areas of this virtual chancery are the flotsam and jetsam of Georgian politics pre-Misha. There is Tedo Japaridze, who was Eduard Shevardnadze's longtime foreign policy advisor, probably the most sympathetic of the crew. Shevardnadze was the last foreign minister of the Soviet Union and the second president of Georgia. Tedo understands politics in the Kissinger sense and practices the courtesy of high stakes versus the viciousness of low ones. The same cannot be said for the rest.

One round-faced woman reminds me that my client, Irakli, once called her sons thugs—he was probably correct—and she wants me to tell him she hasn't forgotten. The one thing everyone in the room has in common is a quest for vengeance against Saakashvili, who tossed them all out of power when he took over. "Misha's a tyrant," they all grumble. Having been a onetime political advisor to the man they are united in their desire to remove, I feel a little outgunned.

Were Misha an actual dictator, I think to myself, *all these people would be either dead or in prison*. But instead, here they are—living ghosts of the power structure he overthrew—in the same rooms where paintings by Mark Rothko sit propped up against the walls, waiting to be hung.

Some are helping themselves to the array of fine whiskeys and French wines sitting on a table in front of a commanding view of the city below, but I remember what Garabashvili just told me about how the master is always watching and abstain. Besides, Georgia is a country known for having some of the world's oldest vineyards, and the very idea of French wine seems somehow treasonous.

In the sixteenth century, politician and military commander Giorgi Saakadze forged an uneasy truce with the Persian potentate Shah Abbas in order to counter the Ottoman and Russian forces who, like the Persians, were tearing his homeland into pieces. Then Saakadze double-crossed Shah Abbas to make a power play for Georgian sovereignty, becoming a national hero in the process.

Saakadze paid a heavy price though. Having been forced to leave his son Paata in Tehran as a hostage, he soon received Paata's head in a box. Stalin also named his son Paata, and when he was captured during World War II, Stalin refused a trade the Germans proposed for one of their generals. "What? Trade a general for a captain?" Stalin is reported to have said of the deal.

By taking the job for Alasania, and now Ivanishvili, I betrayed Misha. What cost will I now be forced to pay for my treachery?

TBILISI, FEBRUARY 2008

George W. Bush flew to Tbilisi in the late spring of 2005 and gave a speech on Independence Square in which he called the tiny country "a beacon of liberty." He was the first American president to ever visit Georgia and might have been the last, had the grenade a crazed Armenian threw onto the stage from which Bush spoke not been a dud.

Eighteen months earlier, Georgians took to the streets to protest ballot rigging by the Shevardnadze government in what came to be known as the Rose Revolution, and the first of the color revolutions that so rattled Russian president Vladimir Putin. Then Saakashvili was one of a triumvirate of opposition leaders who came to power in its wake. He famously stormed parliament with red roses in hand and became the charismatic face of the new, young order.

Then he nudged his corevolutionists aside. Prime Minister Zurab Zhvania died in a gas leak in his apartment, and Nino Burjanadze was pushed into opposition.

Two years after Bush's visit, the bloom had begun to fade from the rose. Now facing protests of his own, President Saakashvili authorized the use of force against demonstrators, which led to mass beatings and a worried pause among his admirers in the West. Friends of Misha urged him to refresh his mandate through new elections, and he hired one of the top US polling firms for Democrats, Greenberg Quinlan Rosner (GQR), to help steer him through these.

Conscious that this Georgian client and his political set were center-right in their orientation, GQR hired me as their man on the ground. I was, they told me, the first Republican they'd ever hired.

It was also my first venture on my own as a political consultant, and I became quickly wrapped up in the febrile environment of the Caucasus, and Misha world in particular.

Smart, energetic, and bent on reform, this crew seemed like the perfect foil to Russia. For instance, the Saakashvili government fired all the old policemen who would routinely shake citizens down for bribes and built new glass buildings for state services that were—literally—transparent. A Russian girlfriend came to visit me from Moscow, which was brave of her, given the mounting tensions.

"Is it true," she asked with widening eyes, "that the police here no longer take bribes?"

Though I was able to sustain her amazement by answering yes, the reality was not quite so simple.

Before the recent protests, Misha seized Imedi-TV and put his former chief of staff and mini-me, George Arveladze, in charge of it. George and I became fast friends. Somehow the fact that the state took over an independent broadcaster became something I was willing to overlook because these were the good guys and modern-izers forging a bold new chapter in the history books.

The first chill trickled up my spine during a bus tour fashioned on John McCain's "Straight Talk Express." We were riding the country-side with the five top names on the parliamentary ticket, our dream team, and assorted Georgian journalists. One of these, a young woman, came and sat with me. After a few minutes of happy banter, she leaned in and said to me, "I'm scared."

Someone must have overheard her, because at the next stop she disappeared. When I asked the logistics guy what happened to her, he looked down and said she had decided to ride the press bus instead.

Then there was the convention. I wrote every minister's speech and choreographed the whole thing to be a pageant of positive energy and progress. Every speaker stayed on script, except one: Misha. Pumped by the look and feel of the event, Misha literally skipped onto the stage, slapping each of his ministers on the back of the head in the process. When he got to the podium, he reached inside his suit coat for his speech and said that his advisors had written him a very nice address before tossing it over his shoulder and declaring he'd speak from the heart instead.

The president went on and on and on. The whole sports arena went totally silent as he thundered away. George had been roughly translating for me throughout the first bit of Misha's improvisation, but after a while stopped. When I turned to ask what the president was saying now, I saw his face was in his hands. I nudged him insistently and repeated my question.

"You know what this means?" he asked ominously. "We're fucking going to war."

This was mid-April 2008. At a NATO summit in Bucharest, Romania, two weeks earlier, the transatlantic powers gave Georgia and Ukraine the bad news that neither country would be granted a membership action plan to the transatlantic security alliance, which Georgia in particular had deeply coveted. Having been a golden child of the West, Misha took the news especially hard.

I telephoned the top man for the project at GQR in Washington, who had worked on Bill Clinton's National Security Council and had a pretty good concept of the larger stakes. He in turn made a speedy visit to Tbilisi, and we did a round of talks with the key figures in the Georgian government.

The national security advisor at the time was an amiable fellow who had come from academia and had run programs for George Soros's Open Society Institute in Georgia before being tapped for Misha's government. He told us they had twenty thousand special-forces troops in position, ready to sweep Abkhazia's Kodori gorge and take it back from the puppet government Russia had installed in the breakaway region.

"Then what?" Jeremy Rosner, the senior GQR man, asked. "Let's say you do in fact seize the gorge, and the next day Russia resupplies by sea to take it back. What are you going to do then?"

The national security advisor looked befuddled. Clearly, no one had thought this through. That evening we shared our concerns with the president, who was slouched in a chair in his darkened office. Misha listened to us with an irritated expression and said he understood. Then he said he had a slew of other meetings and thanked us for our time. We were basically swimming outside our lane—this sort of thing is beyond the scope of advice political consultants are expected to give.

For the next month, until the election, there was no more talk of war.

While I was in Georgia on this 2008 assignment, I was waiting for my paperwork to clear for a speechwriting and advisory job at the State Department. White House personnel told me they were getting pushback from the security clearance team on me—after all, I'd lived in such strange cities as Almaty, Moscow, Baghdad, and now here. I responded with a rhetorical question that implied a challenge: "Are you guys serious about democracy or not?"

It worked. White House personnel pushed back, in turn, on the famously risk-averse security guys, and I was granted a provisional clearance that enabled me to start my new job.

I was safely ensconced on the seventh floor of the State Department on August 8 when Russia launched a full-scale invasion of Georgia. I had just bought a town house on Capitol Hill and was driving back from a Restoration Hardware outlet in Northern Virginia when I heard the news over the radio.

While the Russian-backed government of South Ossetia was responsible for the pretext of hostilities by firing rockets into Georgian villages, the Georgians marched right into the trap by seizing the South Ossetian capital of Tskhinvali on the seventh. Russia's military responded with massive force, quickly overwhelming Georgian defenders. Acts of courage by Georgians were no match for the world's third-largest army, which poured out of the Roki Tunnel and rolled across northern Georgia with tank divisions flying the red Soviet flag.

I called my friends in Georgia to make sure they were okay and to see how they were holding up in the face of this nightmare scenario. Oddly, George sounded elated.

"We're going to win *your* election for you!" he chirped with an enthusiasm that belied the devastation his country was then suffering.

What he meant was the US presidential campaign, through-out which John McCain had been trailing Barack Obama. Old man

McCain had a soft spot for Misha, who played him like a violin.

When Russia invaded Georgia that second week of August, McCain's polling numbers came within striking distance of Obama's for the first—and only—time. Faced with the prospect of a resurgent Russia, against whom we might have to fight, the qualities of the crusty old warrior suddenly seemed preferable to those of the well-spoken but inexperienced and soft young law professor.

The only winner of the conflict was US senator Joe Biden, whom Obama—in a rare moment of panic—then selected as his running mate as a foil to criticism that he himself lacked the necessary foreign policy experience to be commander in chief.

After the five-day war, Georgia had lost a fifth of its territory. International powers brokered a cease-fire, and US secretary of state Condoleezza Rice flew to Tbilisi for the announcement. According to her memoir, she sat Misha down before the joint press appearance and told him to restrain himself in his remarks. But he didn't keep to the agreement. Instead, he laid into the Russians as if Rice's presence inoculated him and suggested he had the Americans on his side. Recalling that episode, Rice wrote that she had never before been so furious in her life.

I visited Tbilisi in 2010 with Freedom House to attend a conference and found the country still tired and demoralized. Gone was the energy and enthusiasm I'd once admired, and absent was the sense I once felt the country was charging forward to seize its destiny. People looked and sounded like they just wanted some rest and relief. This was what the war had reaped.

IMERETI REGION, SEPTEMBER 2011

It's an ugly stub of a thing, this ear of corn. Some kernels are bigger than my thumbnail and an anemic white in color, while others are small, shriveled, and brown. The field is filled with such abominations, this Imereti farmer tells me with desperation. His crop this year is essentially a bust.

"It's a good thing I didn't tell him you're an American." Dato smiles. A onetime youthful minister of finance under Shevardnadze, Dato went to Tennessee to teach economics after being blacklisted by the Saakashvili government. He and I drove out here at breakneck speed when a local informed us about the failing crop so we could see for ourselves. Historically, agriculture has been a cornerstone of Georgia's economy, but in recent years it has withered, in part due to the government's disinterest and neglect.

It is not just the current government to blame for this corn, however. Sprouted from genetically modified seeds produced by a US-based agricultural giant, my homeland is the origin of this alien strain. Maybe it wasn't planted or fertilized properly. Who knows. But even if so, this doesn't mitigate the disaster this farmer and many others like him face as the harvest season approaches.

What we have here is a case of mutant American corn.

I've been living with these guys for five months now, and they've nicknamed me Sam Saburtalinski, a gangland-sounding sobriquet that for all practical purposes makes me theirs. Maybe that makes it easier for me to take off my patriotic blinders. Heck, most Americans agree that not everything we produce or export is good. Take Hollywood, for instance. But this GMO corn is actually doing harm.

On the ride back to Tbilisi, I'm already scripting. We'll hold a press conference outside the ministry of agriculture and demand that heads roll. I fire off a statement, and we manage to attract some media attention. Georgians love to talk, and informal news sometimes travels faster than anything in broadcast or print, so it is here that I break down and join Facebook.

My post about mutant American corn draws the ire of US ambassador John Bass, who comments on my page that I am being an irresponsible fearmonger. Of course he has to say that, but it still stings. Here's the good news though: American diplomats don't vote in the country of Georgia's election.

The underlying message is more powerful than Dato or I originally imagined: Misha and his crew are more invested in sucking up to foreigners than they are in improving the lives of ordinary Georgians. When it comes to such medieval, retrograde pursuits as farming, they just don't care. We push and we push, and finally the government caves and fires the agriculture minister. It's our first win, and the first sign that this government is not invulnerable. In parallel, Ivanishvili pledges $1 billion to strengthening the country's agriculture sector.

Now I'm spending more and more time in the Count of Monte Cristo's mountaintop lair. His communications team needs help, and he is about to launch a political party, the Georgian Dream. Yet we are encountering the same kind of resistance that an opposition party in Russia faces. Venues are afraid to rent us space for the founding convention, television stations are pressured not to carry our material, and the government is even raiding the armored cars bringing cash to and from Cartu Bank, which Ivanishvili owns.

While accompanying one of our candidates canvassing in one of Tbilisi's exurbs, where there is a large prison, I snap a photo of the Gldani penitentiary and post it on Facebook. Almost immediately, one of the government's own lobbyists in Washington, DC, who I happen to know from the Bush campaign, writes me to ask if I'm okay. Misha's own handlers don't trust his impetuousness or lack of restraint.

So much for the "beacon of liberty."

Pressure is also building within the fortress. Each of the small political parties that have been subsumed into the Georgian Dream is fighting with the others to have the benefactor's ear. One of the leaders of the Georgian Republican Party approaches me one day with a hand-drawn cartoon of the letters *BGR* cloaked in the gowns of the Ku Klux Klan—a dig at the southern origins of the firm under whose aegis I am here. "Is it wise," she asks me, "to maintain an association with such a company when America has a Black president?"

It's a dirty trick, meant to highlight the fact that BGR's founders are white Southerners. I wonder if she invented this herself, or if one of BGR's rivals in Washington did. Given the size of Ivanishvili's checkbook, I assume the latter.

With the same focus on detail I'd devoted to Misha's party convention three years prior, I work with Ivanishvili's team to script out the Georgian Dream's launch. As the only one of the crew who has designed a convention of this scale, I work late into the evening with the others diagramming the event, ensuring that each part helped to drive the same message, and explaining to the team why it should be this way. When I return in the morning, no one on the team would look me in the eye—somehow the plan had totally changed in the wee hours of the morning.

The first draft of Ivanishvili's speech I read is a complete disaster. It's a laundry list of complaints, most of which seem whiny and petty coming from a man primed to be the country's savior. Obviously, it's been penned by the bitter old men from the previous government, Eduard Shevardnadze's, who've had years to nurture their grievances. Wanting to break with this, I write an alternative version that is aspirational, weaves together national pride and respect for the human spirit, and sets an agenda for the future.

They end up giving my speech to a national soccer star they'd recruited, and the one Bidzina delivers is essentially the original draft—a long rant. With these guys, it seems always to be one step forward and two steps back.

After the convention, I am pouting in one of the sun-drenched corridors of the castle in the sky, and the count himself appears. He looks at me like a wolf and asks me what I thought of his speech, and I shrug, careful not to say what I really think but also not wanting to give false praise.

"Yes," he says in English, "it could have been better." Then he walks away.

———————

Bidzina may not have stuck to the script—perhaps that is the billionaire's conceit. But Irakli does, and when he does, it is as if the skies have opened and the angels sing.

I wrote it in a thicket in Kakheti. We were boar hunting there, which requires a lot of crouching in the brush and waiting for a hairy wild pig to come crashing in your direction. The gamekeeper gave me a single-barreled shotgun with a grin and said if I miss, I'd just have to reload really fast.

Meanwhile, Irakli is prowling somewhere nearby. Unlike me, he has a 7.57mm carbine with a clip. *Should I miss, maybe he'll back me up*, I think hopefully. At one point, I think I've got a boar coming my way. There is snorting and the crackling of brambles as it crashes through, both noises getting louder.

Until I see it's a hound dog. Later I will learn the dog had once been snared by a boar's tusk. Could that have made it snort forever thereafter?

The only other sounds are my thumbs hunting and pecking on the BlackBerry keypad as I hammer out Irakli's speech for the chamber of commerce tomorrow. Misha has become as tough on small- and medium-sized businesses as the previous regime was, he will explain. The Georgian government might take out full-page adverts in the *Economist* about how tough they are on corruption, but we know a different reality. Soon after he announced his plunge into politics, cash trucks belonging to Bidzina's bank started getting seized by the Ministry of Interior. What kind of message does that send to the private sector? One at odds with the image Misha and his crew have been carefully projecting.

In the long stretches of silence there on a frosty, late November day, I keep thinking of things to weave into Irakli's speech. It is becoming the barn burner that Ivanishvili's was not, embroidered with the bits and pieces I'd witnessed over the preceding six months. It grows devastating because it lays out the case against the government for stifling the market economy and using its heavy hand to reward its friends and stymy its opponents.

When Irakli delivers the speech, nearly verbatim, the next day, it is to an audience at least half of which is made up of foreign investors. Before he even finishes, the room erupts into a longer and louder applause than I've heard yet on the stump. The group's chairman closes out the meeting by saying, "I think we have all just heard history in the making."

In moments like this, I am not just an American advisor. Instead, I am one of them. I am Sam Saburtalinski, and I live in a modest apartment down a dusty street from the party headquarters and spend almost all my time with my clients. I'm proud of my guys, who have yet to be fully absorbed into Bidzina's world. All our hard work might just pay off.

———————

"Big Ears wants to see you," a common friend tells me.

Out of respect to our mutual friend, I agree.

A young Mormon woman with ears that stick out like Mr. Potato Head's and no discernable sense of humor, Big Ears is "attached" to the embassy, but is in fact CIA. Because I am the only American going in and out of the mountaintop fortress, Big Ears sees her chance to write a cable that will get her noticed in Langley.

"We're going up, and Misha's going down," I tell her as she stares at me over tea in a Tbilisi café. To fill the silence that follows, I elaborate with my why: There is more repression and fear going on in this country than any of us realized before. What little attention we do pay to the Georgian government amounts to pity for its having lost the war with Russia. After pumping $4 billion in aid into the tiny country of four million people, America feels we've cleansed our conscience. But all we've really done is temporarily prop up Misha. He's not just an excitable boy; he's an actual menace, and his tactics are becoming more and more authoritarian.

Now the young woman with the big ears looks cross and quips, "Is there anything else you'd like to add? This is your big chance."

My big chance, is it? Oh yeah, I forgot to tell you our secret squirrel strategy.

Should I tell her that Ivanishvili is buying hundreds of thousands of satellite dishes for ordinary Georgians so they can tune into news on channels other than the state-sanctioned ones? He will be fined for this by authorities who claim it is a violation of election law, and he will pay that fine the same way you or I pay an unfair parking ticket.

Should I tell her the Ministry of the Interior, the Ministry of Justice, and the Ministry of Finance of the government we just propped up are colluding on a crooked scheme to imprison ordinary people on spurious grounds and then shake down their families for bail they cannot afford and for which they will mortgage their homes and collateralize all their possessions so they can spare their loved ones unspeakable abuse?

The photo I'd snapped of the Gldani prison was prophetic. In a few months, the election will turn on revelations that authorities conducted the systematic rape of male prisoners, filmed the episodes, and then blackmailed the victims.

Maybe I should tell her that Misha's recent decision to create a Minister of Prisons and Democracy is in fact a leitmotif for everything that is wrong here.

But if she and her colleagues are doing their jobs, they should know all these things. So I stick to the headline: The United States government needs to prepare itself for a change in leadership here. It will be a peaceful, democratic change that is consistent with everything we've been promoting since 1991. I finish my tea and wish her well.

Meanwhile, Bidzina has been courted by another Washington firm, the legendary Patton Boggs, whose chairman, Tommy Boggs, personally flew to Tbilisi, unbeknownst to me, and convinced the oligarch that to be taken seriously in the American capital you need to be a Democrat. Patton Boggs also brought in Burson-Marsteller, the firm I'd beat out with BGR for Irakli's business the previous spring.

When I return to the Free Democrats office, Irakli asks to see me. Bidzina has decided to terminate the contract with BGR. He doesn't like it, he says, but there's nothing he can do. Instead, they are hiring a new firm, but they want me to sever myself from the faraway lobbying firm and make a new contract directly with them. I remember an old saying George W. Bush must have picked up in Texas: "You dance with the one who brung you," as a famous Texas football coach once counseled.

Every time I visited the modern palace on the hill that has become the temporary command center of the new opposition coalition, I find myself in the crosshairs of various competing agendas. Not everyone here shares my enthusiasm for Georgia joining NATO, for instance. And some still suspect my sympathies remain with Misha, even though I am now working overtime to remove him from power. Bidzina's security people tell him I'm either American or British intelligence; they just can't tell which. I'm even a little flattered by their misdiagnosis.

But I'm on thin ice. I can either stay in a situation in which my ability to influence the outcome is shrinking, but rake in more fees nonetheless, or I could fall on my sword for a faraway master.

As if by divine providence, Aizhan calls me at the very moment I'm moving all these factors around in my whiskey-fueled brain to complain that Max, now twelve, has been acting up at school and mouthing off at home. Even though it's late at night in Georgia, it's still afternoon in Virginia, so I call him and play the stern father. He calls my bluff. "What are you going to do about it, huh?" he challenges defiantly. "You're halfway around the world."

With that, I book a ticket on the next flight home, pack my bags, and fall on my sword. Irakli's driver picks me up to take me to the airport and looks concerned at the amount of luggage, but I tell him everything is going to be okay.

When I get back to Washington, as if to add injury to insult, I fall off my bicycle and break my leg. While healing, another mutual friend connects me with Laura Ballman, a single woman my age who has also worked extensively overseas. Laura spent ten years as an operations officer for the CIA but has left and is now a counterintelligence officer for the Department of Energy—a reliable, if somewhat boring, government job.

The Georgian Dream does overcome Misha's various obstacles and wins parliamentary election with enough seats to form the next government. Around this time, Laura takes me to dinner with former colleagues of hers, though apparently at senior levels. During a pause in the small talk, our host looks at me and says, "Maybe now you'd like to explain yourself."

Big Ears must have sent them an indecipherable cable. Had

America "lost" Georgia? Hardly. By the time I'm dining with Laura's friends in Vienna, Virginia, voters in Georgia have swept the Georgian Dream into power. Misha will remain president—for now—but with significantly reduced power. It is probably the first time the Georgian government has changed directly from the ballot box.

As a mercenary—a gun for hire, so to speak—Georgia becomes the first country where I've worked both sides. When you have worked both sides, you see things differently because you know where the chinks in the armor are. I failed my first test, though, by being loyal to the firm. A good mercenary is loyal only to himself.

CHAPTER 6
UNFINISHED BUSINESS IN IRAQ

Other than a three-month stint as spokesman for a long-shot US Senate candidate in Maryland, I haven't worked since Georgia, and my savings have run dry. Were my new wife, Laura, not gainfully employed by the government, things would be even more desperate than they seem.

Sam Amsterdam's father, Bob, has flown me to London to help him with a pitch. Bob had been Mikhail Khodorkovsky's lawyer and specializes in high-stakes, edgy work. Sam worked with me in Georgia, and we became fast friends. His dad reminds me a little of Charlie from the 1970s show *Charlie's Angels* because his law firm is filled with beautiful young women, who have gathered for the firm's holiday dinner.

I'm chatting with one of Bob's angels at a large table in the Dorchester Hotel's dining room when my phone rings. It's a Jordanian number, and I step outside to take the call. It's Munqith al-Dagher, who had been IRI's pollster in Iraq when I was there. Munqith knows I'm looking for work and has a proposal.

Iraq will have new elections at the end of April, and he has landed a Sunni Arab party as his client. In addition to knowing I'm on the hunt for a gig, Munqith also knows I share his view that Iraqi Sunnis got the short end of the stick after the invasion and have not had much success organizing politically since then.

From the dark street, I look through the window at Bob's dinner party looking like an advert from *Cosmopolitan*. The piece of work I'd been discussing with him involved financial and legal PR, and I was having a hard time picturing myself in the project, not to mention among such sophisticated company.

Iraq, on the other hand, is old hat to me. Moreover, what Munqith is suggesting ticks the box of unfinished business. He needs a written proposal as soon as possible. I excuse myself from the dinner and head back to the hotel to write it.

"A large Black man will meet you at the airport," was the last thing Munqith had written me before I boarded a Royal Jordanian flight for Amman. Indeed, Mohammed meets that description, and he makes sure I am settled in Jubeiha before vanishing into the Arabian night. From here on out, it will be all taxis for me.

Getting a taxi that will take me to Jubeiha is a daily struggle, but this far-flung district of Amman has its advantages. At one thousand meters above sea level, it is one of the hilly capitals of Jordan's highest neighborhoods, topographically anyway, so it is a couple of degrees cooler than the rest of the city and offers a nice breeze. When I arrived, there were even little patches of snow here and there.

But it is also remote and at least a twenty-minute drive from the center where I work and eat my meals. While the University of Jordan is just down the hill, I'm now a happily married man, so I scarcely notice the passing young beauties, often in black abayas and always in a headscarf with a bump. The bump, Laura says, is a sign of a woman's fashion status: the taller, the higher.

This is saving Munqith money, since he owns the building, and the ground-floor unit is empty. I am the only westerner in the neighborhood and probably the only infidel. Because Max is a sayyid, though, I figure I'm okay. Aizhan's father, Nurlan, insists he is a descendant of the Prophet, which means Max is too. Harming the father of a sayyid is probably a bad move for devout Muslims, which I keep in the back of my pocket like a get-out-of-jail-free card.

In addition to working for IRI, Munqith had also contracted his services to its Democrat counterpart, NDI, as well as the US Army, State Department, and others. It was dangerous work for his teams, and I can't count the number of letters I wrote on their behalf asking various Iraqi authorities or militias to release one or several of their interviewers from custody for asking too many questions. By now, a decade later, his teams have conducted something like a million interviews in Iraq.

Life in Iraq eventually got too dangerous for Munqith, with death threats calling him a collaborator, so he moved his family to Jordan. Our work will be based here, with occasional trips to Iraq as needed.

By decree, all buildings in Amman are required to be a dusty white color to stand out from the sandy beige of the surrounding desert. There are patches of green at the traffic circles and sometimes in the median strips of the main roads. After a while, it all blends into the same palette in varying shades. I daydream on my way into the center, sometimes about Sarah, who is here, though like me, married in recent years. It is a new world, with new rules.

Saleh al-Mutlaq, an Iraqi deputy prime minister, heads the Al Arabiya list. I remember meeting him in Baghdad in late 2004, and a decade later he seems much older and more tired. Politics, and especially Iraqi politics, can have that effect on people. Mutlaq is a man of contradictions. In 1978 he was expelled from the Ba'ath Party for defending several Shi'a political activists Saddam had slated for execution. A farmer from Fallujah, he told me how one day Saddam had landed in his field in a helicopter to announce he'd be expropriating Saleh's farm.

Now he lives in Baghdad's Green Zone, in a house behind the Republican Palace, where he manages to keep several deer he'd brought there from his native Anbar governorate. When I climb up to his roof, I can see in one direction the Fourteenth of July Bridge that crosses the Tigris to my old neighborhood of Jadriyah, and in the other the Republican Palace's now empty swimming pool, where young CPA staffers used to frolic on Fridays.

He is paying a heavy cost for the official house and job in the Maliki government though. With good reason, our prospective voters hate the government and are now inclined to see Saleh as a sellout, regardless of whether or not this is actually the case.

At first we just see Mutlaq sporadically when he and his crew fly to Amman to talk business. For the most part, our work is done remotely.

The headquarters of Munqith's al Mustakilla research group is near the small canyon in the middle of Amman, where he employs more than a dozen Iraqi expatriates and some Jordanians who work away on their computer terminals. The ten-year-old son of one Munqith's associates comes to work with his father from time to time and helps me with my computer problems. The kid even teaches me how to make better use of PowerPoint. I reconnect with Qutaiba, an old colleague from IRI who has moved his family here, and bring him on to the team.

We dive right in with focus groups, which al Mustakilla's Baghdad office organizes there, while I listen in via Skype as an attractive Jordanian woman named Doa'a translates. It is illuminating, especially to hear participants in the groups talk about the unfairness they experience in their everyday lives.

In the last elections, held in 2010, a secular centrist bloc headed by Ayad Allawi won the most votes. But when it came time for negotiating to form a new government, the pro-Tehran prime minister, Nouri al-Maliki, bent the rules to snatch Allawi's victory. The Obama administration, anxious to get on good terms with the Iranian mullahs, did not object, effectively enabling Maliki's heavy hand.

Iraq is in the midst of its own version of the Arab Spring. In April of the previous year, the Iraqi army gunned down peaceful protestors in Hawija, just west of Kirkuk. The government also raided the compound of Sunni finance minister Rffi al-Issawi, killing some of his bodyguards. What ordinary people see in these events is sectarian discrimination. Sunnis are being disenfranchised.

The US military has withdrawn, pro-Iranian Shi'a parties are having a triumphant moment, and everyone else is getting angrier and angrier.

———————

My head hurts from having drunk vodka in the desert, which always seems to be a mistake. Whether it's the climate or the altitude, I don't know. But there was a good reason Saddam drank whiskey.

When I get down to the lobby of the al Rashid hotel, I see a commotion in the gift shop. From the long marble hall, I catch the occasional elbow and a flash of what looks like silver fly out for a second. A smarter man would walk away, but I'm intrigued.

The closer I get, the more bewildered I become. It's Faisal, in a well-tailored suit by the designer from Brioni he told me he'd stolen away, and he's swinging an antique sword. The shopkeeper is both tolerant—Faisal's family is legendary in Baghdad—and alarmed. The local fixer who meets us at the airport is standing back, looking bored, but then pretending to be amused when my eyes meet his.

Saleh's funder, Faisal al Kedairy, is an Iraqi tycoon whose grandfather was knighted by the Court of Saint James for purchasing a regiment of captured British troops who were slated to be executed by the Ottomans and returning them to London. His family loaned the residence to Iraq's Hashemite king Faisal, who was his namesake. Kedairy owns a bank, a construction company, a pharmaceutical concern, and various other pieces of the country's industry.

Faisal sheaths the sword and hands it back to the relieved shopkeeper. We'd been up finishing a bottle until about 3:00 a.m., so I'm amazed at how animated he is, given that he's a decade older. When he notices me, he takes on a more businesslike air and marches out of the store. "You finally woke up," he snorts. "Now let's get some work done."

Saleh has an interview with the BBC, and for the occasion a friend of Faisal has lent us his house in Mansour, a tony district of Baghdad next to the Green Zone. It's hard to find furniture here that isn't painted gold, so I decide to just own it and let the set that I craft out of the man's living room look a little ornate, but in a distinguished way. Then our host breaks out the quzi, or slow-cooked lamb over yellow rice with raisins and nuts—always an honorific meal. I use the lunch to media train Mutlaq before the journalist and her camera crew shows up.

As they're setting up, I take a cigarette break in the garden and hear some rumbling on the street outside, beyond the wall. Faisal appears out of nowhere and barks at me to get inside and stay out of the front rooms. A rival army brigade is rolling through. Every deputy prime minister—there is one for each major group in Iraq—gets its own brigade. Happily, there is no confrontation, so we start the interview. Saleh performs well, hitting the right notes in his own style.

"Now I'm going to go make some money to pay for this circus, and you're going campaigning," Faisal announces as the crew breaks down and Mutlaq's bodyguard helps me move the furniture back to where we found it.

Even after ten months in Baghdad ten years ago, this is my first time on the proverbial campaign trail—Blackwater security would never have signed off on multiple public events. With our brigade in tow, we hit a poetry contest, a children's beauty pageant, and then walk through a covered market. As we roll through the city in a black Suburban left over from the Americans bracketed by Toyota Hilux pickup trucks filled with machine-gun–toting soldiers, Munqith looks at me and smiles as he asks rhetorically, "Do you feel safe enough?"

In the ordinary campaign context, being surrounded by so many soldiers would be off-putting to the public, but in Iraq this is normal. This is the same country where a local journalist threw both his shoes at US president George W. Bush during a press conference. Bush demonstrated catlike reflexes by dodging both shoes, and in Saddam's birthplace of Tikrit, local authorities later erected a statue of one of the shoes to honor the journalist.

In the market, only one old woman summons the courage to confront Mutlaq about the crooked government as he smokes a cigarette and half listens, not bothering with the theatrical "active listening" of his American counterparts.

After a few hours on the hustings, Mutlaq goes back to his official residence to hold court with the various visitors who gather there, smokes cigarettes, and talks into the wee hours of the morning. Munqith and I go to party headquarters next to the Baghdad Zoo to train candidates lower on the ballot on what they should say when they go door-to-door in their neighborhoods.

The women and men gathered here do not get security for their campaigning, and their neighborhoods—Sunni strongholds like Adamiyah, Yarmouk, and al Rashid—are hunting grounds for who Munqith calls the "vampires." These are heavily armed Shi'a paramilitary units who travel at night in the Humvees we left for them pulling military-aged Sunni males out of their homes and taking them somewhere quiet for extrajudicial executions.

Between rounds of training on our message and answers to what we anticipate to be frequently asked questions, one of the few English-speaking candidates, a well-regarded lawyer named Riyad, takes me aside. "The fact that you're here tells me you must know what you're doing," he says politely, "but please, whatever you tell these people, don't ask them to say or do anything that will get them killed."

It's a sobering thought. In an hour or two, Munqith and I will be on the tarmac at Baghdad International Airport, waiting to take off, while these candidates will be canvassing their districts while trying to avoid the vampires.

At passport control, a border guard goes back and forth through the pages of my passport before looking at me with an altogether straight face and saying, "I see you spent the night this time. Good for you."

———————

The first thing I told Munqith we need to do is create a "war room."

Ever since the 1992 Bill Clinton campaign, everyone in the consulting business has talked about "war rooms." The 1993 documentary by that name featured James Carville, George Stephanopoulos, and Paul Begala running a command center through which all communications and campaign direction went.

Especially when you're working with a firm like GQR—headlined by Bill Clinton's pollster, Stan Greenberg—there is a conscious effort to replicate it, whether you're in Bogata or Kyiv. When I was GQR's man on the ground in Tbilisi three months before the Russian invasion, the future parliamentary speaker asked me quietly if we could call it something else—maybe just the communications room. But that lacked the same sizzle.

As he is a man who was displaced by a war that America started, I'm a little hesitant to use the term with Munqith and the Iraqi immigrants who will staff it, but it still conveys the urgency of the situation better than anything else, so I stick with it. Faisal gives us a whole floor in the same downtown building as his construction company. Munqith doesn't love the degree of interference this allows, but I've come to enjoy the Iraqi tycoon's eccentricities and occasional obsessions. At the end of each day, he calls us up for a chat, which usually goes on for several hours.

On a late afternoon in early February, Faisal cuts straight to the point: "Saleh is going to Washington tonight, and you're going with him. You'd better go now and pack your things."

While seemingly out of nowhere, the trip is sponsored by the US government and intended to engage Iraqi decision-makers and may have been in the works for some time. Mutlaq doesn't want to simply be a yes-man, so Faisal has decided to send us to help him stick to his guns on key points.

In that moment, I recognize I will be in effect lobbying the US government on behalf of a foreign power, so I download the registration materials to comply with the Foreign Agent Registration Act (FARA). This is my second registration; BGR had filed for me when I was in Georgia out of an abundance of caution, as the lawyers say. Often this is a fuzzy line, but to my mind, if I'm sitting in a room with senators helping Saleh make his case, it technically applies to me, even if my actual job is as a political consultant focused on Iraq.

What Washington needs to hear is what Iraqi Sunnis in these focus groups I've been eavesdropping on all day have been saying: what they need is equality. Unlike Munqith, I don't really need to pack, since our business trip is to my home, so I sit down instead and hammer out a 750-word piece for Saleh that clearly conveys the message. To make it relevant, I peg it to the sale of Apache helicopters our defense industrial complex has been pushing.

The *Wall Street Journal* accepts Mutlaq's piece, which begins: "While Washington debates whether to sell Apache helicopters and other advanced weapons to the Iraqi government, my country is engulfed by violence that threatens to spread well beyond Anbar Province, where the black flags of al-Qaeda now fly."

In other words, not addressing the way in which the deck is stacked against Arab Sunnis in Iraq—most Kurds are also Sunnis but enjoy quasi-independence—will give rise to bigger, worse problems, such as the tired remnants of al-Qaeda. At the time of writing, we are nearly six months away from the rise of the Islamic State, or ISIS.

In terms of making your voice heard in America, it is a powerful shot across the bow that attracts the attention of the ranking member of the Senate Foreign Relations Committee and the chairman of the Senate Armed Services Committee. Carl Levin, who occupies that latter seat, tells my client in front of me, "Saleh, every time I open a newspaper, you're in it!"

I beam. Again, the lobbying part is tangential to my job at best, but on the media score I'm hitting it out of the park.

The Iraqi ambassador, who joins us in the meeting with Levin, is not happy with us one bit. He and I argue in front of Levin about whether it is technically possible to attach human rights observance conditions to the supply chain for the state-of-the-art war birds. Knowing relatively little about military hardware, I am bluffing, but I sense the Iraqi ambassador is as well.

"Which is it, guys? Can you or can't you?" the frustrated Michigan senator asks.

The White House isn't happy with Saleh's piece, either, and told him as much. Their number-one foreign policy priority at this moment is cinching the Joint Comprehensive Plan of Action (JCPOA), or Iran deal, and anything that interferes with that— like not selling advanced weapons to the Iranian satrap that Nuri al-Maliki's government in Baghdad is—is very much off message, from the Obama administration's standpoint.

Being a one-man lobbying shop when I just signed up to be a political operative is challenging. One of the State Department–assigned security officers guarding Saleh during the trip overhears me yelling at a House staffer who is not helping me arrange a meeting between Saleh and his boss.

"Take it easy on him," the borrowed bodyguard says, reminding me, "after all, you used to be him." Of course, he is absolutely right. The security officer, meanwhile, used to be a US infantryman in Iraq, fighting the Sunni insurgents who were trying to drive us out. One never knows where one will eventually end up.

By the time we get back to the region, I learn from our media monitoring team that Mutlaq isn't the only one who has been making news. Thanks to my FARA filing, I am too. Wild stories have begun spinning like minicyclones through the Arabic press to the effect that I am some dark, secret weapon whom Saleh is paying tens of millions of dollars to in order to upset the apple cart in Iraq. The next time I see him, Saleh gives me a long, menacing stare before asking for his cut. "Of what?" I ask.

"The forty million dollars I gave you," he says with a smile.

We may not have blocked the Apache sale, but we definitely upset people both in Tehran and Washington.

———

"It" was the original sin of the new Iraqi state. "It" was not de-Ba'ath-ification, disbanding the Iraqi army, or failing to go full throttle on reconstruction from the very outset—these were all America's sins, and collectively they kneecapped the new Iraq from the very start. But it was the constitution, which was for the most part written and ratified by Iraqis, which carved the basic inequity into stone, if you ask most Sunni Arabs anyway.

"Read the fucking preamble, for crying out loud," Faisal shouts when I ask him what the big deal about the constitution is.

So I do. Within a handful of short sentences, the first paragraph of the highest law of the land lays blame squarely on the past regime for usurping the people's freedom and enacting racist and sectarian laws. Depending on how you interpret the past regime, the preamble itself establishes the guilt of anyone who ever served in the Ba'ath Party, which is to say many Arab Sunnis.

Beyond the question of foundational guilt, the constitution fails to define Iraq as an Arab nation and then allows for a system of federalism that, some Iraqi nationalists believe, will lead to the unraveling of the country. These were the issues opponents of the constitution raised in 2005, just before it was ratified. One of those opponents was none other than Saleh al-Mutlaq.

In order to narrowly pass the constitution back then, US ambassador Zalmay Khalilzad, the grinning Pashtun, persuaded my old friends at the Iraqi Islamic Party to support it, effectively splitting the Arab Sunni vote. When we were in Washington the week before last, Saleh was talking to a large group at the US Institute of Peace when he paused to point out Khalilzad in the audience. "I see you," Mutlaq said, and his tone was anything but affectionate.

So now it makes perfect sense to run on the constitution. In politics, you want to own an issue in which your guy has credibility. This is it.

You can say prices or violence or corruption are all more pressing problems than sterile sheets of paper few people actually read, sure. But you can also trace all those problems back to that very same pile of paper.

Still, it's an issue that runs the risk of being too abstract. So you have to know your audience, and we test it as a question on polls. It turns out that among our target voters it's more of a hot-button issue than I ever would have guessed. The other risk is that Saleh is seen as just some old man trying to prove he was right all along, but given the cards we're dealt, they are both risks worth taking.

When you think about it, the logic is clear. Most Sunnis sat out the first election in 2005, which means they didn't get to elect constitution drafters. Their boycott cost them a seat at the table where the current constitution—modeled on America's Transitional Administrative Law—was written. If we go back to the beginning—and we're only talking about less than a decade—our promised "do-over" can correct the wrongs of the past. Besides, it even sounds good in Arabic: *al Dustor*.

How to communicate all of this into the simple language of politics?

Munqith and I write a series of video scripts that tell the story in terms beyond mere logic and that appeal to the basic sense of dignity. Our different approaches reflect our different personalities.

Of the two he wrote, one centers on an old, rural man, dressed in a traditional keffiyeh, who is disrespected by corrupt, cigar-chomping politicians but then set right by one of our supporters. The other has a bunch of boys asking difficult questions of their teacher about why Iraq is the way it is. In other words, his are grounded in the local reality and find their power in understatement.

Mine, on the other hand, swoons toward drama. A young doctor is examining a little girl of eight or so with a wound. This spurs a flashback to when he was a teenager and happened across an adolescent girl being harangued and about to be assaulted. He reaches down to the ground and takes a rock into his fist. We don't know what happened next, but now he is all right. You, too, can be all right if you act now to defend honor, even if you couldn't before.

Yes, mine is a little more confusing, but it is supposed to be unsettling. And together the three tell the story we're trying to convey: even if once threatened, honor can be regained. Faisal is frustrated that we're being indirect, even oblique, and wishes we'd just come out and say it, but not everyone is as direct as he is.

To be clear, the action we're suggesting here is voting—not protesting, not burning government buildings, not targeting government employees. If you want to take the power back into your hands, use the ballot box. In Saleh al-Mutlaq, we are offering you, the voter, a chance to take a principled stand. Some may offer handouts or patronage. We're offering something different—the possibility of reshuffling the deck that was stacked against you not so long ago.

One never really knows how ads will be received by the people they're trying to reach. Sure, one can focus group them and then make tweaks. But ultimately, the best we can do now is put them on TV and hope for the best.

———————

While we are all making ads and working out a frame for the election, Saleh is trying to do the work of a deputy prime minister. With the government's vise tightening on his native Anbar Province, Mutlaq tries to inspect a dam near Abu Ghraib, where authorities have cut the water flow to farms outside Fallujah. Himself originally a farmer, this is something he takes personally.

Protests in Fallujah have been growing, and it seems the powers in Baghdad have been doing all they can to inflame them further. These are, of course, our voters we're talking about. If they're wrapped in the kind of violence to which protests have historically led, they can't very well vote later this month. When we talk about voter suppression at home, we never imagine it being like this.

While approaching the dam, Saleh's convoy comes under fire from uniformed gunners from what is initially reported to be Ministry of Water Supply security. Mutlaq's own security contingent returns fire, and in the ensuing shoot-out three of his bodyguards are injured before the attackers flee.

The story coming from the authorities keeps changing, though the firsthand account of Saleh's team is very consistent. Their attackers were well armed, with truck-mounted machine guns and Humvees, bore the insignia of an Iraqi military unit, and fired first, before melting into the haunted outskirts of Abu Ghraib.

Neither Mutlaq nor the local member of Parliament who is with him to inspect the dam is injured. What remains of the international press corps in Baghdad shows little interest in the story, running the Iraqi government's account essentially verbatim, so I put out a press release on PR newswire: "If the state-influenced media is reporting that the attack on Dr. Saleh today was the work of insurgents, when all present clearly saw and returned fire with a brigade of the Ninth Division, this incident calls into question every report the Iraqi government is making about what is happening in the Anbar governorate."

This is not the first time someone has tried to kill Mutlaq, and to me, he seems unflappable. I remember how, in Georgia, Saakashvili used to go looking for trouble, driving up to the demarcation lines of occupied territories and taunting the soldiers there. In stark contrast to these kind of dramatics, all Saleh did was try to find out why the vital water supply for his constituents' farms had been cut—a legitimate thing for someone in his position to do.

After pleading with a friend at the Associated Press, they run a short piece, as does Al Arabiya, but for the worldwide media accustomed to such things happening in Iraq, it is a dog-bites-man story.

What it does for me is accent the tremendous risk one takes here by going into public life. The examples of loss are everywhere.

Saleh's chief of staff puts up a good front despite the fact his family has been kidnapped. He is hoping to be able to come to terms with their takers and get them back. Still, he is able to joke about the enterprise. On one day trip to Baghdad, he teases me at departure time. "Are you sure you don't want to spend the night? I promise we'll get a very good price for you."

And our voters are being targeted every day. For them, a constant state of siege is the new normal. An anonymous denunciation is enough to get someone picked up and taken away to a holding cell from which they might never return, and even if they do, they will likely be scarred by the experience.

A dark feeling hangs in the air, one that makes politics feel small and even insignificant by comparison. It reminds me of an exhibit I'd seen years ago at the Nahum Goldman Museum in Tel Aviv. In a huge black room, the history of the Jewish diaspora spans the walls, and overhead, obscured by a black catafalque that makes it blend into the room, is a looming presence—a structure that simply hangs like guilt or the drawn sword of vengeance about to strike.

It can be easy to get carried away in other people's affairs while ignoring your own. I've been away from Laura, my newlywed wife, for several months now, save my quick trip to Washington with Saleh and a long weekend visit she made to Amman. Max is about to start high school. And we now have a husky named Pepper, meant to offer Laura a greater sense of security while I'm gone. But instead, Pepper has been pooping all over the house. It's getting to be time for me to go home.

The election comes but brings no good tidings. We lose seats, falling from sixteen to ten. Meanwhile, the more extreme Sunni party, Muthaidoon, picks up ten seats. Allawi's Wifaq (National Alliance), my old client Masoud Barzani's Kurdish Democratic Party, and even Moqtada al-Sadr's party of the streets all join us in taking losses. There's a bad moon rising out there, and at times like these the centrists can fall out of favor. In such times, as W. B. Yeats wrote in *The Second Coming*, "The blood-dimmed tide is loosed, and everywhere/ The ceremony of innocence is drowned;/The best lack all conviction/ And the worst are filled with passionate intensity."

———————

"You should really stay through the horse-trading phase," my old acquaintance tells me. "Now is when they need you the most."

Ahmed Rushdi has grown in girth, and his once dark shock of

hair has turned white since I last saw him in early 2005, just before Iraq's first election since the coup of 1958. But he has the same playful eyes, even if they have been made a little weary by the years. Once the international relations guy for the Iraqi Islamic Party, now he is associated with Muthaidoon—our main competitor for Sunni votes. Unlike al Arabiya, his guys gained seats in this week's voting.

Having lunch with a competitor after an election seems to me like a very civilized thing to do. Doing so before the election is fraught with suspicion and usually a waste of both parties' time.

"No," I tell him. "I'm going home." The only reason to stay any longer in Jordan would be if Laura were to undergo fertility treatment here, which is an option. But I'm tired and homesick. More than four months away is the longest overseas gig I've taken since Georgia.

I'm less depressed about the net loss in seats because what we really did was avoid a total wipeout. Saleh had taken a job in Maliki's government. To most of our prospective voters, that's akin to treason. Right now, the US secretary of defense is former Republican senator Chuck Hagel. My old boss Bill Cohen had done the same for Bill Clinton. Today's Republicans consider both men turncoats, even if they had principled reasons for doing what they did. When it comes to vengeance, Republicans have nothing on Iraqis.

As Ayad Allawi pointed out to me back in 2005, I am not an Arab. The horse-trading is better left to the men who have handled these things ever since Faisal's family controlled the Baghdad chamber of commerce and industry, which dates back further than the seventeenth century.

Something else was bothering me. It was an uneasy feeling that we'd raised a question that hadn't been answered. In all our messaging, we'd told people they would have a chance to rewrite the social contract. If they vote, they could cast their ballots for the square deal they'd been cheated out of back in 2005—though, in a sense, they cheated themselves by boycotting that first election. And here we are, with no plausible chance any of that will happen.

Meanwhile, the *Washington Post* had sent an editor named Richard Leiby out to do a profile on me—that is, an American political consultant advising foreign politicians before their election. Leiby had been bureau chief in Islamabad for several years and had done a piece on an advisor to Chalabi just after the invasion. His piece on me ran at the same time as the Iraqi election as a sort of companion piece, and it dominated that day's style section.

The feature starts out with my insisting on releasing sheep outside Allawi's party office because he refused to debate, causing Allawi's spokesperson to call me "ill-mannered," but then the piece gets closer to my actual take on the heart of this work: "Here's Patten working in Iraq, three years after the withdrawal of US troops. He's chasing Jeffersonian sunbeams in a country where bombs keep going off, yet he adopts a rather sanguine long view. 'People like me are not agents of change,' he reflects. 'We're helpers, perhaps enablers, of a historical process that is going to happen eventually, one way or the other.'"

Saleh just shrugged the piece off, as he'd learned to do over the years with things said in Washington. It is typical of a consultant. I am self-promoting and a gun for hire. That's the difference between Ahmed and me. He is working the system to make life better for his people. And I am now a mercenary, the political version of the Blackwater guys.

Electoral politics are about to become obsolete in Iraq, at least for the time being. It won't really matter who is in the new government, because an even bigger crisis is about to strike.

Of course, neither Ahmed nor I could predict any of this as we catch up over lunch in this Amman café. But it's not beyond the realm of the imagination either. After I left Iraq the first time in 2005, he and I remained in contact.

While I was working in the Senate the next year, Ahmed would send me grisly photographs of tortured and murdered Sunnis, whose skulls had been drilled through with power tools. The interior minister at the time, who had until his official post headed the Shi'a paramilitary Badr Brigades, was nicknamed Black and Decker. These images confirmed the drumbeat then that a civil war was coming.

That was nearly a decade ago.

The fact that we're now having a peaceful lunch, discussing what went right and wrong during the campaign like a couple of political scientists at a conference, amounts to nothing more than a calm in the storm. It will get worse, much worse, before it gets any better. But for now, I'm just going home.

————————

Four months before my return to the region, ISIS militants kidnapped an American aid worker named Kayla Mueller in Syria. The twenty-six-year-old Arizonan had crossed into the war-stricken country from Turkey with her Syrian boyfriend one day before she was taken from the city of Aleppo. At the time, I was a newly married man, worried about more mundane concerns altogether—where I could find a stable job and how I could hold up my end of making ends meet in this new partnership. The abduction of a young woman who'd been helping war refugees was not on my radar screen.

Soon after reimmersing myself into the world of Iraqi Sunnis, the dangerous imbalance in the region started becoming clearer to me. Peaceful protests in the Anbar Province were becoming less so. People in our focus groups said outside agitators were slipping in among the protestors, and the pro-Iranian Nuri al-Maliki would send Shi'a paramilitary units into the predominantly Sunni province to confront the protestors with force.

As I try to understand the current moment, I flashback to my 2004 visit to Rushdi's Iraqi Islamic Party, when one of the party faithful chased my car as I left the compound, pressing pictures of slaughtered civilians against my window, or Rushdi's own graphic images two years later.

A deep grievance was building among the Sunnis, more serious than the slights embedded in the new constitution. Then the United States responded with a "surge" of military activity that incorporated the "Sons of Iraq," or local Sunnis with tribal ties willing to join the fight against al-Qaeda in Iraq. This strategy of focusing like a laser beam on the bad apples and getting the buy-in of everyone else then helped avert an all-out civil war.

Now history is repeating itself, just a couple of years after America's withdrawal of troops in late 2011. Except there no longer exists a counterweight to the sectarian government of al-Maliki.

Sure, Mutlaq is "in government," but without any real power—save advocating for farmers as best he can. Muthaidoon is also in coalition, and while bigger than us, they are also essentially just window-dressing. This is where ISIS, as the international community calls it, creeps into the vacuum. Iraqis call ISID Da'esh. Their Iraqi-born leader, Abu Bakr al-Baghdadi, is a veteran of al-Qaeda in Iraq and US military prison camps. Baghdadi aims to create a new caliphate that stretches from Iran's border to the Mediterranean Sea.

Less than two months after the election, Da'esh begins to seize more and more Iraqi territory—Anbar; Diyala; Kirkuk; Nineveh, where it made Iraq's second-largest city, Mosul, its capital; and Salahadin. In many instances, the Iraqi army simply dropped its weapons and ran. Its black flag will fly over 40 percent of Iraq at the so-called caliphate's zenith.

Baghdadi will torture Kayla Mueller in unspeakable ways, a rescued Yazidi woman reports. This will continue for a year and a half, until he will claim she was killed by a Jordanian air strike in 2015.

Four years later, a US air strike will kill Baghdadi himself in an operation named for Kayla. Her parents will then disregard the advice of the FBI and travel to the region and meet with one of their daughter's captors to see if there is any chance Kayla is in fact still alive.

Mueller's ordeal brackets the span of Da'esh's monstrosity. Her suffering put that of the Iraqis into some understandable context for Americans. Thinking of her reminds me of Marla Ruzicka. After I placed a piece by Mutlaq in *Foreign Policy*, the publication insisted on paying the Iraqi politician an author's fee of a few hundred dollars. With Saleh's consent, I ask FP to donate the fee instead to a foundation set up in Marla's memory.

Once home, the disaster that follows the 2014 Iraqi election seems a world away. I stay in contact in Munqith, who is amazingly still able to conduct polls in Da'esh-controlled Iraq, and help him get audiences when he comes to Washington to share his findings.

Maybe the future will hold some chance to fix this mess. But for now, I can't shake the feeling I've been the inverse of what former secretary of state Dean Acheson called "present at the creation," which is to say, an accessory to yet another disaster.

CHAPTER 7
IT'S NOT MOTHER'S SILVER, IS IT?

"I don't know why, but she just makes me nervous," Laura tells me with furrowed brow after we bid farewell to our brunch guest. Since my wife is a trained counterintelligence officer, I should probably pay closer attention to her instincts but instead just assume she's being jealous.

My college friend Anna Miller has always been stunningly good-looking, and the years haven't dulled her shine. Straight, dirty-blond hair crowns an oval face with narrow brown eyes and a hint of Slavic extraction, though she's always been more focused on her connection to the late socialite Edie Sedgwick, who was a muse to Andy Warhol in the late 1960s and died tragically when I was four months old.

The last time I saw Anna I was newly separated and living in the rathole behind the Hawk n' Dove bar, and she wasn't impressed. She also thought my job at the time, speechwriting for a senator, was as boring as my accommodations were subpedestrian—which, of course, they were. We've long been close, and to me what Anna thinks, even if fatuous, matters.

If I'm going to write my book, she said back then in the rathole days, I would need some sunlight. Well, I've checked that box somewhat. As for the humdrum job, things have been looking up since I've been back in the field again, doubling down on my trade as an international man of mystery.

For at least the last several years, Anna has been living in Geneva with her young daughter, sired by a Serbian prince. She's done with all that, she says, and is moving back to New York City. The *Washington Post* piece caught her attention, and she says she has shared it with a friend of hers in London named Alexander Nix.

Originally a finance guy who now heads a British political consulting company called SCL (Strategic Communications Laboratories), Nix has the look of one of Anna's guys: blond, thin, and blue-blooded. SCL works in Commonwealth countries, where they can leverage their public-school connections. Nigel Oakes, who chairs the firm, was a lover of Lady Windsor and once shocked Her Majesty the Queen when she discovered him being smuggled into Saint James's Palace.

According to Anna, much of SCL's campaigning abroad consists of mailing dildos to their clients' opponents in Caribbean elections and then doing press on it—that sort of thing. *But there had to be more to it than just a bunch of public-school tricks*, I reasoned.

"You might really help him up their game," she says, getting up from the dining-room table of my better-lit house as a life-size portrait of the Prussian general von Steuben looked down at us quizzically. The mercenary baron had given it as a remembrance to a van Rensselaer ancestor of mine who commanded the New York regiment during the Revolutionary War. "Alexander will be in touch with you very soon."

Sure enough, the next day I get an email from Nix, who says he'll be in town this week and asks if we could meet for a drink on Thursday.

Knowing the kind of guys in Anna's orbit, I suggest the swanky bar in the basement of the Hay-Adams Hotel off Lafayette Square. The small park between the hotel and the White House is home to statues not only of the French Marquis de Lafayette but also the Comte de Rochambeau, Polish general Thaddeus Kosciuszko, and my personal favorite, von Steuben—all foreigners who fought for America's independence from Britain.

What better place to meet with a Brit seeking to take over America's Republican Party than alongside these earlier "foreign agents"? The elegantly lit and velvety walls of the Off the Record bar give the impression of having heard and kept many secrets over the years. I'm right—he seems to love the place.

"SCL has taken microtargeting to the next level," Nix explains. Microtargeting is the use of both quantitative research (polling) and data analysis to identify very specific pockets of potential voters to target. They could be soccer moms who are unhappy in their marriages, for instance. What Alexander is talking about is overlaying psychographic profiles on top of all this to identify what sort of person you are targeting and how best to motivate that person.

In fact, he says, SCL has developed a computer platform to put all of this at the average campaign manager's fingertips, and he's trying to sell this to the Republican National Committee and affiliated campaign groups. But there is resistance, of course. The Koch brothers have already foisted their own platform on the Republicans, and their money talks.

Spending time with Lance and Tony after the first Iraqi election, I learned how crooked the consulting marketplace is in America, for both parties. A handful of powerful firms dominate, and most business is referred to them. Sometimes they hand out scraps to the little guys, but basically we're talking about cabals run not on performance but connections. It is a risk-averse, unimaginative lot united mainly by greed. Being a little quirky, I've always found it hard to break in, so Nix's situation—and his willingness to fight the odds—appeals to me.

Our meeting was a happy blur. We drink so much that later in the evening Alexander is nearly off-loaded from his flight back to London but manages to talk himself out of it. Waking up in chains in the Penobscot County Sheriff's jail in Bangor, Maine, has long been a nightmare of mine, as that's the fate that lies in store for anyone so drunk and disorderly that their transatlantic flight has to make an emergency stop there to eject them.

After a week or two, he writes again. This time, he says, they've got something concrete. SCL is signing up real campaigns, for the US Senate, in Arkansas, North Carolina, West Virginia, Colorado, and Oregon. This will be the trial run of the RIPON platform, named after the small town in Wisconsin where the Republican Party was formed in 1854. He asks if I would like to train with them to be a "message architect"—that is, the guy who figures out what kind of messaging to use for the segments they identify.

But first I fly to London for ten days of "onboarding." SCL's office is on the first floor of an out-of-place academic sort of building tucked down an alley in Mayfair, a couple of blocks from Shepherd's Market. Here is a motley crew of a few data scientists and a dozen or so young public-relations types. There is an all-nighter, crashing-before-the-pitch sort of feel to the office, which runs to a hum of frantic scrambles. Together with me, there are a handful of Canadian Liberal Democrats.

We learned about psychographic profiling and the OCEAN (Openness, Conscientiousness, Extroverted-ness, Agreeability, and Neuroticism) scale and how it encompasses all personality traits in the same dominant-recessive way as the Myers-Briggs profiles. People in North Carolina, for instance, tend to be agreeable, while people in New York City can be neurotic. Of course, these are gross generalizations, but if you have a large enough sample—say, one hundred thousand interviews—you can start identifying psychographic pockets and tailoring your message to these when they overlap with your likely or persuadable voters.

The sort of things one could be neurotic about include limiting gun rights, allowing unchecked immigration, or raising taxes. Of course, we're just talking about Republicans, but for Democrats the same can be said about ending the constitutional right to abortion drawn from the 1973 *Roe v. Wade* decision by the Supreme Court, blurring the line between church and state, or expanding police powers. Again, these are generalizations, but attaching issues to voters' psychographic profiles gives us something on which to train.

I see Alexander only sporadically while in London, but when I do, he smiles and sometimes winks before promising, "When this is done, we're going to send you absolutely everywhere," adding for emphasis, "We're totally going to wreck your marriage."

———————

More than twenty years ago, I'd spent a summer in London as an intern for a member of Parliament for Kensington, J. Dudley Fishburn, who also happens to be my godfather. In his youth, Dudley went to Ethiopia and became an advisor to Emperor Haile Selassie. Perhaps this is where I originally got the idea of being a political advisor to foreigners.

Sitting in Hyde Park having a picnic lunch with my SCL colleagues, a somewhat older Indian woman produces a bottle of wine, and my mind flashes back to the early nineties, when I was nineteen.

Maybe it's the bow tie, I think. A ruddy-cheeked, balding Englishman is staring at me with a puzzled expression, and I am wondering why. I'd just learned how to open wine bottles without tearing off the metal wrappers because the old ladies who frequented events at the Kensington Conservative Association can be impatient. If it's not the tie, maybe I left a piece of tin in his glass.

"That's Nicholas Soames," a musty-smelling man who writes obituaries for the Daily Telegraph *tells me. "He's the member of Parliament for Crawley, out by Gatwick Airport, and more importantly, he is also Winston Churchill's grandson."*

Boozing up the crowd and half-listening to the speakers is par for the course at these things. I'm a nineteen-year-old intern for J. Dudley Fishburn, member of Parliament for Kensington and my godfather. Most of the time he has me in the Conservative Party constituency office in swish Kensington.

The musty-smelling man and I are thinking about the same woman: Cordelia Honeycutt, a fringe theater actress whose pregnant sister Carlotta is Dudley's "party agent." He may know who Nicholas Soames is, but he doesn't know—not yet anyhow—that Cordelia and I have been intimate for a week now. She's in her late thirties, and our affair is the most exciting thing I've ever done.

I look at my watch. In less than thirty minutes, she is getting out of rehearsal and taking me to dinner with friends of hers. Artsy types. Tonight I could use some fun. Earlier today, I was canvassing a housing project in North Kensington, above Portobello Road. An angry man in a soiled tank top took offense at the double indignity of being disturbed by an American working as a lackey for the Tories. He'd released his dog on me. Thankfully, I managed to outrun it.

La Femme de Fer, Margaret Thatcher, stepped down as prime minister last fall, toppled by an intraparty coup. John Major, who replaced her, is a comparatively mild-mannered guy—even milquetoast, as some at the fundraising dinner are grumbling. Greatness has been struck down as Gulliver was by Lilliputians.

Cordelia is happy to see me. The production she's in involves a lot of writhing on the stage while moaning, something I don't like to watch in public, especially when it stars a woman with whom I'm intimate. But actresses play roles.

At dinner, I play my role: young American who must be good at something. It doesn't matter what I say, really, as long as I look good. That's why I'm wearing the bow tie. My dad's old suits that Joe had tailored for him on Savile Row when he was my age fit me, more or less. Most of Cordelia's friends are gay men. French prime minister Edith Cresson had just said at least half of all Englishmen are gay, to which Major rejoined that a quarter of all Frenchmen are rapists.

I can't wait for dinner to be done. We take a taxi to Cordelia's small row house in Islington, which has yet to become fashionable. She leads me up the narrow staircase to her bedroom. Though the room is dark, moonlight filters in, and I can make out her Modigliani-shaped face with a long nose she inherited from her ancestor Robert Peel, who last served as prime minister under William IV.

While this association with a nineteenth-century prime minister would not seem sexy to most, for some reason it does to me. We kiss and undress and make love. Soon her body shakes, and I leap back, afraid she is having a seizure or I have done something terribly wrong.

"No," she laughs. "You've done your job just right," she tells me, caressing the side of my face with her elegant, cold hand. She looks at me with detached affection, and then she looks away. Is she feeling something despite herself?

Cordelia's parents live in the country, in a stone manor house sitting beside a field. She'd taken me to meet them the weekend before, and we stayed in separate rooms. In the morning, her father took me walking in the field with shotguns, through the mist and dewy tall grass. I had the feeling he was about to ask me my intentions, but he didn't. After all, I'm only nineteen. We drive back to London in silence, neither really knowing what was going on in the other's head.

On the marriage-wrecking score, at least, Alexander makes little progress. Laura comes out to visit me in London for the weekend during my training, which overlaps with her birthday. We have tea at the Ritz, go to the theatre, and play with the swans, again, in Hyde Park. She did the same when I was in Jordan earlier in the year, and these trips help keep our connection viable and strong. We've both had to travel a lot for our respective jobs and need to be creative to make our marriage work.

EUGENE, OREGON, AUGUST 2014

When it comes time for assignments, I draw the short straw and get sent to Oregon. Coming from a state that also has a city named

Portland, I've been curious about the offbeat state that helps form the other northern corner of America.

Still, it is far from Washington. The work will be intense as well. This is not generally a Republican-friendly state, and SCL's American entity, Cambridge Analytica, has signed three races here: a congressional, the gubernatorial, and a US Senate bid. Our six-man team is split between them, but the one that offers us the warmest reception is based in Eugene.

Even before I meet him, I form a liking for Art Robinson. An idiosyncratic, paleoconservative who lives on a compound in the southern part of Oregon, where he homeschooled all six of his children—most of them by himself after his wife, Lauralee, died of a liver infection in 1988—Art is also the chairman of the state GOP. But Republicans in Oregon were more or less hobbled around the same time the feds shut down the timber industry by declaring the native spotted owl to be an endangered species.

This is Art's third run against entrenched liberal Democrat Peter DeFazio, and it is a long shot at best. The very left-leaning, small city of Eugene accounts for more than half the district's votes, with the rest scattered all over the southwest of Oregon. There may just be enough people like Art, contrarian conservatives living off the grid, for it to only be a plus-four Democrat seat. But the last time it sent a Republican to Congress was 1974.

As background viewing, I watch a clip of an interview Art had unfortunately agreed to do with Rachel Maddow before our team entered the picture. Predictably, she tore him to shreds, ridiculing his life's scientific work seeking strains of liver disease in urine samples. A world-class scientist, Art's work isn't all that risible. In fact, it has expanded the frontiers of medicine. But from a New York television producer's standpoint, he makes a perfect target: kooky, out-of-touch Republican. *Damn*, I think, *this is going to be hard*. Honest men tend to do poorly in politics.

One of my colleagues makes a graphic of Art's disarrayed white hair and puts a smile and a pair of Ray-Ban Wayfarers across his sturdy face. It's a totally original meme, and we are even two years ahead of Bernie Sanders getting made into a cult figure. It is a noble effort to make Art hip.

Meanwhile, the much-vaunted RIPON platform is still under development. Art is the least uptight about this; he's happy to get what help he can. This amounts to all of us improvising. Yet Alexander has promised similar staffing levels for the two Portland-based campaigns, requiring four of us to make a painful, daily commute from our little burrow in Eugene. Pere, a Canadian Brit, identifies a dead sheep in a pasture as a road marker, which we look out for to mark our progress there and back in grueling sixteen-hour days. Compared to the others on the team, I'm an old man, like Art, and I'm feeling it in my bones.

In Portland, we have two candidates: a Mormon state senator in his sixties running for governor against a popular incumbent who had spent time in Bhutan studying the secrets to human happiness, and a female pediatric neurosurgeon in her fifties running against the relatively new Democrat incumbent Senator Jeff Merkley. While the Mormon had his trusted team in place, headed by an ex-driver for Mitt Romney, the brain surgeon had just fired her entire staff, which until then had been headed by the same ex-driver for Romney.

Apparently, when confronted with allegations that Dr. Monica

Wehby had stalked her ex-boyfriend, the well-rounded ex-driver cum campaign manager had said something to the effect, "At least she's persistent. Now just imagine how tough she'll be on Obama!"

The team of ringers the National Republican Senatorial Committee strung together for her has no idea what to make of us. Shouldn't we be wearing lab coats, they ask—if we're data scientists, that is, they snicker. The Republican consulting class in America is not known for their imagination. To be fair, we are quasi-absurd players in a Kabuki dance over a yet-to-be-delivered campaign platform. In this sense, they are not wrong to be skeptical.

I try to make myself helpful around the office drafting various things for the communications director. Among these is an op-ed by two married men who sued for their right to have a civil union and are endorsing Dr. Wehby. If I'm not mistaken, this is the first instance in America of a Republican candidate campaigning on—as opposed to simply tacitly approving of—gay marriage. There's no way we're going to win this race, but at least we're making history.

A prospective client flies me to Washington one weekend in early October for a pitch meeting, and when I land in Portland, I open my email on the tarmac to find a forwarded note from Jones Day, the law firm retained by the NRSC, firing us from the Wehby campaign. The Mormon had already canned us the week before.

So now our entire team returns to full-time focus on Art, whom one of the Canadians has bizarrely persuaded to own the issue of rape victims' rights because it might soften his image. This is two years after Missouri congressman Todd Akin tanked his own campaign to unseat a female US senator by talking about "legitimate rape." None of this is tethered to science, and in this case, our advice is actually flouting the actual, real-world lesson about why old, white Republican men should never talk about rape in political campaigns. By this point, the outcome of the race is all but preassured. It's time for me to go home.

My last act of service to Dr. Robinson comes in the form of the Foreign Policy Roundtable of Coos Bay. The deepest water port between San Francisco and Seattle, Coos Bay could have been the nexus between Canada and China in the liquefied natural gas trade had DeFazio and his environmental cronies not interfered, so it seems like a fitting place to consider how foreign policy impacts the Oregonian. Art's faithful travel from near and far to hear him tackle issues of a global scale as dusk settles into night over the Pacific.

And with that, my role as a guinea pig for Cambridge Analytica goes into snooze mode. The other races Alexander had sold me on—Arkansas, West Virginia, and Colorado—never signed up, yet Republicans go on to win all three without Cambridge Analytica. One of my team, a burly former kickboxing champion, gets sent to North Carolina, where he goes on to help elect a relatively decent US senator. *Lucky him*, I think. But for me, this will not be my ticket back into American politics after all. It's time for me to try something new.

MCLEAN, VIRGINIA, NOVEMBER 2014

I'm no stranger to far-out political campaigns, and this is fitting, really. That vanilla guy with the chamber of commerce stamp of approval, Colgate smile, and perfectly curated life running for office *x*, *y*, or *z* is, like the Mormon in Oregon, probably going to find me unacceptably weird. But the unconventional candidate, well, with good reason, he or she is becoming my niche.

Rob Sobhani was not a conventional candidate. Born in Kansas to Iranian parents, he grew up in Tehran until the 1979 revolution. His parents wisely fled just before the Islamists took over because his father had been head of military intelligence for the Shah and was studying with the American military in Leavenworth when Rob was born.

Chased from his ancestral homeland by the Islamists, Rob worked hard to establish himself in the States and was even an adjunct professor at Georgetown University before supporters of the Islamic Republic managed to stir up enough antipathy on campus to get him fired. Meanwhile, he established himself as a regional energy expert in an area close to my own experience.

I'd read about Rob in my friend Steve LeVine's book *The Oil and the Glory*. When the Soviet Union broke apart, the new leader of Azerbaijan took a shine to Rob and brought him on as an advisor for early energy deals. Rob's first advice to him was not to go into business with the British, but with the Americans instead. Where American oil companies go, our flag follows, he reasoned. A new country wedged between Russia and Iran could use a powerful friend like the United States, so Azerbaijan chose to go with Amoco on its first, big oil deal.

Marty Youssefiani, a mutual friend who also left Iran in the wake of its revolution, connected me to Rob after he'd already launched his campaign for the US Senate in Maryland. The professor and I hit it off when we met in 2012. He hired me to be his spokesman. His opponent was entrenched Democrat Ben Cardin, whom I had actually lobbied when I was at Freedom House to introduce the Magnitsky

Act, the only major bill he had to that point passed.

Rob was running as an independent and submitted over two hundred thousand signatures to get on the ballot. Just as Rob may have fancied himself a future prime minister of Iran should the Shah's son, Reza Pahlavi, ever return to the Peacock Throne, I fancied myself Rob's chief of staff should he be elected to the Senate. As we now know, neither of these things happened.

Yet we stay in touch and continue to hatch plots. For instance, Rob sent me to the *Washington Times*, owned by the family of the late Reverend Sun Myung Moon, founder of the Unification Church, with an offer to buy the conservative-leaning newspaper. They politely told me it was not for sale. Or we developed a plan to create a Farsi-language broadcasting company to beam content into Iran, and then prospective funders lost their nerve.

We're sharing a Turkish lunch at a restaurant in McLean, Virginia, when I get a call from London, and Rob signals I should take it, which I do. It's Alexander, and he's got something new that he's excited about.

How would I like to relocate to Houston, Texas, and be Cambridge Analytica's man on the Ted Cruz for president campaign? Rob, who can hear from his side of the table, nods enthusiastically, but I'm more reserved. I try to picture myself in this scenario and just can't. If I'm not willing to do it myself, Alexander insists, find someone who will.

My protégé, Jason, fits the bill perfectly. He belongs to the same church as Cruz and speaks fluent Spanish. More conservative than I, he will fit in well with the Texas crew and happily break the workday for prayer as they do. Plus he's young and ambitious and looking for a job after IRI sacked him for no legitimate reason, though I later learn it was to free up a job for a cabinet secretary's son. On my recommendation, they will hire and send him down to Houston.

I look at Rob and wonder if I'm more like him than I originally realized: one foot in one world and the other in another, trying to make things fit that never will, and constantly reinventing myself. Or am I lazy and, like my State Department boss Paula Dobriansky had once said of my speechwriting, only really excelling at the things that interest me and not plowing hard enough into the things that don't but are still important all the same? Maybe, like Rob, only the politics beyond our shores really get me, and vice versa. Or he, like me, is a stepson of the time.

When I look at Rob, I become anxious. He reminds me of a line he read in one of his own television commercials: "We are running out of time."

Ted Cruz is just too in-your-face for me and too extreme for a New England RINO, such that I am, I think to myself. Surely another horse will come along—with or without Cambridge Analytica.

ABUJA, NIGERIA, JANUARY 2015

The Nigerian passport control officer's round, dark face is beaded with sweat as he gestures for me to lean in closer.

"What are you *really* doing here?" he asks with big, incredulous eyes and a hint of conspiracy.

"Like my visa says," I tell him, "consulting on matters of sand and gravel."

With an irritated grunt, he waves me on as I go to see if my baggage indeed followed me to Abuja. To get into town, we drive around Aso Rock, behind which lies the presidential compound.

I know this because it's not my first visit to Nigeria. Just before my wedding eighteen months ago, Sam Amsterdam flew me here to media train his client, a wealthy businessman who dabbled in politics. It was a surreal week spent on the man's compound in the Niger Delta. Sam is certainly following in his father Bob's footsteps with this client.

Sam's client was my introduction to Nigerian politics. He'd been governor of Abia, one of the country's thirty-six states, and sought to be seen as the leader of the Igbo people—one of Nigeria's three major tribes. To top it all off, he has the improbable first name of Orji, which is pronounced a little differently than its homonym. Though his time as governor was cut short by corruption charges, Orji insists these were politically motivated. Regardless, Orji was definitely an *oga*, which among Nigerians means "big man" (not unlike *oligarch*).

While we were his guests on his compound, with most of the fittings of a modest country club, rent-seekers of all sorts would come and wait in one of the various sitting rooms for an audience with the oga. Just meeting him could be enough to change the future of any of the many hangers-on, you'd think from the sheer number of people who did it.

There was also an engaging and articulate man about my age whom others called the Honorable and was, by his telling, a senator. He'd been elected in a nearby state but had never been formally given this mandate, so he was suing for his seat. With a clipped Oxford accent, he would advise Orji on matters of the upmost importance and, if he wasn't by the oga's side, could be found strolling the grounds in a tailored linen suit.

I later heard he eventually got his seat, and then Orji won his own after switching political horses. If politics in Nigeria were a game, these men were players.

It is just before Christmas 2014, and my gift from SCL and Cambridge Analytica is a last-minute reelection campaign for President Goodluck Jonathan. Contrary to his sanguine name, the winds aren't blowing Jonathan's way, as voters in Africa's fastest-growing country are hungry for change.

The team is already ensconced at the Hilton, which boasts an enormous kidney-shaped swimming pool, which I hope will give me some occasional relief from the campaign. Once in my room, I switch on the television and can see a rally for Jonathan's opponent, General Muhammadu Buhari, in the north of the country. There are tens of thousands of people gathered on a plain. Some are waving brooms, and all are stomping their feet in unison. I can almost feel the ground shake all the way down in Abuja. This is going to be hard—maybe even impossible.

Nigeria has never had a peaceful democratic transfer of power. Jonathan, a zoologist who legend holds was so humble in his origin that he was once shoeless, literally lucked into the job when the sickly Umaru Yar'Adua, a Muslim from the north, picked him to be his vice president. By the informal agreement that has kept the peace since civil war from 1969 to 1970, the North and South take turns at the presidency, and this is a northerner's turn. Jonathan, though, is from the South—the Niger Delta, to be precise—and now that Yar'Adua has died, he is serving out of turn.

London has contracted a former BBC correspondent to do the media, and we immediately begin collaborating on a script for a

TV ad. Really, we're working in the dark, without a poll or focus groups to orient ourselves. So we start soft with a thirty spot called "Stay on the Path." It's so soft that it's nearly anodyne. For it to work, enough Nigerians would have to believe they are already on the right path, and while there has been piecemeal progress under Jonathan, poverty and corruption persist.

"They're more American than we are," a former US ambassador to Nigeria told me when I was doing my pretrip research, "and that rattles us."

What he was talking about is the ambition and hustle that actually does characterize many of the Nigerians I meet from the very outset, including a cop who pulled us over when we'd been out drinking and told my friend who was driving, after a drink or two himself, "Brother, I'm thirsty."

Too many are thirsty and hungry. We've got just a little over a month until the election. After a tepid response to the first ad, we get the message quickly. We need to be bolder to even have a chance at not failing. So I call in my old mentor, Tony Marsh, who has a knack for getting to the heart of the matter.

Buhari had been military dictator of Nigeria in the 1980s, at a time when there were serious human rights concerns. There was an urban myth that he would horsewhip civil servants whom he considered to be slacking and lock up anyone who criticized the state—including a pop star named Fela, whose imprisonment angered the youth. Had the worm turned though—did Nigerians today long for the strong hand Buhari had exercised in the past?

Our team is already working on some radio spots that use the audio of a cracking whip to remind of Buhari's past abuses. It doesn't occur to me that plenty of people would like to see that whip applied to crooked, ineffectual government players. Tony and I take a slightly different approach. We lay hands on some old footage of gross human rights abuses from the mid-1980s, and by *gross*, I mean literally. Footage of the atrocities that took place in the 1980s is gross—no more Mr. Nice Guy. The infomercial-length piece ends up looking like a short horror film.

Again, though, context is everything. Earlier this year, the Islamic extremist group Boko Haram kidnapped 276 Christian schoolgirls from the northern town of Chibok. Buhari, a Muslim from the north with a military background, was promising to have all the girls back in a matter of two weeks. For Jonathan, this crisis is comparable to what the US hostages in Iran were for Jimmy Carter in the late 1970s. It makes him look very weak and useless.

I report on the grim situation I am seeing to London. Soldier through, they say, and do the best you can.

Poolside, I run into an old colleague who is there with the British PR giant Bell-Pottinger, contracted by another backer of Jonathan's to do the same thing with an exponentially bigger budget. This is what sometimes happens when people panic: they make a big show of how hard they're trying to stave off disaster.

"We've got a massive TV campaign we're about to drop. It's going to be a game changer," one of the Bell-Pottinger guys tells me with a straight face. "We're calling the campaign 'Rolling Thunder,' just like Vietnam. Catchy, eh?"

But for my efforts to coordinate, we would be working at cross-purposes. In addition to a healthy budget appropriate for a national campaign, they have polling as well. For the most part, the research they're willing to share bears out our initial instincts: this is a change election, and we're with the incumbent.

One of the benefits of being a consultant is that I can come and go. I'm courting a new client in Eastern Europe, and this gets me out of Nigeria for a week. The crew that is holed up at the Hilton is, understandably, edgier than I. According to an account I will later read in the *Guardian*—albeit one that was drummed up as an attack on Cambridge and chock-full of exaggerations—some members of the team were fearful for their lives. This part of the story, at least, is true.

I'm on my second Bloody Mary waiting in the Frankfurt airport for my flight back to Abuja when Faisal from Iraq calls just to check in. When I tell him where I'm going, he pauses.

"Special services," he says enigmatically, "are scrambling all the private aircraft they can lay hands on for a possible mass evacuation from Nigeria. Be careful!"

I have a third drink before boarding.

At the same time, US secretary of state John Kerry is making the first of two visits to Abuja. "Respect the will of the people," he tells Jonathan. We're going to lose; you can just feel it in the way people seem to wince and cringe despite themselves when they talk to you, seeming eager to escape.

"Stand tall, look strong," a governor of one state or another tells my friend in the Hilton's bar one evening as the ominous election nears before hurrying away himself with a mobile police escort.

The hotel has only one Mamba APC, which is an armored vehicle with run flats, making it the only vehicle capable of getting to the airport even in the midst of melee and hostile fire. Yet there are hundreds of foreign guests who might also want to be evacuated should things go, as the Brits say, "tits up." At this point, the best we can do is hope they don't.

Now a senior consultant, I'm not in country by the time the election comes. All you have to do to be a consultant, one of my early mentors joked, is blow into town once a month, have a couple of martinis, and shoot the shit. Obviously, it's a little more involved than that in practice, but you get the idea.

MEXICO CITY, JANUARY 2018

Standing between Chapultepec Park and a three-story bronze statue of a dancing Aztec man, facing the posh neighborhood of Polanco, the InterContinental Presidente seems like a solid place. I've been in this racquet long enough to know that looks can be deceiving, but I need the work. For want of anything permanent, this will be my office.

By the time I get to Mexico City, Cambridge Analytica has already been at this for some time. The previous team had run up something like a year's worth of expenses and still not signed the PRI, Mexico's long-standing party of power. It would be a big fish, certainly. I'm part of the new bait.

Alexander has now brought on Mark Turnbull, whom I'd known in Iraq as one of the Bell-Pottinger men running publicity for the interim government, to professionalize the "Rest of World" division of Cambridge Analytica.

Now there is the US division, the biggest, and the "Rest of World," into which I am, ironically, a better fit. Mark's brought his right hand, James, to organize a reboot of this expensive and time-consuming pitch.

As usual, Cambridge Analytica has assembled a motley crew of a couple of Mexican consultants, an American doctoral student who has essentially gone Mexican, James to keep a tighter leash on things, and yours truly as the Machiavellian strategist. I feel it would be better if I spoke Spanish, but London doesn't seem to care.

A few months ago, we pitched the Spanish government on combatting the Catalonian independence, but that never gelled. You miss every ball at which you don't swing, and I may have been overvaluing being an expert on the country where you work. I'd downloaded several political histories of Mexico and done my best to catch up since this prospect arose two days ago.

Mark's a company man, which, like the solidity of the hotel where we've gathered, is reassuring after all the smoke and mirrors. If Mexico becomes real, it will be my fifth campaign with Cambridge Analytica and certainly the biggest. It will be a year's work, and for that it will even be worth learning to speak Spanish. This one we'll do right, he promises.

PRI doesn't have an easy path forward. Morena, its opponent, literally means "dark-skinned" and is led by the charismatic populist Andres Manuel Lopez Obrador, who speaks the language of the streets and maintains PRI stole an earlier victory from him. The new American president Donald Trump, whom Cambridge Analytica claims a role in helping to elect, has said unpleasant things about Mexico and threatened to tear up NAFTA, so Mexicans reasonably want a tough guy who will push back, not a milquetoast toady.

And then there are the violent drug cartels, which have only grown in power. PRI's claim to fame had been stability and security, yet neither of these things seem to exist in the country today—beyond

Polanco anyway.

Plus we're still trying to figure out exactly what PRI has already been told. Brittany Kaiser had been heading the never-ending pitch until last week. Alexander blew through town just before my arrival and yelled at her in a restaurant, making her cry. Where he found her, I'm not sure, but she struck me as a big talker—a Sandra Bernhard ringer in her early thirties who claimed to be tight with everyone from the Obamas to the inventors of blockchain. What precisely the client may have been expecting could have been unclear, but it is our job to change all that.

Mark has set up a new modus operandi, and we're retooling the scope of work. As with all campaigns, this requires seizing control of the narrative. In any contest against the larger-than-life AMLO, that is going to be a serious challenge. The bigger challenge, of course, will be projecting a sense of strength and order in a country where drug cartels run rampant and de facto rule various regions. But that's a future problem, now we just have to secure the account.

There's a lot of hurry up and wait. Good thing I brought so much reading.

Every few days I'm moving hotels. James usually gives me the heads-up a day or so ahead. Already I've been checked in and out of three, and now, at long last, they're putting me in the InterContinental, reducing my morning commute to an elevator ride. I feel almost too lucky.

But in the longer view, though, neither Cambridge Analytica nor I are all that lucky, either in terms of Mexico or more broadly. We're both about to experience major upheaval on parallel though separate fronts. PRI is already bracing for a loss to Obrador and is cautious about engaging a firm that has been darkly tied to Trump.

James calls to tell me London is pulling the plug. He's headed out that evening and has booked me on a flight back to Washington tomorrow morning. Would he meet me in the hotel bar for a last drink, I ask?

We are leaning against the lobby bar, laughing about the various absurdities of this mission to hide our disappointment that it has come to naught.

And then a gut-rumbling shake under our feet snaps us back to the present. Beneath the massive concrete and marble slabs on which we are standing, the earth just moved. Literally.

"Did you feel that?" James asks.

I nod. Others in the lobby also stop talking and look at one another as a moment passes before the siren sounds. Walk—don't run—as you exit the building, an announcement advises. I put my bourbon down on the bar and follow the throng of hotel guests and visitors up to the lobby and out onto the street.

The massive forty-two-story building shakes but does not fall. Everyone gathers around the dancing Aztec. It occurs to me the statue stands on only one leg, really, with the other tucked behind its calf. Instinctively, I step back. "Hate to leave you like this, but I've got a flight to catch," James reminds.

I help him find a taxi, we shake hands, and I say I'm sorry it didn't work out.

"Not Mother's silver, is it?" he says with a smile as he slips into the cab.

I am not sure exactly what that means, but James is gone before it occurs to me how puzzled I am by the phrase. He likely meant the value of a thing is subjective and never entirely clear based on its appearance alone.

When the all-clear sounds, I follow the crowd back into the hotel. My drink is still sitting on the bar, and I pick it up. This is it, I sense, as I take a long sip. *This is my last rodeo with Cambridge Analytica*, I tell myself, unaware that it really is, irrespective of my own will. In a couple of weeks, there will be revelations that the company was harvesting data from Facebook in violation of privacy rules, leading to a massive scandal that will nearly tank the social media giant and from which the London-based consultancy will never rebound.

Steve Bannon, who once sat on Cambridge Analytica's board, will tell me a few weeks later that he is skeptical the company could ever do what it promised. Jason, the young man I recruited as my body double for the Cruz for president campaign, will tell a reporter that he quit the company "because I got tired of lying every day." When he does quit, I will get him another job in Moldova—this time for a Democrat firm that made its name on the Clintons. So there are questions as to whether the psychographic modeling ever really worked.

That's not all. In a month's time, Alexander and Mark will be caught on tape during a sting by Britain's Channel 4 boasting about all the dirty tricks they can offer two journalists pretending to be middlemen for a Sri Lankan political party. Honey traps with hookers, Nix promises as Turnbull intimates MI-6 connections. It's a caricature of the kind of exaggeration one often uses in pitches. While Alexander may be all pitchman, Mark—whom I met in Baghdad more than ten years earlier—is a solid professional of the old school.

So it's not just an earthquake I survive in Mexico City but also the implosion of a high-flying, too flashy for its own good political consulting enterprise. Still, I can't quite shake the idea it was an experiment worth doing, especially given the belief so many have that we now live in the age of disruption.

CHAPTER 8

UKRAINE AND THE PRELUDE TO WAR

OCTOBER 2014

The steel door had been torched earlier in the year. Russian journalists had holed up here during the government-toppling events of February, and I suppose that made sense. It is a conveniently located apartment with a narrow view of the nearby Maidan—Kyiv's central square, where protestors camped out during the winter months both in 2004 and 2013. Now the door is still charred, with bits of black and rust-colored metal flaking off if you close it with too much force. But it served its purpose then, and the landlord sees little point in replacing it now. I've just gotten used to it and handle it gingerly.

Looking up as I climb the stairs, I see three men in leather jackets standing right in front of the door, ringing the bell and waiting. That's a bad sign, which I suddenly connect with the guy standing by the entrance and the van parked in a way that almost blocked the building's front door. Instinctively, I keep climbing past my landing, pretending not to notice the men. One of them must smell my fear and starts to follow me up the stairwell, but the man in charge tells him to hang back. I keep climbing up several flights, though I feel I'm just going deeper into a trap.

Breathlessly, I'm standing on the fourth floor, with my limited options racing through my mind. I can keep going, though access to the roof is probably locked, and what would I do up there anyway? I could try to talk my way into one of these apartments to hide, but "frantic foreigner" just isn't a good look, and this option is likely to draw even more attention to me. Or I can bolt, using the only practical technology at my disposal: an old-fashioned elevator with a wall-less cab. That's my best bet. I press the button to call for it.

At first none of the leather-clad door lurkers below notice as I descend in the humming and clanking old elevator behind them. Then, just as my head is level with their feet and almost entirely out of their view, one catches sight of me out of the corner of his eye, and I hear him rally another to join the chase.

The door opens, and I run for daylight, bursting out of the building's entrance and cutting a sharp left up the hill. I've already been jogging nearly an hour this morning, and I'm both loose and anticipating the hill, so I'm already a couple of blocks up by the time my pursuers get onto the street.

Neither the Canadian embassy nor a large Catholic church that I pass is likely to protect me, so I keep climbing. I'm more focused on running than looking back. Darting across a street without stopping, I dive into the park at the top of the hill and straight for a trail that cuts through to another part of town.

Once I'm in the park, I know for sure I've lost them. Who could they have been? The government? Maybe they were hired thugs there to settle someone's score with me? Whoever it was, they almost got me right where I was living. I make like I am jogging to the Hyatt Regency in Sofiivska Square. Once inside the Hyatt's protective cocoon, I allow myself to get angry. My first call is to Kostya.

"I'm not getting paid anywhere near enough for this kind of shit," I bark into the cell phone, trying vainly to sound cool when in fact I am terrified.

"Are you sure this really happened?" he asks.

Kostya's question sends me into a fit of rage. "I'm not going to debate what I just experienced," I tell him. Instead, why doesn't he use whatever resources he has to figure out why the fuck this just happened and make sure it doesn't happen again. I'm now spluttering into my iPhone and drawing attention in the hotel lobby.

"Of course," he assures me. But it might be a good idea for me to hang around here at the hotel until he does, Kostya prudentially suggests. So I check into the spa and swim for an hour in an effort to calm my nerves.

Still dripping wet, I hear my phone ringing, and when I answer Kostya tells me it was all a misunderstanding, and there will be no further problems. I can go back to the apartment now, he says. It's safe. For some reason, I just accept what he's said at face value and head back to the dimly lit *podyez* (hallway in an apartment building), charred door, and IKEA-furnished, sunny little flat in central Kyiv.

This is a test, I tell myself as I walk back down the hill. *Just a test, and I'll pass it like the others. Everything is going to be okay.* My mind flashes back to a conversation I wasn't meant to understand soon after I arrived here.

Together with my translator Sunshine, I was meeting a shady guy who Sergei calls Michael. He is in charge of printing and distributing pamphlets attacking our enemies. These pamphlets are based on the scripts I'm writing with Sunshine's help. Under his breath, Michael asks her in Russian, "Is this guy strong enough?"

My heart sings when, after a beat, she tells him that I am indeed. Now the gauntlet has been thrown again: Am I going to let a botched kidnapping, followed by Lord knows what, throw me off task? Or am I going to be the guy Sunshine just said I was? That guy would neither bend nor buckle. He would take whatever danger and difficulty thrown in his path in perfect stride.

Two weeks earlier, I'm loitering outside a dreary campaign headquarters, staring at a cross-fit gym in a garage with open doors as I suck down a cigarette in the parking lot of the strip mall outside Portland, Oregon, when my phone registers a Ukrainian number calling. With the US Senate campaign Cambridge Analytica attached me to here flailing, it's only a matter of time before the candidate fires us like she did her last team. At that moment, I was desolate and dejected enough to take a call from anyone.

As it turned out, it was Konstantin Kilimnik, or Kostya, calling. Would I be interested in a short-term gig in Kyiv for a month? Laura has planned for my being away through November elections anyway. It's as good an escape as any, and unlike the Brits, Kostya's guy there is ready to pay above my rack rate because of the short notice. That's $30,000 for three weeks. They want me on the ground ASAP.

Kostya had been my deputy in the IRI office in Moscow. He had since hooked up with a heavyweight, Darth Vader–esque American political advisor Paul Manafort, and landed a significant piece of work steering Ukraine's Party of Regions through parliamentary and presidential elections. The man Manafort helped shape into Ukraine's next president, Viktor Yanukovych, had once served time in prison for stealing a hat. If Manafort could make an ex-con president, he must be a magician.

Up to a point anyway. Manafort was able to persuade Yanukovych the president to make his first foreign trip to Brussels, not Moscow— an important signal of intentions. But that was 2010, and by 2013 Yanukovych's government needed cash and forbearance on gas debts badly, so it switched gears, putting the European Union membership dream of many Ukrainians on hold indefinitely.

Slamming the gears into reverse like that sent a shock wave through the increasingly westward-leaning country. It was headed somewhere bloodier than the Orange Revolution had been in 2004–2005.

I'd crossed paths with Kostya seven years before when I was doing media work with Tony for the political party of Victor Yushchenko, the appealing central banker who was poisoned before pro-Russian consultants tried to rig the election for Yanukovych in 2005.

The backlash to these events became the Orange Revolution, in which the protest crowds swelled in central Kyiv despite the harsh winter. The authorities then folded in a deal brokered by an ex-Polish president. Yushchenko took the presidency, and Yulia Tymoshenko, a comely blonde with a Princess Leia hairdo, got the prime minister's chair—both promising reforms.

That defeat then prompted a group of Donetsk-based eastern Ukrainians to switch their own approach west by hiring Manafort instead of Russian "political technologists." I don't know what precisely Paul did for Ferdinand Marcos, or Jonas Savimbi, Mobutu Sese Seko, or Abdul Rahman el-Assir, who reportedly hired him on behalf of French presidential candidate Eduard Balladur in the 1990s.

But what he and Kostya did for the eastern Ukrainians was essentially party building—something Paul knew about ever since age ten, when his dad got elected to the New Britain, Connecticut, board of aldermen and Kostya from his years of translating for IRI in Russia. While my old boss David Kramer told the *Guardian* "advising Yanukovych is like putting lipstick on a pig," there was actually a bit more to it.

As it tends to happen in Ukraine, one side pushed too far. Yanukovych had jailed his likeliest opponent, Yulia Tymoshenko, allowed even more flagrant corruption than usual to take root, and was now saying no to the one thing that allowed Ukrainians to overlook those first two offenses: a European future.

In mid-November 2013, crowds of mostly young protestors encamped on Kyiv's Maidan, or central square, and refused to leave until Yanukovych reversed course or stepped down. Over the next couple of months, the demonstrators grew in numbers and began occupying central Kyiv in larger and larger droves. In late January the next year, blood spilled down the little hill on which the presidential administration stands after snipers picked off protestors in the crowd. A "Holy Hundred" were killed as protestors tore cobblestones from the streets to build barricades, and the street started shooting back.

That's when Sergei Lyovochkin, Yanukovych chief of staff, resigned in protest. INTER, the Eastern-focused TV station he co-owns with exiled oligarch Dmitro Firtash, showed continuous live broadcasting of the events on the square and played a role in shocking a nation's conscience. When Yanukovych's government fled under the cover of night, there were those who went to Russia with the toppled president and those who stayed behind. It's the ones who didn't run who hire me, on Lyovochkin's recommendation.

Lyovochkin and Kostya are tight because my old deputy is now the link between Manafort and his clients. If he needs to know what the "wise old owl" thought about something, Sergei goes to Kostya. This made him more than a translator and, as Manafort told me, "a powerful little dude."

Manafort and Kostya kept their office just a block off the Maidan throughout the "Revolution of People's Dignity." I wondered how the angry crowds would react if they knew that this dark, Machiavellian advisor of Yanukovych's was tucked among them, probably peering out his window at the mounting unrest and hoping he wouldn't be recognized. Or maybe he wasn't all that worried, because he knew everything was not quite as it seemed.

In the immediate aftermath of the revolution, I got an offer to go to Kyiv and work for the acting president, Petro Poroshenko, and help him on his campaign to win his mandate formally in snap elections. I was already working for Saleh al-Mutlaq in Iraq at the time, and tempted though I was to return to Ukraine at another historic moment, I was not going to ditch one client for another.

Now the Party of Regions is gone, dissolved. Manafort is now counseling the Opposition Bloc, comprised of some of the old parts but, as the name informs, is no longer in power. At the time I arrive in October, they are polling at less than 5 percent. Manafort would handle the party side of things, Lyovochkin explains, and I will run a parallel "minus" campaign against the handful of parties most primed to steal our votes. I title the plan I quickly wrote up for his approval "Operation Clawback." The title makes him smile.

By Sergei's design, I don't report to Manafort. But I am now practicing the dark arts of negative campaigning so Manafort can focus on the positive case for Opposition Bloc. As such, I'm doing Darth Vader's dirty work. Kostya tells me they had initially planned to hire Manafort's old business partner Roger Stone for the gig, but then he got busy with something in New York, opening the opportunity for me.

———————

I'd already switched sides once, in Georgia. In Iraq last year, I was working for people who didn't necessarily love Americans. But in coming here to work alongside Manafort for the remnants of the Party of Regions—those dubious, "pro-Russian" people—have I not truly crossed over to the dark side? Did it matter?

In my first meeting with Sergei, I try to give him the elevator speech about who I am, but he just waves his hand.

"I already know," he says, "that's why you're here."

For me, this is already a cliché—former Soviets acting like they have dossiers on everybody—so I give him a wry look, and he clarifies. The *Washington Post* story about me told him everything he needed to know, he says. Even if we both know that's not true.

But I pretend for a moment it is. Just like Cambridge Analytica had, Sergei had summoned me because he thought I was the best available option. That makes me a prized commodity. *After so many years of struggling professionally, my moment has arrived*, I think. But let's look at this gift horse a little more closely.

Lyovochkin quit Yanukovych on what appears to have been principle. Some might liken it to a rat leaving a sinking ship, but narrative spins are cheaper than actions. The worst of the worst, which is to say the most criminally corrupt, have fled to Russia with the toppled president. By default, that means the ones who stayed behind to fight for the equal rights of Russian-speaking Ukrainians who dominate the southeast of the country are in fact the real deal.

Western Ukrainians want to join Europe and are good, while eastern Ukrainians are stuck in the past like Slavic trolls, or so we think in the North Atlantic community. Yet Misha in Georgia caused me to question the Manichean light-versus-dark take on all things Eurasian. The truth is often more complicated.

If Ukraine is going to work as a country, the West and the East will have to reach a better accommodation than the one we've got now. Just recently, the speaker of the Rada, an ardent nationalist of the Western bent, referred to Russian speakers as "subhuman." That's the same kind of rhetoric that usually precedes genocide.

Had followers of the nationalist leader Stepan Bandera not cooperated so enthusiastically with the Nazi occupiers when it came to exterminating Jews in the 1940s, one might not recoil as quickly from such rhetoric today.

But not all western Ukrainians are Banderistas, and not all easterners are Russian serfs. Political rhetoric that plays on these old wounds is worse than the ever more polarizing messaging we're hearing at home. There was a time, only seven years ago, when I was producing ads making fun of the very people I'm working for now.

JULY 2007

"What y'all are seeing now is the effect of staying on message," political commentator and strategist James Carville is telling the dour-faced room full of Ukrainian functionaries as he points to a chart of polling results over a period of several months. Tall, thin, and bald, the Ragin' Cajun strikes an unusual profile on Bankova, the street where the Ukrainian presidential administration sits.

Carville is about to expand on his point about message discipline—and perhaps even refer back to his famous "it's the economy, stupid" communications guidance on the 1992 Clinton campaign—when the red-faced Roman Bezsmertniy, deputy chief of staff to Ukrainian President Viktor Yushchenko, stands up from the head of the huge elliptical table around which the assembled company are gathered and walks up to Carville, taking the marker out of his hand.

"No." Bezsmertniy—whose name in Russian literally means "without death," or" immortal"—emphatically contradicts the American guest, takes the Sharpie out of his hand, and draws an X through the section of the slide that showed a recent uptick. "It is summer, and in summer polls in Ukraine go down. Not up," he explains.

Celebrity political couple Carville and his wife, Mary Matalin, are here for GQR's dog-and-pony show meant to wow the clients and engage the top level, which in this case means the president and his key staff. Local teams can be stubborn and resistant, everyone in our little racket knows, but this is pretty remarkable even by those standards. Carville shakes his head in amazement.

"I've heard some stupid shit in my time," the thin, bald Cajun shoots back, "but that is dumbest motherfucking shit I have *evah* heard!"

Until now, I've just been a fly on the wall, sitting back and soaking in the subtle cultural differences in how the GQR team is delivering the presentation and how the locals are receiving it. To everyone else in the room, Bezsmertniy is essentially the top dog in the president's administration. He helped organize the Orange Revolution that brought the whole crew into power. Dissing him, as Carville has just done, is a big deal—and not in a good way.

I look at my watch. There's a shift change for the guards in five minutes. Time to snap into action. When the guards change their shifts is the only time our foreign advisor team can enter and leave the presidential administration on Bankova Street since we were never supposed to have been there in the first place, so I seize the opportunity to steer Carville and Matalin toward the exit and into a waiting black Mercedes. From the astonished look on their faces, I can tell they haven't been fully briefed on Ukrainian politics. One wonders whether the fly-through folks ever really are.

We are fighting a two-front war here. Ostensibly, our enemy is the Party of Regions, which controls the parliamentary-led government. We are trying to wrest that away from them and give Yushchenko enough clout in the Rada to push his agenda through and modernize Ukraine.

But there is actually more intense infighting within the Orange coalition, especially with the Princess Leia–looking Yulia Tymoshenko. She and Yushchenko loathe each other, and this becomes more obvious with each passing day. Ordinary voters, our research shows, are getting angrier and angrier about this because they see the Oranges fighting each other instead of improving people's lives. They're getting even angrier than Bezsmertniy just was with Carville.

Our message is simple: no one is above the law. To get more of a handle on Ukraine's free-wheeling, alliance-shifting parliament, Yushchenko has proposed ending the immunity from prosecution that deputies enjoy and which in fact incentivizes crooked businessmen to become deputies in many instances. It is almost like we are stealing a page from Newt Gingrich's 1994 *Contract with America*, in which he promised to make Congress more accountable to the people.

Sitting in a grungy bar somewhere in the downscale Podol district, where our production studio lives in a modest basement—in between elections they pay their rent copying porn on DVDs—Tony and I hatch a script that tells the story well: What if the politicians had to live like us for a change?

Imagine if, instead of living on plush estates, Rada deputies had to live in crummy, small apartments like us. Imagine if, instead of chauffeured foreign cars, they had to cram like sardines into outdated buses like we do. Imagine if, instead of dining in fancy restaurants, they had to eat cutlets in the cafeteria like us? And so it goes. We see a pompous politician get his comeuppance when he has to live like the rest of us. It's aimed squarely at the pissed-off electorate and gives them something to smile about. We invite voters to fire the fat cats in government.

That is understandable, even if the intricacies of Ukrainian politics can make your eyes glaze over as you try to follow the allegiances of convenience and double or triple hitting by most of the players. You can't honestly just say these guys are "pro-Russian," and these folks are pro-freedom or reform or European integration or what have you.

A year after this episode, Yushchenko will accuse one of his allies—possibly even the one footing GQR's handsome bill—of having been involved in his 2004 dioxin poisoning. It is all so forbiddingly opaque.

When the election comes at the end of September, both Our Ukraine and the Party of Regions will lose seats while Tymoshenko will gain them. She will become prime minister, and more than two years later Yushchenko will support Yanukovych's bid for the presidency over hers.

If I've learned anything about Ukraine this summer, it is just how little things are as they appear. When I board my flight home the day after the election, I will do so with an overwhelming sense of relief. But relief is just the dominant emotion; there is a surging mix of others as well, and it often includes tears.

OCTOBER 2014

"She looks like a witch," the older man growls at his deputy, Rick Gates, as Kostya and I look from a little distance at the threefold brochure with a photograph of a gnarled, rural woman of advanced years on its cover. What Manafort is being asked is to sign off on one of the party's fliers for door-to-door distribution. The intended recipients, like Kostya and myself, see a grandmotherly old woman, perhaps a little worse for wear given the tough times.

Gates shakes his head dejectedly and leaves with one of the party's lieutenants to come up with a graphic of a less "witchy-looking" babushka. Quietly I smile and wonder if Manafort isn't missing the point. Witches, I'm beginning to learn, seem to be a big deal here.

My job is the "minus," Sergei has made clear. Making the

Opposition Bloc look like it's on the side of the people is Manafort's job, while mine is simply attacking Sergei's array of enemies. I do this well—well enough that someone sent a welcome party to thank me.

The internet ads I make with Sunshine's help are all bleeding edge. Our ads underscored the lies baked into our major competitors' claims, for example: a rival oligarch who also said he represents the people was sunning himself on the French Riviera while dozens of our target voters were burned alive during political violence in Odesa, or one of the former president's sharpest critics is seen taking a knee and kissing the ring of the very man he piously rebuked in public. As a matter of gravity, it's easier to tear things down than it is to build them.

"You earned your money, kid," Manafort tells me over dinner the night after the election. Opposition Bloc won about 10 percent, which is more than twice what they were polling at when I arrived a month ago. When you consider our guys were overthrown in a revolution less than nine months ago, it actually does seem like an achievement of sorts.

When he talks to me about his role in Ukraine, it's largely in the past tense. He's proud of how he's integrated with the client—"They consider me one of them," he tells me—and he has played some role in geopolitics, he says wistfully. He's checked out of this place, it seems to me. Either he's headed off to retire on a golf course somewhere, or he must have some new, better gig in the offing.

Kostya explains the clients are no longer in a position to pay Paul's princely fees, especially now that they are in the opposition. The new government is squeezing them in the yin-and-yang flow of Ukrainian corruption, and they're going to have to do more with less. This being the case, he says, they are pleased with my performance at a fraction of Paul's cost. This can be long-term work if, he pauses, we can somehow manage the divorce.

As best as I can understand how the divorce goes, there are two camps: Lyovochkin and everybody else. Of course, like everything here, it's more complicated than that. They are the Donbas guys, oligarchs in steel and metals and construction and manufacturing. Sergei pulls together everybody else.

He would finance his share with proceeds from energy assets, but these are under siege, so he just hustles, and this breeds resentment among the Donbas crew. They've not only lost territory to separatists but they're also getting stuck with the bill. To them, Sergei is a political pimp.

Yet he is also the guy who, as one heavyweight told me, "is always playing three-dimensional chess," and that's an asset everyone needs. In practical terms, that means Sergei is the prospector for new political real estate and the broker of alliances and ententes.

Ever since that last dinner with Manafort in late October 2014, a sword of Damocles hangs over the Opposition Bloc. It's a lost opportunity, too, because OB is one of the few players that probably could pull off local elections in those parts of the East, where "separatists" fight the Ukrainian state. This is an unmet requirement of the Minsk Accords that are supposed to set the framework for peace, even as sporadic fighting continues.

Sergei now flies me in every six months or so to present poll findings and make strategic recommendations. Invariably, they are headlined: "Put aside your differences and position yourselves to make a common attack here, there, and there so as to win the next election." But that first part never happens.

Walking out of one of these recurring, almost identical shadow politburo meetings, I turn to Kostya and ask him if he's seen *Groundhog Day*. He hasn't, so I explain the idea, in which Bill Murray is a TV reporter who ends up reliving the same day over and over again.

"Yeah," he says, "I guess that's pretty much it."

During these visits, I meet with other political leaders to advise them on their particular situations, often with Sergei's encouragement. He arranged for me to see the woman who intrigued me from the start: Yulia Tymoshenko.

The fact that she would see me at all, given that Sergei was the chief of staff to the president who had imprisoned her, baffled me at first. But now I get it. This is the protean nature of Ukrainian politics, which are constantly writhing, shifting, and evolving. There are always surprises, and sometimes even witches.

"Be careful of Ukrainian women," Kostya's wife, Katya, a Muscovite through and through, tells me mischievously over dinner one night. "They're all witches." Despite a pained expression on Kostya's face, she elaborates. "For instance, if you're having dinner with one, the moment you look away she will slip a drop of her own menstrual blood into your wine, and when you drink it, you'll be in her thrall forever!"

It seems obvious Katya is teasing here, but to her point, the old ladies who campaign for Tymoshenko on the streets are trained in hypnosis. One political heavyweight in Ukraine told me she casts spells over men. But with me, she doesn't bother—I'm just a consultant.

I share with her some of the research we've done and point out some vulnerabilities that her party, the Bloc of Yulia Tymoshenko, may face from others trying to take what she considers her share of the vote. She listens politely and then asks a few questions that suggest a keen mind for politics. *Maybe she'll be my client one day*, I think to myself.

The tour continues.

Another Ukrainian oligarch whom Sergei sends me to see is known to have given nearly $10 million to the Clinton Global Foundation. It is the summer of 2015, and I take some pleasure in telling him I think Hillary, whom he considers a friend, will lose the coming presidential election.

"Oh, but I also give to Republicans," Victor Pinchuk defensively says as he reaches for a photograph of himself playing golf with George H. W. Bush. Now he smiles, having evidenced that he is in fact a true player. A few months later, he will donate $150,000 to a Donald Trump charity for the reality TV star and now presidential candidate to speak at the annual "mini-Davos" he hosts each fall in Kyiv.

"You're like an expensive watch," Kostya tells me. "He wants everyone to see he's got it." That is around the same time Kostya starts introducing me to people as the "New Paul." At the time, I don't really have much of a sense where any of this will lead, except possibly to another gig.

FEBRUARY 2015

Of the three epic knights who in legend defended the Kievan Rus from attackers both from east and west, Ilya Muromets is the best remembered. Tall and strong and good-hearted, he rises from the stove on top of which he had been convalescing his entire youth at age thirty-three to defend the motherland. The one figure on Ukraine's political horizon who most reminds me of Muromets is former world heavyweight champion Vitaly Klitschko.

Just a few days older than me, Klitschko came onto the political scene after my first campaign here for Yushchenko. The man is built like a brick shithouse and keeps up his prizefighting form even though it's his brother Wladimir who now holds the title. And people know where he got his money: he fought for it fair and square.

I heard him tell a group of students how a crooked bureaucrat tried to stiff his mother out of his late father's military pension. Had she paid the apparatchik a regular cut, he would allow her to get some of what was rightfully hers.

"When he became president, Yanukovych asked me the name of this man and promised to find and destroy him," Klitschko told the kids, "but I said, 'No, Viktor, it's the whole fucking system that is crooked. It needs to be torn down and rebuilt.'"

I haven't lost my soft spot for underdogs or political heroes in waiting. My old friend Boris Nemtsov is now marching on the streets of Moscow for the freedom of assembly and an end to the war in Ukraine. Irakli Alasania had recently been Georgia's minister of defense and is back in opposition there now as Bidzina, like Misha before him, becomes less democratic. Klitschko is big enough to speak truth to power in this crooked country. Maybe the future should be his.

I meet Klitschko in January 2015, playing hooky from a Nigerian campaign to do so. He is finishing his first term as mayor of

Kyiv, putting together his reelection team. A second term is by no means assured—Kyivans are restless and angry the way only those in a capital city can be.

Low-intensity war drags on in the east, but you wouldn't know it walking down the city's central Kreshatyk Avenue, with its expensive stores and high-end European autos illegally parked left and right. The city's residents have high expectations, and with things falling apart everywhere else, it seems somehow more important to deliver now than ever.

Klitschko and his kitchen cabinet hire me, and I bring on a couple of US pollsters with experience in Ukraine. We are basically plugged into a team of Ukrainian consultants, and for the most part everyone gets along. At my inspiration, we call our headquarters the "bread factory," because it is there we take the raw ingredients and turn them into a necessary product. It's a uniquely hybrid setup, where the integration of foreign and local consultants can as work smoothly and effectively as any I've known.

It is only on return from a trip to set up the bread factory in late February that I learn Nemtsov has been assassinated in front of the Kremlin in Moscow. He was shot five times in the back by people who knew where the security cameras were planted and when a passing snow removal truck might lend them cover.

I'm devastated because even though I hadn't seen him in a number of years, Boris was a friend who cared about me as I did him, in whom I had seen a brighter vision for Russia's future. It is searing not only that it happens but that it does just after I started working for yet another figure in the region, who to my mind is also offering something different and better.

At the time of his killing, Nemtsov was about to release a report on the Ukraine war that would throw water on the claim that the so-called "separatist" regimes in Donbas and Luhansk were anything but Russian puppets. He had been here for Maidan and earlier during the Orange Revolution. The girlfriend who was with him when he was shot is Ukrainian. Klitschko announced he is changing the name of the street in Kyiv where the Russian embassy stands to Nemtsov Street, which wins me over more than anything he has said or done so far.

Now Klitschko's reelection is my raison d'être. I spend a month working with him on what we call the "big speech" that lays out an agenda for the city in his second term. We identify that young to middle-aged women are open to him but not yet sold, so we create a program that gives them something they really value: free English lessons. It's good for the city too.

We strong-arm the actual bread factory to keep prices down and show the people we're plowing the snow from the streets as soon as it begins to fall. Critically, we give the Ukrainians what they deserve: an elected official who is in touch, down-to-earth, and driving comfort and progress.

Some helpful "friend" snaps a photo of my giving Klitschko pointers on the margins of a public event and leaks it to the press. It's a funny shot. I'm standing on a ledge so as to be able to talk into his ear. What's less funny is the wild speculation throughout the rest of the local news piece. It suggests I am the dark mastermind behind almost every political event in the country for the past decade, giving me way too much credit.

Now I'm flying back and forth to Kyiv at least once a month and sometimes every other week. My enthusiasm for the campaign becomes so great, Vitaly has to tell me to hang back more and be less visible. In a local cabinet meeting, where I'm lurking in the eaves, the head of the city's SBU, or state intelligence, also whispers something in Klitschko's ear that prompts him to whisk me out of the room. "Go back to the hotel," he tells me. "It's safer there." He knows this because he owns the hotel.

When October comes, Klitschko beats a pack of more than a dozen opponents with a commanding plurality of 40 percent, but since it's less than 50, there is a second round three weeks later. Finally, he wins with a little more than two-thirds of the vote. This is almost ten points higher than his initial victory in 2014. When I think back over all the campaigns I've fought up until now, this win is somehow the most satisfying.

Six months later, when passing through Kyiv to see Sergei, I catch a glimpse of Klitschko riding around the city on his comparatively tiny bicycle, with no cameras in tow, looking for potholes to fix. I'm in a taxi and terrified of what would happen if his huge frame tumbled from the small bike, so I don't call out to him but just watch instead. The guy is really trying. I hope he really makes a difference. In all the time I knew him, I don't think I ever heard him lie, which is very strange for a politician. Ukraine can use more politicians like him.

JANUARY 2017

Tickets to Trump's inauguration are the last thing I need to worry about right now; I'm trying to get out of Congo alive. Why not ask Manafort, for crying out loud? Kostya is texting me between flights and asking on Sergei's behalf. He tells me Sergei is trying to build some distance there, so it would be great if there were any way I could possibly arrange it. "Fine," I tell him, "I'll look into it."

Which, should I have paused to think about it, is a ludicrous statement. Manafort is a trusted consigliere of the newly elected American president, and someone whom Sergei and his lot have paid millions of dollars. But I didn't pause; I just considered it an irritating client request and did it anyway.

Ukraine is one of three projects on various burners right now, and as of late it has been the least active. The warring factions in Opposition Bloc are still trying to sort out their business. Trump's election is big news, especially given all the Russia talk during the end of that campaign. Is Manafort going to be a Cardinal Richelieu presence in the White House now? Or, as ex-US ambassador to Russia Michael McFaul tweeted as the news of Trump's victory settled in, is Ukraine going to be the biggest loser now?

The other two projects—communicating through a peaceful transition of power in the Democratic Republic of Congo and determining whether there might be a second life for the Committee to Destroy ISIS—seem more immediate and are therefore top of mind. But the Congo project is nearly over; I just have to make it out all right. I'm going to spend a day in Vienna on the way home and explore the Middle East avenue a little bit further.

Why all the fuss over inaugurations? I wonder. I went to George W. Bush's first one because I'd worked on his campaign and because that connection allowed me to get rack-rate tickets for a dozen or so friends and associates on the Hill. But when we were finally in the receiving line for both the new president and First Lady and the Cheneys, Aizhan complained that her shoes hurt. I was irritated, but agreed. Pomp and circumstance has never been my thing.

What I would love now is just a little time to decompress, having spent the last few months in Kinshasa hoping the city wouldn't explode. It was 4:00 a.m. there when the media called the US presidential election for Trump. To make it even more dramatic, no sooner had the news crossed the lips of the BBC anchors on the ancient TV set in my room than the screen went to fuzz and then black as a puff of white smoke emerged from behind it.

There was nothing I could do about it.

At home there is no peace in the air. And now, instead of relaxing with Laura and Max, I need to play host to Sergei and whomever he brings. Also, in order to get the tickets, I need to attend the ball myself, which I'm not at all enthusiastic about doing. The things we do for clients . . .

Washington, though, is looking more like Kinshasa than I remembered. There are Humvees and armored personnel carriers in Lincoln Park, down the alley from our house, where I walk Pepper. Some Trump supporters but many more protestors are flooding into the capital from all over, and there is more tension in the air than usual. In our house, we host both groups.

My aunt and uncle, Lizzy and Frank McNamara, are in town for the inauguration—Frank headed the Trump campaign in Massachusetts, which seems sort of Sisyphean. Then my sister Eliza, cousin Katy, sister-in-law Britt, and some others have come for the pink hat march the following day. In our home, anyway, we manage to be civil.

Kostya and I watch the "American Carnage" speech in the lobby of the Mandarin Hotel, where he and Sergei are staying. The expensive tickets came with preferred seating to the speech, but it's raining, and Sergei wants to spend the afternoon in the gym instead, so I give those seats to my aunt and uncle, who are delighted.

My Russian Ukrainian partner and I look at each other in amazement as Trump delivers his inaugural address. "I never thought I would hear such a thing in America," Kostya says. The random assembly of itinerants also taking shelter in the hotel bar looks similarly mind blown. As former president George W. Bush, who is there in the grandstands, puts it best: "That was some weird shit."

When it comes time for the ball, Kostya tells me he's not going, because he doesn't want to run into Paul, so it will just be Sergei and me—arguably a strange couple, but it's Washington in 2017, so perhaps not that odd after all.

The Washington Convention Center is built for big events, but not for counterprotests. On one traffic island in front of it stands a pretty Carnegie-built library that is now a construction site, as it's being turned into an Apple Store. Parallel fencing provides a corridor for us "penguins"—in black tie and ball gowns—to wait in line before going through security.

It feels a bit like a processing center on the Hungarian border, made worse by the fact that an angry mob of protestors stands on the other side of the chain-link fence, which they're clawing at and pressing against while screaming terrible things at us and spitting.

Sergei finds humor in various aspects of the evening, like the bountiful clouds of marijuana smoke in the air as we sat stuck in traffic for an hour, or now the increasingly confrontational standoff with angry demonstrators.

"This all looks very familiar to me," he says with a wink.

It does look and feel a bit like the Maidan. And for a moment, it seems like the barbarians have breached the walls of Rome, undoing all of that republic's efforts to impose a civilizing effect on the empire. The authors of *The Federalist Papers*, including my ancestor John Jay, were concerned about mob rule back at the founding. In 1788 Jay and Alexander Hamilton were nearly stoned by the crowd during the New York Doctors Riot. For all practical purposes, we are witnessing a certain degeneration of a democracy—just not an unprecedented one.

In front of us, a little girl attending the ball with her parents is less conflict-hardened than my date. She is dressed like the princess from *Frozen*, but the virulent hatred hits her harder than it does her parents, Sergei, or me. She breaks down in tears on the sidewalk. Instead of having a moderating effect, this spectacle only makes the crowd more vicious.

By the time we've all moved up toward the security station, they have nearly toppled the fence. The sight of the crying girl has no effect on the mob. They're angry and letting it be known that violence churns in their hearts. There will be lots more of this in the years to come.

Included with the $12,500 entrance tickets, Sergei and I each get a coupon for one free drink. At the bar, we meet another Ukrainian businessman with a breathtakingly beautiful wife and make small talk as we wait for our drinks. The newly inaugurated president and First Lady arrive, are announced, and share the first dance on stage to Frank Sinatra's "My Way" while we all watch.

202 — SAM PATTEN

The fact that something feels off in an uneasy way—the same kind of feeling I often had in Iraq on my first assignment there—is no surprise. I didn't vote for Trump and am in essence behind enemy lines, but I'm doing it for my client. When the song is over, Sergei smiles and says, "That's it. We can go now."

I don't know it at the time, but this will end up being an even more expensive party than I thought. For now, I'm just relieved to go home.

CHAPTER 9

THE COWBOY DAYS ARE OVER

Now closed for counter service, the little venue is filling up as its comfortable lighting reflects on the darkening sidewalk outside. Laura is hosting a party to open an exhibit of her modernist paintings at a coffee shop in Washington's Dupont Circle neighborhood, and it's turning out to be a gathering of our combined circles of close friends and associates.

I am trying to conceal both the rage pulsing through me on a client matter into which I've gotten too deeply involved and the fact that I am pretty drunk. I think I'm doing a decent job, but we always kid ourselves about these things. What matters, though, is that we both look good. After all, this is Washington, where that is usually the bottom line.

Steve LeVine has been like an older brother to me since I met him in Kazakhstan in the mid-1990s. Back then he was the correspondent covering Central Asia for the *New York Times*, the *Washington Post*, and *Newsweek*. Now he is the Future page editor at AXIOS, and he's here with his wife, Nurilda. I was his best man at their 2003 marriage in Almaty. My conversations with Steve are often intense and boisterous, and the fact that I'm lit only fuels that dynamic tonight.

As Steve arrives, I'm talking to Rinat Akhmetshin, another close friend to whom Steve introduced me back in the 1990s, when I wanted to help the Kazakh opposition. Conspiratorially, we're laughing about one absurdity or another when Steve gives us both a wry look. Then he reaches out and clasps the lapel of my deconstructed Brunello Cuccinelli blazer between his thumb and index finger and says appreciatively what a beautiful jacket I've got.

"You have to work for very bad people to wear such good clothes," Rinat snaps back at him, almost as if he's defending his protégé in the practice of dark arts.

Steve had witnessed my wide-eyed idealism when I first arrived in the former Soviet space and has known me since my early adulthood. Despite his Soviet origins, Rinat is someone I've come to know over the past two decades as a Washington operator. A journalist, Steve is always looking for the full story, while Rinat is a spinner of narratives. Both men were guests at my last wedding, which was an intentionally close-knit event. They represent different parts of me, really.

And that is why Rinat's rejoinder to Steve's compliment hit me hard.

Whether I'm a political mercenary or a highly bespoke whore is really just a matter of opinion. Look at my dance card and judge for yourself.

For the last several months, I've been working on a couple of Middle East projects, neither of which is reaping much return. One is Faisal's Committee to Destroy ISIS, and the other is a Farsi version of Breitbart—both hinge on Steve Bannon. On an entirely separate front from Bannon, Cambridge Analytica is about to send me to Prague on an attack campaign against a pro-Russian billionaire monopolizing

Czech politics. When I come home from that, I will venture on my own dime to the Deep South to try and keep an extremist, accused pedophile of going to the US Senate. And there are those who by now have become a constant client of alternate intensity, the Ukrainian Opposition Bloc.

Think what you will of Bannon; the paranoia-driven politics of the Middle East; or carpetbagging below the Mason-Dixon Line, where I'm actually working against the candidate Bannon endorsed. I don't think I'm working for "very bad people." In some cases, I'm helping quite good ones. But still, this is a murky stew, and one that I suppose could rise to suspicion for anyone actively seeking a conspiracy.

If you want unalloyed virtue, go build houses for the poor in Central America. I'm moving pieces on the global chessboard. I'm *un homme sérieux*, if a shady one. And as my old friend Steve LeVine has just affirmed, I dress like the werewolf of London. Yet I seem ever more tortured and unhappy. Things feel like they're spinning out of control and heading somewhere very dark.

The room is lit like a courtesy lounge in a European airport, even though it's in the think-tanky corner of Washington, DC. Splashes of blue and pink or yellow and green, Laura's paintings are expressive and lively.

I look across the room, and there is Laura, full of life and laughter as she talks to our guests about her paintings, but I know there's something eating her too. We're really just winging it, aren't we? If you do that too much, you crash.

———————

Faisal had a vision come to him as a "eureka" moment about Iraq's future and called me while I was scoping out another opportunity in the same time zone to tell me about it. Peace can only be achieved by splitting the country into three largely autonomous "ministates."

"Let the Kurds go their own way as they wish," he explains, "and divide the rest into East and West Iraq, just like the allies did to Germany after the Second World War."

Strangely enough, this is an idea Joe Biden had pushed when he chaired the Senate Foreign Relations Committee. When he was vice president in the Obama administration, he had to change his tune because the president he served had different ideas. But things in Washington have changed.

When you think about it for a moment, it becomes clearer still that Faisal's idea, or Joe Biden's, actually makes a lot of sense. The Kurds have been chafing at Baghdad's chain for at least a century. A West Iraq would give Arab Sunnis something to build and develop and take any wind out of the sails of terrorist extremists, like al-Qaeda and ISIS.

A stable state bordering Saudi Arabia, Jordan, Syria, and Turkey would push back at the chaos that ISIS had unleashed by exploiting weaknesses in Iraq and Syria. East Iraq, and its overlords in Tehran, wouldn't love the plan. But frankly, who cares?

Other than the Obama administration, that is. When Faisal and I first discussed his idea in 2016, the White House was fully intent on securing Obama's Iran deal, and that meant doing as little as possible to irritate Tehran. But the Trump administration hates the Iran Deal, so what better moment to dust off our plan and put it out there for both candidates to consider taking on board? That is what we agree to do. It feels historic, and we celebrate—even if it is a moon shot.

Faisal's plan requires eradicating ISIS, as they're now occupying much of what will be West Iraq. For this, we propose arming local defense units in much the same way the US military took back Iraq's Anbar Province from al-Qaeda during the surge of 2006–2007, when it trained and equipped the Sons of Iraq.

Ever since Paul Bremer dissolved the Iraqi army and endorsed a de-Ba'athification policy soon after the 2004 invasion, military-aged Arab Sunni males have been unemployed and angry about being burdened with the blame for Saddam's crimes—not to mention being pulled out of their homes at night by militias, tortured, and sometimes killed. If ever there were a recruiting pool for terrorists, this is it.

So we call ourselves the Committee to Destroy ISIS. Not long after I register with the House and the Senate as a lobbyist for the committee under the Lobbying Disclosure Act, a friend at the Pentagon reaches out to let me know that Intelligence Online is now calling me the ambassador for the Anbar sheiks. I like the ring of that. We can put the idea out there, but we lack the resources for a full-scale lobbying effort.

It was in first promoting the idea back in 2016 that I met then Breitbart publisher Steve Bannon, who interviewed me about it on his satellite radio program. Now Bannon is the chief political advisor to President Trump and has carved out for himself an unprecedented role on the National Security Council, so I approach him again to give the committee a second try.

If I can demonstrate there is an open ear in the White House, perhaps I can build some momentum in the region to push our plan.

Faisal has his people, and Bannon his. This hybrid approach would be an improvement on the past. After all, the pen that carved up the map of the modern Middle East via the 1916 Sykes-Picot Agreement was wielded in Europe. Winston Churchill was reportedly blotto drunk when he scribbled down what Jordan's borders would be at that time. For good or for ill, external influence has played a huge role in the region for the last century.

Bannon is generous with his time. He convenes his "war council," consisting of Sebastian Gorka and Erik Prince, founder of the now-defunct security firm Blackwater, though he's just proposed a plan for privatizing the war in Afghanistan. I arrive at the meeting with rolled-up maps of how the new arrangement will look under my arm and feel for a brief moment like an architect of history.

As I enter the Old Executive Office Building with my maps, I get a stern look from National Security Advisor H. R. McMaster, whom Bannon calls Mini-Mac, which telegraphs the unasked question: Which one of the freaks are you, and what kind of weird-ass mischief are you up to?

The war council endorses my plan. In fact, Prince says it's actually his plan. I just smile and think to myself that imitation is highest form of flattery. Gorka eyes the Hudson Institute paper I had commissioned evaluating our plan on Bannon's desk that I'd just brought him and snatches it while the man *Saturday Night Live* parodies as the Grim Reaper is telling Prince that he'd been too busy writing the "American Carnage" speech back in January and hadn't had time to focus on foreign policy until just recently. But he agrees it makes sense.

Then comes Charlottesville, and Bannon is forced to resign from the White House. Establishment foreign policy type, a.k.a. "the

Blob," balk at the plan for having too many problems: angering Iran, encouraging Kurds in Turkey to seek independence, and upsetting what the balance in the Middle East is supposed to be.

When the United States declines to back the Kurds in their September 2017 independence effort, I am outraged and write to Bannon asking why this administration has no more guts than the ones it has succeeded.

"We betrayed a friend," is all he wrote in response. Yes, I suppose that is true, even if it is sort of obvious. This is certainly not the first time we've seen this movie. We let the Kurds down in 1991 when, having backed Saddam against the wall, we didn't let them declare independence. Before us, the British had given them a raw deal.

So much for the "best-laid plans of mice and men."

———————

With at least a crack in the door's reach into the new administration, it would be a shame to lose the chance to steer policy in a constructive direction. It is at this moment my friend Rob Sobhani, whom I'd worked for when he ran unsuccessfully for the US Senate from Maryland, approaches me with his plan to set up a broadcasting network to beam into Iran.

Rob's father had been a high-ranking military intelligence official in the Shah's regime. His father-in-law ran the Shah's state television channel and, though in his nineties, is still alive and mentally acute. He ran Voice of America's Persian service until Obama shut it down in 2009. Who better to guide us on creating something new? We bundle him up and bring him to the "Breitbart embassy" for a strategy session.

Broadcasting independent information into Iran is not a new idea. Already there is at least one Saudi-funded channel doing this out of London. But its programming wheel consists mainly of cooking shows and "soft stuff," suggesting a long-term strategy to build audience share before getting more revolutionary in its message.

Ours, by contrast, will be more hard core and to the point. Sure, we will include some documentary programming from before 1979 as nostalgia of a freer society that once existed there. But there will also plenty of hard-hitting news from Washington.

I bring in one of my old colleagues from those days, a Serb, who has been working with Iran's opposition digitally. Bannon produces an attractive young woman of Persian Jewish heritage to be a face of the operation. All we need now is funding, and for this we rely on contacts in the Gulf—the same sort of people Meghan O'Sullivan had counseled me to contact ten years ago. But this is where the trail ends. We're relying on Bannon to make connections we should have ourselves, so it fizzles.

"I could have told you it wouldn't work," says my old friend Marty Youssefiani, another Iranian who fled to the US as a child because of the revolution. It was Marty who introduced me to Rob, and his father had been minister to OPEC. Now Marty is an unofficial spokesman for Reza Pahlavi, the "crown prince," who lives in Potomac, Maryland. "Every few years there is an effort like this, but almost always they fail for one reason or another."

Marty and I worked on a polling project funded by the State Department in 2006, before the crowd anxious to make nice with Tehran came into power. He'd run our call center out of Los Angeles, from which we were able to dial into phone lines across the country to gauge how Iranians thought on key issues of the day. As it is for Rob, regime change in Iran is intensely personal for Marty.

Both in the cases of Iraq and Iran, I am promoting other people's dreams. Whether it's for Faisal, Rob, or Marty, I'm trying to elevate the visions of others who see what they are convinced is a better way of doing things. They may indeed be right. But like aircraft carriers or oil tankers, we are talking about huge vessels set on their respective course, and these are hard to change. In each case, it will take a great deal more than little old me. I am exhausted and weighed down by what seems like the inevitability of defeat.

———

Prague is a plum assignment for a guy like me. Young American expats my age flooded into the city in the early 1990s, just before I went further east to Kazakhstan, and then I envied them a little bit. Commonly referred to as the Paris of Central Europe, Prague seemed mysterious, rich in culture, and sort of a halfway point between East and West. Like Vienna, it is a cosmopolitan meeting point for shadowy figures.

In what will later be shown to be fabricated out of whole cloth, the infamous "Steele Dossier" has just been thrust into the American media, political spin cycle, and even the Justice Department. The salacious report claims Donald Trump is Russia's Manchurian candidate—a toady, a stooge, and a traitor. One component of this "dossier" holds that Trump's lawyer Michael Cohen held secret meetings here with his Russian handlers. Cohen had not in fact been to Prague, but you wouldn't know that if you believed the increasingly frothy US media.

William—a lanky young fellow who seems either shy or just perennially disinterested—doesn't talk much. I call him Silent Will. He's the social media guy Cambridge Analytica sent here with me to Prague. It's just the two of us, and we share an office with our translator, Tomas, who is in his later middle age and has a long gray ponytail. As is often the case, our existence is supposed to be a secret, so it's probably for the best Silent Will rarely speaks.

Our work here is a hit job, but unlike in the movie that's just come out titled *Anthropoid*, in which a ragtag group parachutes into Prague during World War II to assassinate an SS leader, this job is political. But like the 2016 movie, it's also for the good guys.

The target is a ferret-faced billionaire, whose party is poised to win the coming election, making him prime minister. The concerned businessmen who hired CA know that the well-funded "Yes" party will win but want to at least weigh down the margin of its victory. So every day in our quiet little office I am writing script after script, which Tomas vets and translates into Czech, while Silent Will builds the social media infrastructure for our campaign.

Based on an old Czech saying, one ad reminds the audience "if it looks like a weasel and acts like a weasel, then it's probably a weasel." The name of our campaign is Stand Tall, Czechs! More substantive ads look at the ferret's business empire, which has shady written all over it. There is plenty with which to work.

Ordinarily, this would be a fun assignment. The last place Cambridge sent me was Kosovo, which, while fascinating in its own right, has nothing like the Charles Bridge, the castle overlooking the city, or the extraordinary astronomical clock that Prague boasts. But I'm tired and worn out and gloomily wondering if I'll ever be able to convert my peripatetic work life into the nine-to-fiver I'm beginning to crave. The round-the-clock revelry of English football fans swilling beer in the cobblestone streets here and screaming some happy exclamation just as I fall asleep only reminds me of how much I miss home. In earlier days, I might have taken the party in the streets as a summons to let the good times roll. Perhaps I'm just getting old.

When we were married four years ago, Laura and I vowed to make a gentle kingdom of our lives. She had also spent her young adulthood overseas in sketchy places, but as a CIA clandestine operations officer, journalist, and volunteer. Now she also wants a more rooted existence.

Laura has just left her job at the FBI and joined a global financial services consulting firm, where she is trying to build an art-asset management practice. Maybe I can find a steady job somewhere at home. We've been trying to adopt a child for a couple of years now, and the prospect of being a stay-at-home dad is something I find appealing. Somehow I sense that here, in the city of Franz Kafka, my life is about to experience its own metamorphism.

Though advancing years have me turning in earlier and earlier at night, the racquet on the street outside keeps me from sleeping. Given my present state of mind, I might as well be on another planet. Haunted by distant worry about what the next gig might be, I get up out of bed, dress, and head out for a walk around this seemingly magical town. As I drift by, I stare morosely into the windowpanes of closed shops and pause outside a toy store.

There in the window is Krtek, an upbeat cartoon mole who is the hero of Czech and other Eastern European children. The life-size stuffed animal smiles at me reassuringly. He reminds me of when

Max was two or three, and I took him on our first-ever trip together, just the two of us, by train from Moscow to Vilnius, where I was to speak at a conference and renew our Russian visas.

On the second day, Max started crying inconsolably and panicked. I took him into a bookstore, where I bought him the story of Krot, Krtek's Lithuanian persona, because this creature looked like he could help us out.

"Read it," the sniffling Max demanded. But the text was in Lithuanian, which presented me a challenge. Rolling with the illustrations, though, I ad-libbed. While Max might have suspected I was making it up, he showed his appreciation for the effort by calming down. This mole had bailed me out before. Could he do so again?

What if the ferret kidnapped the mole? I suddenly think. Sure, it would be a joke, but if done right, maybe we could make him a villain even to children, giving their superstitious parents pause before casting their ballots. I snicker at my devilish plan and kid myself into believing it is brilliant. Of course, Krtek will eventually be rescued by good Czechs who stand tall, but we'll save that until the end. My mood improves, if only for the moment.

Cartoon characters aside, our own ads are pretty tight in that they pack a punch and support what they say factually. CA even hired one of those Mayfair private-eye firms to vet their content for libel or slander.

Now if only we can get our array of contrast advertisements on people's screens, they might move the needle.

It's getting harder and harder to get Facebook to host our ads. Eager to remain anonymous—because the ferret is ultimately going to win, after all, and will have ample opportunities for revenge down the road—the client gives us cash cards for the ad buys. But back in America, the Russia investigation, seeded by the Hillary Clinton campaign, has given rise to new levels of caution, indeed paranoia, by the Silicon Valley social media giant, which, like Russia, is also being blamed for Trump's win. Fantasies are sometimes easier to believe than the truth, I guess.

That is why Facebook looks at our efforts to buy ads in Eastern Europe with cash cards very skeptically. The Stand Tall account keeps getting frozen, sending us back to square one every time we start building momentum. One of the many ironies here is that the ferret is the candidate closest to the Russians, so putting our account on ice effectively aids Moscow's regional friends.

Frustrated by this two steps forward, two steps back routine, Silent Will and I head out on a Friday night to tie one on and have some fried cheese, greasy duck, and purple cabbage. Broken down by the liquor and dark humor surrounding our current situation, Silent Will finally begins to talk, which amazes and delights me. I ask him how the clandestine collective of hacks calling itself Anonymous actually works, and Will starts to explain it to me in terms even a Luddite can understand when my phone rings.

"It's Jim from the Senate," the caller tells me brusquely. "You had better check your email." I look at my watch, do the quick math, and realize it's 5:00 p.m. in Washington.

I ask, "Jim who?"

Reluctantly, he tells me he's the chief security officer with the Senate Select Committee on Intelligence, or SSCI (an acronym aptly pronounced "sissy").

Then I tell him I'm in a loud, crowded pub in Central Europe and can barely hear him, or really understand what he wants from me.

"Just check your email," he repeats in a tone heavy with ill intent and hangs up.

This has a sobering effect on me, and I share with Silent Will what little I could decipher from the call, as if he, knowing the workings of Anonymous and Lord knows how many other secret societies, could somehow elaborate.

"The cowboy days are over," he prophetically announces.

What a Delphic statement from a man in his midtwenties. Now I start to worry, so I pay the bill and head back to my rented flat, where I can have some quiet and focus on whatever it is I'm supposed to read.

This Russia investigation has been spinning in circles since the Clinton campaign started screaming about it fourteen months ago. Senior Clinton policy advisor Jake Sullivan reportedly spent much of the 2016 Democratic convention driving from one press tent to another in a golf cart urging, prodding, and pleading reporters to give it more attention. On losing the election to Trump, they only doubled down on these efforts in the media and with their friends in Congress.

As soon as I break out my laptop, I learn it's not good news. The SSCI is asking me to submit all communications with Manafort, his deputy Rick Gates, and Kostya, and then, if they feel like it's worth their time, submit to an interview with the committee's team of investigators on Russian interference in the 2016 US presidential election, SSCI chair and vice chair Richard Burr and Mark Warner write.

I'd seen how this array of blame-hungry investigations had consumed people I knew, like Rinat, and was afraid of getting roped into the tripe hunt. At the same time, I have some faith the investigators will be smart enough to distinguish between smoke and fire. After all, both Maine senators—including Susan Collins, who I've considered a fact-focused public servant—sit on the committee. Surely the staff are not all hacks. *Can I do this without a lawyer*? I wonder, cringing at how much a firm will charge. Having done nothing wrong, why should I have to lawyer up?

Any honest assessment of the facts would rule out me being involved with the Russians installing Trump as their stooge. It's well known I like neither Trump nor the Russians. Sure, I happen to know Manafort and Bannon and am at this moment on an assignment for the increasingly notorious Cambridge Analytica.

Despite these various threads that could be tempting for a conspiracy theorist, I suppose, a clear-eyed look at me would quickly reveal that I play no role in whatever elaborate scheme teams of narrative shapers have been conjuring for America's media and probe-happy politicians. But these are not honest times. Ill winds are blowing back at home. The initial version of the committee's letter to me, for instance, asks me to produce all communications with any Russian I'd ever met. This is patently absurd, and when I object, they narrow the scope a little.

So now there is a new, bigger worry than how this Czech project develops. There is a chance I'm going to end up as chum in a feeding frenzy back home. Logically, this would make me more interested in staying in Prague for as long as possible, but it doesn't. With Manafort now in the crosshairs, I'd worried something like this might happen. Might as well just face the music.

Every few days Facebook cuts us a break and lets us run our campaign just long enough for our audience to begin growing again before they shut us down. Is this what is meant by *Kafkaesque*? Before Silent Will and I have time to elaborate that thought, we get a call from London.

"Pack your things now," an implausibly good-looking Slovak assistant of Mark's tells us sternly. "We're pulling the plug."

Apparently, Facebook won, ensuring the ferret would too. The Czech campaign comes to an abrupt halt, and I head home to an uncertain welcome.

———

It's been several weeks since I returned from Prague, and I'm still looking for the next gig or, better yet, a conventional job that doesn't require the kind of travel I've been doing. Laura is giving me that worried look but doesn't need to, because I'm plenty worried myself.

In October I submitted about one thousand pages of emails that I printed out and stamped "Confidential" to make it harder for them to leak than an e-copy. Fittingly, on Halloween, I hand-delivered them to "Jim from the Senate," a.k.a. James Wolfe.

Wolfe didn't look me in the eye when he took the box of print-outs I handed him, and instead of saying "thank you," or "received," he simply grunted like a malevolent beast. With him was an equally unfriendly young woman named Vanessa Le, the committee's counsel, who told me they'd email me a receipt when they got around to it. She seemed irritated I'd even asked for one.

Will they leak them? The part of me that was once an intern for Bill Cohen and who looked at the SSCI as a cool thing because he was on it hoped that no, they will act professionally. That part of me is what Freud called the superego. My id, however, understood that of course they would be leaked. While the superego wanted to believe if only I could get in front of those nonpartisan, seasoned investigators I could explain I'm not involved in any of this, the id laughed bloodlessly at my own naivete. *The storm clouds won't pass you by*, it taunts. *No*, it says, *they'll drown you.*

This would be a great moment for something new and engaging— anything, really—to take my mind off the mounting sense of dread.

A story in the Daily Beast catches my eye. It's about a retired marine colonel who has thrown his hat in the ring to run against the Reverend Roy Moore, who just won the GOP primary in Alabama. Lee Busby spends his retirement casting bronze busts of fallen marines, and the one on which he is currently working is of George Alexius Whitney, or Lexi, my second cousin.

When Laura and I were first married, I was still licking my wounds from Georgia and struggling to find paying work. Lexi offered me an easy gig that consisted simply of being interviewed by him about a region of interest to the firm where he was then hanging his hat. He had been a marine's marine, specifically attached to Force Recon, which is the corps' equivalent of the navy's SEAL teams. Like Laura, he also worked for the CIA. His transition to civilian life was arguably harder than what I was facing, as I am a figurative gun for hire, and he was a literal one.

After a brief period in the private sector, Lexi went back to government service as a contractor. In December 2016, while America was still slack-jawed over the election of Trump, and I was in Congo, Lexi was killed in action in Afghanistan. He'd sacrificed himself so his team could escape an ambush.

The fact that this retired colonel and write-in candidate is making a bronze of Lexi right now seems like a message from God. I have to find this man and help him, so I invest $19.99 to upgrade my LinkedIn account to premium status, which allows me to direct message him. How can I help—other than writing a check, because the $20.00 I just spent more or less maxed me out—I ask him, and within the hour he responds.

"Come on down to Alabama," he invites.

Laura is traveling for work anyway, so I pack Pepper in the car, and we drive to the heart of Dixie, arriving in the early evening at the colonel's home in Tuscaloosa.

———

Petey the pit bull growls at Pepper on arrival, but the soft-spoken colonel is very courtly and welcoming. Busby is wearing Ray-Ban aviators and is chomping on a cigar as he works on the bust of Lexi in his garage. *Is this guy really running for the Senate?* I wonder. Here's a guy who served as a top aide to General John Kelly (now Trump's chief of staff) in the Anbar Province of Iraq during the surge. You might say such a man is unflappable.

Other than the colonel and Petey, the team is pretty sparse.

There's a young man named Andrew, who just graduated from the University of Alabama, where he was a member of the colonel's fraternity; a fellow named Jason, who sells tiny houses and lives closer to Birmingham; and occasionally a few law students preparing for the marines' JAG program who come by to help out. That's it.

Alabama Republicans like Andrew are angry that Roy Moore is the nominee because they believe he's too Far Right—even for this very red state. Moore is a caricature of what the elite north of the Mason-Dixon Line expect southerners to be like, and that rubs Andrew and many like him the wrong way. Jeff Sessions's seat opened up when Trump appointed him US Attorney General, but the establishment-vetted stand-in with the unfortunate last name Strange couldn't win the primary, even with the considerable advantage of having been acting senator for nine months.

The irony, of course, is that Luther Strange lost the Republican primary to the much stranger Judge Roy Moore, who was a fringe extremist even before stories about his stalking young girls at the Gadsden Mall began to percolate. He was twice removed from the Alabama state Supreme Court for judicial misconduct, once involving his refusal to remove a monument to the Ten Commandments from court property.

By the time Pepper and I get to Alabama, three women have claimed Moore sexually assaulted them when they were underage, and others have come out of the woodwork claiming he made unwanted overtures to them, too, while they were under the legal age of consent. All of this goes back to the 1980s, when Moore was a local prosecutor, and if true, that only compounded the crime because of the abuse of power element it raised.

Being a predator of young women is enough to agitate marines to take action. Colonel Busby didn't have to tell any young men to go grab their rifles—metaphorically, that is—it was just one of those situations where men see a clear course of action. The press dubbed Busby the "hold my beer" candidate, because he stepped forward with neither a history of past political work nor any long-standing ambition to join the world's greatest deliberative body.

Even though Mitch McConnell is saying the Senate won't seat Moore if he wins, President Trump and Steve Bannon are actively campaigning for the judge, whom they dress up as a cowboy and put on the back of a horse. For them, Moore epitomizes the lesson of the *Access Hollywood* episode in which it was revealed at the eleventh hour that Trump had bragged his celebrity status allowed him to "grab [women] by their pussies." Then it was Bannon who pushed the unapologetic approach while establishment Republicans, like RNC chairman Reince Priebus, were telling Trump it was all over and time to fold his cards.

Most Alabamians I meet are tired of having their state be the butt of other people's jokes in a more refined sentiment along the same lines as that expressed by Lynyrd Skynyrd of Neil Young in the 1973 song "Sweet Home Alabama": "A southern man don't need him around anyhow." Roy Moore, the thinking goes, would only drudge up the past that ordinary folks want to put behind them. Defeating him is therefore a state-riotic enterprise.

"People think that courage is only the kind that this man exhibited on the battlefield," Busby told a VICE News team that comes to watch him spend the Saturday before the election finalizing another bronze bust in a casting studio he borrows on the University of

Alabama campus for the final stages of his art. "It's not. People here in Alabama have the chance to exhibit their own personal courage in their own everyday life and take twenty minutes and go out and vote for whoever they feel best represents them."

At home, Fox News is on essentially 24-7 in the colonel's kitchen. We both rise early and make coffee; sometimes his mother comes in a bit later and makes us breakfast. Then we go about a guerilla-style campaign that consists primarily of getting as much free media coverage as we can.

National—and some international—media made a big splash of Colonel Busby's announcement. But that won't matter much to voters in Alabama, we understand. So we try to go as local as possible. We hit the road and travel to Huntsville, Birmingham, and Mobile to make it as easy as possible for the local stations to put him on—that is, just showing up at their studios after I call them to say he's campaigning in town. He offers a sufficiently interesting angle on the big story that most stations oblige and put him on air.

As one does on campaigns, however improbable, I fantasize about the unlikely outcome of the colonel somehow getting elected. He's an honest, moderate, and sensible fellow who is unlikely to embarrass Alabama. But it's almost statistically impossible for him to win. Still, when you're sitting in the shadows on a TV set watching an interview in progress and taking heart in how well the candidate is making his case, you sometimes let your imagination run away with you.

Unbeknownst to me at the time, a tech firm that the SSCI had hired for its own research on Russian meddling was also inserting itself into the Senate election in Alabama. New Knowledge's Jonathon Morgan, in an "experiment" called Project Birmingham, which is funded by LinkedIn founder Reid Hoffman, is seeding a "false flag" information campaign online stating that Roy Moore was being promoted by Russian botnets.

In other words, it appears Morgan is weaponizing the "new knowledge" they gained from their contracting work for the SSCI's investigation in a US election—the cynicism of this "experiment," as they call it, is galling. Whether or not it is legal is another question. Hoffman publicly apologizes. While decrying disinformation, SSCI's research firm is actually producing it. All of this, though, I will only learn much later.

Alabama's senior senator, Richard Shelby, a Republican, makes a statement just before the election encouraging his fellow Alabamians to opt for a write-in rather than Moore. It's a powerful statement from a man who has chaired the Appropriations Committee and steered more federal dollars to the state than anyone in recent memory. As a result of his shoveling pork home, Alabama surpasses my home state of Maine in terms of average GDP. His word carries weight.

While this isn't an endorsement of the colonel, Shelby is saying choose anyone other than Moore. Likely the popular coach of the university football team, Nick Saban, will get many of these votes. But Busby will get some too.

There's not much left for me to do after the colonel votes. So I pack my things and load Pepper into the car. I wish him well and drive back east. It is only on the radio I learn that Democrat Doug Jones narrowly wins. It came down to twenty-five thousand votes, and about five thousand of them are for the colonel. Success has many fathers—and mothers. Alabama native Condoleezza Rice came home in the final days to rally votes away from Moore, and NPR gives much of the credit for the upset to Black women.

All of that aside, it feels good. That might have something to do with its being the right thing to do. There are moments when, as the colonel said repeatedly over those few weeks, character really matters. From his perch in the great beyond, I hope Lexi is proud of the work he inspired.

PART
THREE

CHAPTER 10
BECOMING RADIOACTIVE

"We're totally nonpartisan here. In fact, you probably won't be able to tell who works for whom," says the young man leading me into the Senate Select Committee on Intelligence's conference room for what they have said will be an "interview." It doesn't take me long to figure out he works for Senator Tom Cotton, a hawkish Republican.

On the table sits an upside-down Chitrali cap popular among Northern Alliance fighters in Afghanistan. It is filled with candy, and another investigator invites me to take a piece. I remember the old warning about not taking candy from strangers and politely decline. Inside I bristle at the casual way SSCI staffers are treating this cap from a war-torn region where we've been mired for nearly two decades. I wonder if they are this blasé about everything.

Michael Bopp, my lawyer, used to be Susan Collins's legislative director. He is now a partner at one of DC's top law firms, and I've retained him for this interview because, even though he tells me the SSCI is interested in me as a subject-matter expert, I have a bad feeling based on the escalating hype surrounding "Russiagate" that things could spin out of control.

Committee Chairman Richard Burr (R-NC) had given an

interview I'd heard on the radio in which he seemed to indicate he understood the degree of exaggeration out there. The Russians had bought Facebook ads and messed around with fake rallies and the like, trying to stir people up based on long-standing divisions.

But these were not huge buys, and they were poorly targeted at deep-blue cities and states, suggesting a real lack of sophistication and seriousness, he pointed out. When I heard it, I was struck by how much it tracked with my own thinking. Maybe there are some out there who see this thing soberly. I don't discount that there was some hanky-panky, but as Burr seemed to appreciate in that interview, the impact of such efforts was marginal at best.

It is early January 2018, and Trump has been president for nearly a year. SSCI's investigation is just one of several brewing on Capitol Hill, and because Trump fired FBI director James Comey in May of last year, Attorney General Jeff Sessions had little choice but to appoint a special counsel, Robert Mueller. It now seems like at least half of Washington has some stake in proving Trump is a Russian asset.

Looking at the low level of Trump's Russian contacts, such as those in the Trump Tower meeting, including Rinat, I'm becoming more and more skeptical that there is any fire beneath all this smoke. The rumors I'd heard are that the big boys in Moscow were in the tank for Clinton, but I discount these as well because they are just rumors, right?

What is becoming clearer to me, though, is the real risk of being hung up on nickel-and-dime charges by an investigation that is clearly running out of steam and needs to claim some scalps. Knowing the terrain and the players in Eurasia, the more I read and hear about Russiagate, the more manufactured it seems. And a good conspiracy needs fall guys. All the charges that have been speculated about so far have been for process crimes.

Have I registered as a foreign agent for my work in Ukraine? This comes as the first question of the interview, which clearly violates the ground rules. In negotiating the terms of my appearance, Michael tells me he has an agreement from the committee's lawyers that they will not raise questions about the Foreign Agent Registration Act (FARA) of 1938, because we both understand that might be an area of technical liability for me.

Had I been seriously lobbying for the Ukrainians? No. But had I technically crossed the line by making inquiries on their behalf? Possibly, yes.

Either SSCI is ignoring its agreement with my counsel, or they just don't care. I tell them that I have filed in the past when I believed my work fell under that statute—that is, lobbying the US government. But my work in the main is for foreign politicians in foreign countries, which does not require registration. I am not working on behalf of any government as a lobbyist on Ukrainian matters.

What is also clear from my production, though, is that I drafted some of Sergei Lyovochkin's communications with US government officials as well as a few op-eds that ran in US publications. Technically, I had crossed a line in doing so, but any reasonable review of what that involved would see the infractions as minor.

Rather than skirt the question, I try to be straightforward, but this violation of our agreement has rattled me at the very outset and gives me a sense of significant foreboding. They are not simply interviewing me as an expert with close subject-matter knowledge as they'd told Bopp. No, I am actually now a target, I intuit.

232 — SAM PATTEN

Most of the one thousand pages of emails I voluntarily turned over to them last Halloween are my interactions with Konstantin Kilimnik, or Kostya. Some of these exchanges use off-color, ribald, and politically incorrect language, for which Michael apologizes on my behalf.

When someone takes what you wrote as private exchanges with a business associate and makes them a basis for discussion and debate, it makes you feel incredibly exposed, especially when your words and thoughts are taken out of context. I'm in part a PR guy, after all, and I give careful thought to how I say things publicly, but what this experience is making me realize is that I was too naive, as there is really no such thing as private anymore.

Looking around the table, I can easily see that at least half of the investigators have already made judgments in their mind based on the intrusions they'd made into my business and personal matters. While I try to not let this bother me, it does.

The staff had singled out about one hundred of the emails for discussion and asks me about them one at a time. I tell them what each means—what I was thinking at the time I wrote it and what I understood the situation to be at that time. In these encounters, it is best not to speculate or imagine, but simply to say what you know. Even though I am careful not to editorialize too much about my skepticism of this whole enterprise, my underlying sense that this is bullshit might be coming through.

We break for lunch, and Michael and I go down to the Senate Chef in the basement of the Hart Senate Office Building for a breather. I'm not hungry. Instead, I am troubled by the shade various investigators seem to be casting on me and on my work. But Michael tells me I'm doing a great job, and it will all be over soon.

Back in the secure room, the interrogation goes on. It's increasingly clear these people are grasping at straws. Their lines of inquiry and specific questions underscore this. At times I feel they're just going through the motions. Other times they lean into various email exchanges I'd had and interpret them in ways that are far removed from the actual context. To call it violating would be an understatement. I am not just feeling exposed; I'm being used.

Given the range of connections I have from Manafort to Cambridge Analytica and to Bannon—not to mention Rinat was in the famous Trump Tower meeting—I stand a very high risk of becoming one of those straws. In fact, I probably already am. Their fixation on Kostya also strikes me as misguided.

Through the afternoon, a dozen investigators pore through my email inbox, pausing every now and again to read a list of names and ask if I know any of them. As we approach hour five, they've run through all the emails and now have "just a few more questions."

It cost me $10,000 to retain Michael for this interrogation. Hopefully, they're getting my money's worth. One staff aide to Senator Mark Warner leaves and returns to the room at least three times, which strikes me as odd because he seems too young to have prostate problems. Then they run out of things to ask me. After a pause, a corpulent young man named Raj at the end of the table asks, "Did it ever bother you?"

I look at Michael, who shrugs.

"Did what ever bother me?" I ask the lumbering Raj for clarification's sake.

"You know, Russia's annexation of Crimea and then the Russian interference in our presidential election."

I look again at Michael, who seems mystified, then I look around the room at the other investigators, who all shift in their seats or otherwise look embarrassed as if to signal, "Oh, don't mind him. He's new." It is such an odd question, which seems to reflect the absurdity of this whole exercise. Am I supposed to feel responsible for either event? What does this man mean?

Senator Cotton's staffer who led me in begins to collect his papers in a sign we're done. Later I will read the transcript and see that they just scrubbed Raj's question. One wonders what else they selectively scrubbed.

Absent from this whole exercise is James Wolfe, a.k.a. "Jim from the Senate," the committee's chief of security. What no one tells me, or presumably tells my attorney, is that since the time I handed Wolfe the cardboard box filled with printouts of my emails as well as some business banking material, he was being interviewed by the FBI about allegations that he leaked sensitive committee material to a much younger BuzzFeed reporter with whom he'd been carrying on an affair.

They don't tell us that the FBI came to this very same office a couple of weeks after I handed in my production and before my "interview" to seize Wolfe's phone. If the clownish nature of the Senate inquiry wasn't clear before, this fact alone puts their whole exercise in perspective.

Throughout the time frame of the SSCI probe, a former aide to the declining senator Dianne Feinstein named Daniel Jones is heading up a spin operation called the Democracy Integrity Project, reportedly well financed by George Soros and "Meathead" actor Rob Reiner. In this capacity, Jones—fresh from having been a top SSCI staffer himself—actively pushes the Russia collusion narrative across all US media.

Had I known either of these things, I might have been more hesitant to sit for the voluntary interrogation in the first place. It was sinking in that this might be the beginning of the end of my career.

———

"Goddammit, Pepper! Quit barking!" I grumble to myself in my dungeon of a basement office as I'm putting the final touches on an op-ed for the *Jerusalem Post*. I'm on deadline and can't be disturbed.

My wife, Laura, left her job at the FBI a couple of months ago and has begun working for a global consulting company, which in practical terms means she works from home now. *She'll deal with Pepper*, I think as I reread the piece quickly before hitting send. But Pepper is on a tear.

Almost always a mild-mannered husky, something about the dog's insistence troubles me. Whatever she's agitated about is at the front door, and my office has its own entrance just beneath. Expecting a call from Kostya, I clutch my phone and step into the front yard to see what all the fuss is about.

Three men in suits are arguing with Laura about something. Seeing me, Pepper stops barking, and one man shows me his FBI badge as another points at my phone. "That," he says, "is what we're looking for."

I'd already had a bad feeling lurking overhead like a dark cloud for about a week now. Coming home from a trip to Florida, I got two calls waiting at baggage claim at Reagan Airport's terminal A.

One was from Ken Vogel, an investigative reporter at the *New York Times*, who told me that Russian oligarch Viktor Vekselberg had just had his phone seized by the feds at JFK Airport. The other was from my son, who was at home and had just answered the door to men in suits who did not identify themselves.

"I think they're with the government," my son said. When I asked why he thought that, he reasoned, "Because of the suits."

More pressing on my mind than Russiagate was the fact that Cambridge Analytica had nearly destroyed Facebook days before. CA is one of my major clients and had sent me to Mexico just two months prior. As the establishment lurched for someone to blame for the election of Donald Trump, the London-based data analytics and political consulting firm seemed an easy target.

"Not without a warrant, you don't," I say defiantly, still trying to figure out what's going on. The cockiest of the agents presents a warrant with a smug grin and tells me they're taking my phone whether I hand it over or they have to resort to other means. With that, I ask them inside to continue the interaction more privately. They beckon over a couple of technical specialists who are waiting in a nearby truck.

"You know, if you had resisted, we'd have used overwhelming force," the cocky agent says. "It's better this way. We just want to talk."

"Not without his lawyer," Laura interjects. She is smarter than I am. Never, ever talk to the FBI without a lawyer. Just ask retired Lieutenant General Michael Flynn. During his brief tenure as Trump's national security advisor, two FBI agents central to the Russia investigation interviewed him in his office with the express intent of "making him lie," court documents later showed. With this, the mood darkens.

I offer them coffee, but the cocky agent makes a show of declining.

"We'd prefer not to," he says, mimicking what I'd told them when he asked me how I came up with my iPhone password. Sometimes with law enforcement, the movies suggest, there is one officer or agent who displays the need to push his or her dominance gratuitously, and this was that guy. Perhaps he's an understudy to Peter Strzok, the agent who set up Flynn after famously boasting to his mistress that he'd stop Trump from becoming president.

I'm not the only one who finds this guy to be a dick. Laura points out to him that until recently she also worked at the bureau.

"Oh yeah," he says dismissively, "we knew that. You were a contractor."

In government bureaucrat talk, this is a put-down.

Slowly, I realize the dick is not in charge. There's a quiet little blond guy named Brock who is actually the senior agent, and others are deferring to him. "Do we have to put up with this kind of abuse?" I ask Brock. He thinks for a moment and then instructs the dick to wait outside.

Meanwhile, the techies are downloading my phone on to some kind of computer they have built into a fat metal briefcase. My contact list shows up on their computer's screen as they scroll through it, stopping for a moment at the Bs when they see Steve Bannon's digits, looking at each other and smiling.

Is that what this is about? I wonder. I'd had dinner at Bannon's house several nights before. Is that what triggered this visit?

Suddenly, I remember Kostya and I had been chatting online just before the raid. *This would be the wrong time for him to pop up on the screen*, I reason. I borrow Laura's phone and send him a brief note letting him know what's happening.

Another agent asks me if I have a pen, and I lend him my green Waterman.

"Just like in *The Americans*," I say, jokingly, referencing the FX series in which Soviet spies infiltrate the FBI via a pen with an embedded microphone.

At this they all look at me in unison. "You watch that show?" one asks, intrigued.

Oh, come on, people, my look says. *Get real.*

As they finish their download and prepare to leave, Brock pretends he just remembered something and hands me a paper. It's a subpoena signed by Special Prosecutor Robert Mueller summoning me to appear before a grand jury.

Fuck, I think. *They really are that desperate.*

———————

This has to be just a misunderstanding. Once the authorities learn all the facts, it will surely get sorted out, I hope. But my gut says otherwise. If you turn on a television anywhere in America, you will see and hear that Trump conspired with the Russians to get elected president. Who but Paul Manafort could have been the critical lynchpin in making that happen?

Scandals sweep through Washington the same way hurricanes do Florida in the third quarter of just about every year. At the time they hit, they're all-consuming maelstroms causing fear and destruction.

But if you know they're coming, you build your house to withstand them. In Washington, this usually amounts to keeping your head down and keeping your distance from people who might get caught up in the thing. On this score, anyway, I had already failed miserably.

Michael Bopp tells me—politely, of course—that I can no longer afford him. He refers me to a criminal lawyer, which at this point is what I'm going to need anyway. Stuart Sears is five years younger than I but already has a receding hairline, which I guess is what practicing law can do to you after a certain period. Stuart had represented Trump's bodyguard, Keith Schiller, when he went through the gauntlet of committees of inquest. But in that case, the Republican National Committee picked up the tab.

Maybe Stuart will be able to set things straight—or so I hope.

That hope is short-lived. After his first conversation with deputy special counsel Andrew Weissmann, Stuart asks me to come into his office for a chat. "It's better than the phone," he advises. In fact, I need to be careful of whom I speak to, about what I say, and should probably assume everything I say is recorded, he adds. I am no longer a subject-matter witness; I am now a subject of a criminal investigation, and it's not just any investigation. It's a nuclear-powered one, and any person it touches becomes radioactive.

"It looks like you're going to have to take a charge," he tells me solemnly.

I already know I have some FARA exposure—nothing egregious, but I did step over the line by placing op-eds for Sergei Lyovochkin in US media outlets and asking some friends on the Hill to see him when he was in Washington. We're talking about driving sixty-six miles per hour in a sixty-five-mile-per-hour zone. This is usually a case of prosecutorial discretion.

There's more, he continues. Weissmann and the special counsel team are also considering charges of obstruction of justice and money laundering.

When I was scrambling to accommodate Sergei's request for inaugural ball tickets, I asked a friend to help out because I was traveling abroad, and my friend was better connected. Even though Kostya was cc'd on some of the emails with this friend, I didn't turn them over on the first production. To my mind, there was no need to embroil this friend, who'd simply done me a favor, into the mindless meat grinder the Russia probe was becoming. Moreover, how I got ball tickets for Ukrainians struck me as irrelevant to an investigation on Russian interference. But I guess I missed the point: the investigators weren't looking for facts, just scalps.

My buying tickets to the inaugural ball for Sergei and friends and then allowing them to reimburse me could be called money laundering, Stuart explains. It is a stretch, but often money laundering is what the government says it is. I had violated a rule of the inaugural process by allowing foreign money indirectly into the system, but the breaking of that rule has never before been prosecuted in America, so they are considering using a money-laundering statute against me instead.

"This is insane," I protest.

"Yes," Stuart agrees. "These are crazy times. If Trump hadn't fired FBI director James Comey, none of this would have happened, but he did, and here we are. If we go to trial, I could probably defeat one, maybe two, of the charges, but not all three."

As he watches my countenance melt into despair, Stuart tosses me a hopeful line. We can seek a deal, he suggests. If he can tell them I'm "on Team USA," they might reconsider the charging arrangement they have in mind. Is there any reason for me not to cooperate, he asks me. I can't think of one. I'm pretty sure the Russia collusion narrative is made up, but even if it isn't, I'm not involved.

Also, I have no particular love for Trump and no reason to fall on my sword as a demonstration of unyielding fealty. If I can assume this is an honest inquiry simply trying to parse through the storms of innuendo "the resistance" keeps generating, it may just all solve itself.

Still, the ill winds are troubling. A couple of days before the FBI came to my door, my old friend Noah Shachtman, who is the editor of *The Daily Beast*, called me saying I needed to talk because a story was coming out anyway, and it would be better to be in front of it. It was about my relationship with Kostya, and I'd already swatted down a bunch of media requests that had been swarming me during the weeks after my SSCI interview and before the FBI raid, in almost synchronized waves, with the same questions. But because it was Noah asking, I agreed and talked to his reporter. That story came out literally one day before the FBI arrived.

Then, a day after the FBI "visit," a second story came out in *The Atlantic* by a journalist named Natasha Bertrand, who prides herself on her relations with Capitol Hill leakers. So the FBI visit was literally bracketed by stories in major news outlets the day before and after in what can generously be called a heck of a coincidence.

Since it is no longer in my interest to speak out, one evening I draft a "mock-ed," or op-ed, just for immediate family so they might understand what's about to happen. It's called "How the Russia Probe Pushes Me into Trump's Corner," and in it I remind my rabidly

242 — SAM PATTEN

anti-Trump close relatives that I am not a Trumper, but I have serious questions about Russiagate, and things are about to get a whole lot worse. In addition to my parents and sisters, I send a copy to Stuart. His law clerk then mistakenly includes this "mock-ed" into the production, or ream of materials I am providing the special counsel at their request.

In other words, my mock-ed goes to Weissmann.

At least my initial bias against the probe has now been established in black and white. It's full disclosure, as it were. Even though Stuart asks that the piece be recalled, and the special counsel's office agrees, it's kind of like telling a jury they didn't see or hear an inadmissible piece of evidence.

As if they didn't before, they now know I'm a skeptic.

"April is the cruelest month," T. S. Eliot's *The Wasteland* begins. Mine is certainly proving the poet right. Even before the special counsel dropped a bomb on me, I was already in a professional crisis as I was wondering whether the only roads my current horizon offered are dark ones.

On the evening of the fifth, I had dinner at Steve Bannon's house with my longtime friend Anna Miller, who had introduced me to Alexander Nix and is now close with the "honey badger," as I'd come to think of the former Breitbart publisher and Trump strategist. Over dinner, he'd reiterated his offer to me to manage his work with the right-wing European parties.

That offer had been torturing me. In the obvious sense, it was awful because some of these parties are pretty awful. Ultranationalists and fascists like the Netherlands' Geert Wilders, France's Marine Le Pen, and possibly even Germany's Allianz für Deutschland populated the new vacuum the old establishment parties have left, and some of these are the guys and gals Bannon is talking about.

On the other hand, it is a compliment of sorts. Say what you will about the honey badger, but he sure is stomping on the terra. Moreover, if these parties could be steered in a more constructive direction, surely that would be better for everyone. If someone had been doing the same in Germany in 1933, could the Holocaust have been prevented—or so my thinking went.

I turned to my friend Steven Moore for advice. "What should I do?"

"How much more pain are you willing to take?" he asked. Coming only a week or so before the hammer dropped, the frame he offered me for thinking about that particular offer was perfect—and in a broader sense too.

Cambridge Analytica could be crazy at times, and now it has spectacularly imploded and nearly taken Facebook down with it. Of the firm's claim to have four thousand data points on every voter, most of these came from Facebook scrapes. In other words, they reportedly purchased user data from Facebook. CA was neither the first nor the last marketing firm to do so, but because of their association with Trump and the fact they are "foreign," they made a great fall guy for the media. From the time the story broke in late March, share prices for Facebook plummeted by billions of dollars.

So imagine that level of crazy times ten. *That's what Bannon's European project was likely to be*, I figured.

Now, of course, it will be easier to say no. I arrange to go by and see Bannon at the "Breitbart embassy" behind the Supreme Court and tell him face-to-face of my woes. He listens as I outline how my situation has just gotten a lot worse, and then I say thanks for that Europe offer, but it's just not going to work.

He gives me a surprised look. "You think you're too radioactive for me?" he asks.

When I respond yes, he just smiles broadly and simply says. "Wow!"

None of my other prospects are much brighter. Leads in Africa keep fizzling. Ukraine continues on its slow burn. There will not be another election until next year, and the most promising candidate is actually a television comedian whose program parodies the country's presidency. I've got a few lines into his team, but my newfound radioactivity will surely put that on pause. I'm helping Sergei's wife, Zinaida, promote her art, which is ridiculous, as I know nothing about the art world, but at least he's throwing me a bone. What will I be doing next, selling arms?

Another change is coming. Max is about the graduate high school, and college is next. In a few weeks, we'll go visit the University of Southern California to see its film school, at which he's been accepted. But first, as his graduation present, he wants to visit a female monastery on a small island in Puget Sound and make a short documentary about it for the Benedictine brothers at the abbey in Washington, DC, where he's been a high school student up until now.

Our Lady of the Rock stands on the high-ground interior of Shaw Island, where less than a dozen nuns run a farm and a monastery, which captured my son's imagination. As we wait by the tiny general store next to the ferry station for one of the volunteers to pick us up with the mail, a middle-aged woman not all that much older than myself emerges from the woods. She is good-looking, though covered in a light coating of white dust and looks as though she's been roughing it for a little while. Because Max and I are the other ones standing out on what must pass for the little island's town square, the woman makes a beeline for us.

Did we just come on the last ferry? Why, yes. Had we seen her friend Tom on the boat? No, but it is not that we could have recognized him even if we had. Now she stares at me for fifteen seconds, as if she she's trying to connect the dots in terms of how I relate to something. Her handsomeness distracts me momentarily from the obvious conclusion that this woman is not entirely mentally well. Then she gets it.

Do I sometimes write about foreign policy, she asks. As a matter of fact, yes, I tell her, happy to be recognized in such a far-flung corner of the country. She thought she recognized me from somewhere, she said, adding that she's read some of my stuff and likes it. Even Max is surprised. Finally, I've found my audience!

Before I can ask her which of my articles she found the most insightful, a pickup truck driven by a gaunt young man with a grown-out beard pulls up, and the man gives our new friend a forbidding look, which causes her to retreat back toward the beach. *What will become of her, my only fan*? I wonder.

"You're the ones coming to interview Mother Hildegard, right?" the young man not much older than Max asks.

We nod, and he gestures for us to hop in the cab. "Kind of a sad case there," he explains as we drive off. "She was with us for a while, but then we had to ask her to leave. She's struggling with other issues."

Just like me.

———————

I'm no interior designer, but if I had to describe it, I'd call it sugar-cookie yellow. Benjamin Latrobe had a Greek revival vision in mind when he designed Saint John's, which has come to be known as the church of the presidents because it stands at the intersection of Sixteenth and H Streets Northwest, across Lafayette Square from the White House.

We've adopted a pew about halfway up the nave on the west side of the main, center block. It is maybe a half dozen pews back from the one where presidents and their families sit, should they come to worship.

To the left is a narrower column of pews alongside the church's western wall, and several rows ahead of us, to the left, sit Special Counsel Robert Mueller and his wife. I'd noticed him a couple of years before, when he was the FBI director, on the Sunday after the school massacre in Newtown, Connecticut, which I found particularly chilling because it was the first major school shooting in New England.

I'd hate to be in his shoes now, I then thought. What an awful responsibility it must be to keep America safe. I was sympathetic to the burden I imagined must be on his shoulders. Now, of course, it's different.

Not wanting to see the back of his head, I look up. There is a shallow dome of a ceiling painted in a light sky blue, brightened by small windows built vertically into the cupola. Particularly during the sermons it is this celestial crown that draws my eyes, and if the minister should see me staring at the ceiling, he will simply assume I am thoughtfully receiving his words of spiritual guidance.

To a paler degree, this yellow and blue are also, by coincidence, the colors of the Ukrainian flag. I notice this, of course, but I wonder if he does.

When Mueller was an assistant US attorney in San Francisco in 2009, he convicted a former Ukrainian prime minister of money laundering and sent him to prison for several years. Now he is investigating alleged Russian interference in the 2016 US election, but many of the people he is indicting have more to do with Ukraine than with its northern neighbor. Does an old prosecutor just end up trying the same cases over and over again?

My uncle Frank McNamara beat him out for the US attorney job in Massachusetts during the Reagan administration, but surely he won't make that connection. Whenever I ask Frank about Mueller, he would mutter something about the "viselike grip of bourgeoisie." I think what he means is Mueller is like a dog with a bone, but I've never been quite sure.

As we're in church, I'm giving more thought to my prayers. The litany helps with this, sort of steers you along the way. In an Episcopal church, the Prayers of the People call on the congregation to pray for the president, along with other high officials. At this moment, I would enjoy seeing Mueller's lips, but I can't. I pray for justice and, more specifically, that I will not be charged with a federal felony. Stuart has already predicted I'll have to eat a charge, but maybe when they get to know me and learn the truth things will be different.

What better opportunity could God be offering than this to "turn the other cheek?" Surely there is some sort of message here; I'm just not getting it. Simply going to church has become an act of will, for Laura as well as myself. It would be easier to skip it.

But this is the same church where Joe Alsop's memorial service was held, and I remember at eighteen years of age standing next to his brother John on the steps afterward. Ted Kennedy pulled up in a black car, too late to properly pay his respects and smelling strongly of rum. Scanning the people exiting for a familiar face, he saw John, made a beeline toward us, and bodychecked me out of the way so he could say hello to an Alsop.

"No, I'm not going to let Mueller force us out of church. Let him see what he is destroying," Laura says. "If they send you to prison," she added for morose effect, "I will continue to come to church, but alone so they can see that too."

I've already made the decision to cooperate. They have not yet made the decision whether to charge me with something, or with what. I've taken a leap of faith and fully admitted to crossing the line on FARA, helping the Ukrainians buy a few tickets to the inaugural and deleting the old emails. My hope is they will see my transgressions for what they were—mistakes that I would not repeat if given the chance. I'm an ordinary guy who screwed up and is willing to make amends.

My prayer and my plea are different, but parallel. My earliest memory of church is at age five, playing Isaac in a Sunday-school prayer for the congregation in Charlestown, Massachusetts. Abraham is willing to sacrifice me to God, and the actor playing him has a prop knife. But it's too real for me, and my faith at that tender age not yet established, so I run offstage. Is this all a redo? *If I am to be sacrificed,* I pray, *let the cause at least be worthy.*

————————

"Something has got to change," Laura and my lawyer say to me in unison as we sat around his conference table a week before my arraignment.

There had just been an incident in the firm's bathroom. I started screaming at a gnomelike man in a suit who was peeing at the urinal next to mine. Somehow, in the polite men's-room chatter that eases the discomfort of two males standing next together and holding their penises while shooting urine at a rubber target, Mueller's name had come up.

The older man, who I later found out to be Bob Bennett, who had been Bill Clinton's impeachment lawyer, said, "Bob's a good man." That was enough to trigger me. Good man, my ass. Fortunately, by lucky coincidence, Stuart was in a stall at that moment and able to tamp down my yelling spat before it got too far out of hand. Even though this was a late-morning meeting, I was already pretty drunk, having had at least two very stiff screwdrivers for breakfast.

"Okay," I glumly agree. They're right. I'll quit drinking. Right now, I am staring down the barrel of growing world-class resentment.

I've just been "arraigned by information" for not filling out a form, and when I plead guilty in front of a federal magistrate in about a week, I will be the ninth American ever convicted of violating the Foreign Agent Registration Act, which was enacted in 1938 to track the Nazis' influence campaign on America. If it is such a great law, why don't they enforce it more regularly?

When I ask my former lawyer, Michael Bopp, how he squares his agreement with the SSCI not to raise FARA questions in my interrogation with the fact they went ahead and did so repeatedly as if agreements have no bearing on them, he tells me the SSCI told him nothing I said in their interrogation was used in my prosecution. Their statement is preposterous.

Resentment feeds on alcohol, especially whiskey, my drink of choice. At this moment, I begin to see that this resentment is going to kill me if I don't get in front of it. After all, I'm here being briefed on the terms of my surrender.

By the time I get to the Prettyman US District Court, which sits at the base of the hill on which the Capitol stands, I've gone almost ten days without a drink. I mention this in response to a question from the clerk as they're processing me. Technically, you have to be sober to be arraigned.

Mueller's press spokesman is sitting in the front left row, where the defendant's family usually sits. His arm is draped over the seat that should be reserved for Laura. I ask Stuart if he can do anything about it, and he asks an officer of the court to reseat the flak. On the other side is Andrew Weissmann, next to the US attorney and some FBI agents.

A young, bald white guy from the FARA unit at the Justice Department is sitting at the prosecutor's table, looking a little confused. His office does little if any actual enforcement, and this case was handed to him tied with a red bow from the special counsel. "Who the heck is that?" I ask Stuart.

"Doesn't matter," he tells me, but then notes that he'll probably get hired at a law firm later based on my scalp.

I give Laura a quick look but am careful not to hold it too long, as I'm afraid it will make her cry. If there's one thing you can't take away from a WASP, it's a stiff upper lip. Devastating though all this is, we are going to maintain our dignity.

Now the bailiff announces Judge Amy Berman Jackson, the woman who will determine my fate. She told a Dutch lawyer who had done some work for the now toppled Yanukovych's outreach efforts in Europe, and whom she had sentenced to thirty days in prison for lying to the FBI, that he was not "a gentleman of Moscow" earlier this year.

That prompted me to read a story about a czarist-era aristocrat who was trapped under hotel arrest in the Metropol after the Russian Revolution. The Dutchman had been complaining that his own long hotel stay leading up to arraignment prevented him from leading an ordinary life. I also took this as a cue that I should use my time between now and sentencing to do good works.

Weissmann and one of the FBI agents come by my table, and I shake hands with them. The media begin murmuring four or five rows back.

"This is the hardest part," Weissmann says. "It will be over soon."

After some formalities, Judge Jackson asks me to approach the bench. Before she accepts my plea, she asks me the pro forma questions: Have I had competent counsel? Am I under the influence of any substances or duress of anyone? Then she asks one that surprises me: "Just so you understand, if the statute you are pleading guilty to having violated is later overturned by the Supreme Court, your conviction will still stand."

I wasn't expecting this and pause for a moment. Is she admitting what shoddy law FARA really is? A top FARA lawyer once told me the statute could be found to be "void for vagueness." It also has some First Amendment problems. Were I a very wealthy man, I could declare war against the law itself by pleading not guilty. A DC jury would still likely convict me, but then the appeals would begin, and there exists a real chance to kill the law. It would cost millions.

So am I under the duress of poverty? In a figurative sense, maybe I am. But I've made my decision, and I'm sticking with it, so I snuff out this last doubt that Judge Jackson stirred in me and nod. Then how do I plead?

"Guilty, Your Honor."

Judge Jackson sets the terms of my release until sentencing. She notes that I've recently quit drinking and urges me to keep it up. So now it's an order from the bench, if you will. It will either get me into trouble or stiffen my resolve. As I leave the courtroom, a Kris Kringle–looking spectator wearing a three-piece suit stops me with a look: "You know who I am?" he asks.

I don't.

"I'm the sign guy." He's referring to the signs that read "Traitor" or equally unpleasant things you see on TV behind Flynn, Manafort, and others as they enter or leave court. "I had a feeling you're different, so no sign today. Don't disappoint me."

CHAPTER 11
RECKONING

In the days before refrigeration, a human corpse had a harder expiration date than it does today, and after a short period it would begin to rot and decompose. That must have been the logic behind the Congressional Cemetery, I figure. In addition to the likelihood that if someone has stayed in Washington for too long, he or she has likely been forgotten at home.

I started to regularly visit the Congressional Cemetery because they allow dogs to run off leash. It's becoming a daily exercise, so I've become more familiar with the markers I now routinely stroll by. Once you pass the wrought iron gate, there is a company of austere obelisks all dating back to the early nineteenth century. One of these reads: "John Quincy Adams, Representative."

The sixth US president, who had been his father's envoy to the Russian court at Saint Petersburg when he was fourteen years old and after serving his own term as president stood for a House seat from Massachusetts, literally died in Congress.

J. Edgar Hoover is laid to rest there, as well as the Lakota chief Sitting Bull, and DC "Mayor for Life" Marion Barry. So, too, is the now deceased Tom Lantos, the leonine congressman from California

254 — SAM PATTEN

to whom I once quoted Chekhov at the US ambassador's residence in Moscow.

Further to the left, looming over some shrubbery and up over a graduated boundary, is DC Jail. Because Washington is not a state, it doesn't have its own penitentiary, so DC Jail doubles as that too. There are inmates serving sentences longer than a year, which is usually the cutoff for a jail.

If I am to be incarcerated, I tell Stuart, my preference is not the "club fed" facility in Cumberland, Maryland, where they sent SSCI leaker James Wolfe, but here. If indeed that's what they're going to do to me, let it be real.

Narrow slits like the windows in a castle peer down from the jail on to the cemetery, with its walkers and romping hounds. Will I be looking out at this scene in a few months' time? It is hard to imagine I'll be sentenced to more than thirty days, especially as I am cooperating in good faith, but stranger things have happened. Now more than ever, people seem to be going out of their way to make a point.

These are the questions I brood over as I follow Pepper through the headstones. Sometimes steam appears to leak from the earth in the wintry months, and I imagine it is a ghost passing by to keep us company here with the incarcerated and the dead. At least no one is judging me here, and for forty minutes or so each day I can find a little peace and let Pepper be as she otherwise might in nature.

After all, what kind of lunatic would mess with a political corpse?

————

As fate might have it, former Georgian president Mikheil "Misha" Saakashvili—someone I had both worked for and against—has chosen this moment to pile on yours truly. On top of everything else, I now have to contend with an attack from the exiled politician and onetime golden boy of the West.

Just before my arraignment, I'd written a short mea culpa and posted it on Facebook. It was earnest and straightforward, and in it I took my lumps and apologized for the trouble I'd caused. Social media was probably the last place I needed to be then, but it seemed expedient. I should have just left it there.

Instead, I impulsively go back to the social media app to see what kind of reaction my statement is getting. That's when I notice that whoever controls Saakashvili's Facebook account has taken my mea culpa and turned it into a meme. The account is pushing out a screenshot of my statement with red scribbling on the margins about how I'm a Russian spy, a traitor, and the like. Misha's followers and trolls then make a swarm attack on my Facebook page, posting vile images, Putin's face, blood, and exclamations like, "Die, traitor! Die!"

Talk about kicking a guy when he's down.

So I write Misha's former chief of staff—and my former friend George Arveladze—in the Facebook messenger app: "Tell Misha to knock it off, call off his trolls, and clean up the mess they made, or else there is plenty of stuff I could say he'd prefer I didn't." It is stupid, but I'm now under an unfair attack on top of everything else. This strikes me in the moment as the most expedient way to solve the problem, but it isn't. I've just taken the bait.

Saakashvili, now a man without a country, capitalizes on the news hook of John McCain's recent death in order to get on CNN. Instead of sharing heartwarming memories or expressing gratitude for all the love and favoritism the late senator had lavished on him over the years, Misha produces an altered version of my exchange with George and tears into me, claiming I have just threatened his former chief of staff "using KGB-like blackmail methods."

Surprised, the CNN host lights up when she catches wind of a Mueller angle and asks the now wild-eyed Misha to elaborate.

I had worked for him long ago, Misha admits, before lying that he "had to let me go for performance reasons."

I was not fired. In fact, his party won a supermajority in parliament as a result, in part, of my efforts.

Then he says I worked for a pro-Russian oligarch against him because Moscow was desperate to get him out of power. To top it off, he demands that I be charged with criminal threatening. Misha is a Columbia-trained lawyer, thanks to the Edmund Muskie scholarship, so he knows how the US legal system works.

On Monday, I am called into the Justice Department for an urgent conversation. "What the hell is Saakashvili talking about?" the understandably mystified senior prosecutors ask me. Did I actually threaten him? No, I tell them, and then explain the backstory.

Once you go into a cooperation agreement with the government, you are discouraged from talking about that cooperation in any substantive sense. Neither in this book, nor anywhere else, have I shared what I was asked and/or how I responded. Under penalty of law, I told the truth, as I do without the risk of perjury anyway. But this flare-up is outside that agreement. It is also wildly ironic and paints a good picture of how vultures descend on carrion in political life.

Misha was not acting alone. A young American woman named Christina Pushaw has attached herself to him in exile, even describing herself as his representative. By 2018, he's already been kicked out of Georgia—or rather been charged with crimes against the state from which he fled—and volunteered for the new Ukrainian government. But soon he managed to wear out his welcome in Kyiv. Policemen even had to coax him off the roof of his apartment building, next to my old one with the charred door, off the Maidan.

I am connected with Pushaw on Facebook. She has a large number of common friends and seems very interested in the otherwise obscure political developments in the former Soviet space. We've never met in person. She's regularly liked things I've posted in the past, which is the sort of thing the vain notice. Now she's attacking me, perhaps because I'm easy prey.

Following Misha's CNN tirade, Pushaw reportedly approaches US authorities and demands that I be charged with threatening her "client." She is an American citizen; he is a foreign political figure. By demanding action on his behalf of the US government, she is more blatantly violating FARA than I ever did. She hasn't registered either. Pushaw is currently press secretary to Florida governor Ron DeSantis and was allowed to register post hoc in 2022.

What would I have said about Misha that he would have preferred I didn't? There is quite a bit, actually.

For starters, he lost 20 percent of his country's territory to Russia in an unnecessary war that he recklessly provoked. Then there is the fact that he was a human rights abuser who lost his last election when the systematic rape and torture of prisoners in the system he claimed to have "reformed" became known. Firsthand, I could share how I'd witnessed a culture of fear he cultivated while he was in power. That he was a failed ex-governor of Ukraine's Odesa oblast, who was less capable of hoodwinking the savvy Ukrainians than he was his own people for a time. The list goes on, but my point is, he's the last person to screech about threatening.

It is the first time a former client has used me as a news hook. Together with being untrue, the things he's said about me aren't very nice. But I'm also being taught a lesson about switching sides: it carries a cost.

To avoid other such lessons, I freeze my Facebook account.

———

I was sound asleep when, late in the evening of September 13, the US Senate voted 99–0 to turn over the transcript of my interrogation by its intelligence committee to defense counsel for Paul Manafort.

Already convicted of eight financial crimes—of the eighteen with which he'd been charged—after a trial in a US District Court in Virginia, Manafort was to be arraigned on additional charges, including failure to register under FARA, in Washington, DC, the following morning. As he had in Virginia, the expectation was that he would plead not guilty.

In a surprise move, Manafort pleaded guilty instead on the morning of the fourteenth and entered into a cooperation deal with the special counsel. I'd always hoped my debut on the Senate floor would be to some worthier and nobler effect. Yet there it is.

The fact that the Senate voted on releasing the transcript of my

SSCI interrogation strikes me as misleading theater. After all, ever since my encounter with the SSCI, I'd been fielding waves of media inquiries about the very issues we'd discussed on the condition of confidentiality. The committee's own chief of security had been removed between the time I handed him a box of documents and my interrogation.

The official story just doesn't seem to add up.

That is why I file a complaint against the SSCI with the Senate Ethics Committee. Months later, a staff lawyer for ethics will write me to say they see nothing requiring further investigation. Three of the Ethics Committee members also serve on the SSCI, so I wasn't banking on a fair hearing there. Still, I believe you have to give the system a chance to do right no matter how cynical you are.

By now, the Senate is done with me, and I'm chum for others.

MSNBC's Rachel Maddow develops an odd fixation on me after my arraignment. In the nine-month period of my purgatory between pleading and sentencing, she devotes four segments to my being a possible "missing link" in the vast Russia conspiracy she has been hawking on her nightly program. I think back to Tony Marsh's somewhat amazed reaction when I told him of my legal troubles: "If they're coming after you, then they really don't have anything."

As my cooperation with the feds continues, Maddow's tone becomes a bit more hopeful. Surely I'm giving them the goods, she optimistically speculates. What becomes clearer to me about this whole investigation is the media's role in it. It is as if they are telling— or trying to tell—Robert Mueller and associates what they ought to be thinking.

Some in the media see their role not just as reporting the news but also as guiding Mueller's team forward, pumping them up and constantly raising the stakes. Others might call it projection, or "gaslighting."

Meanwhile, I'm on a strict no-media diet since the flap with Saakashvili.

In an act of hubris, I agree to give Olivia Nuzzi at *New York Magazine* an exclusive for a feature article, provided she not run anything until after my sentencing. She seems to have an appreciation for the weirder elements of the drama unfolding every day in Donald Trump's Washington, and I hope that maybe she'll see something others don't.

I'm wrong. Not only does she not get me; I come to realize she's not even trying. In Olivia's world, her subjects are just freaks in the circus. It seems as though she's going through the motions, but with little curiosity. Laura and I take her to church with us, and in the article she ends up writing she just makes fun of Laura's outfit, suggesting that she looks like a creature from Dr. Seuss.

Nuzzi also shows little interest in how overseas political campaigns work. I offer to put her in touch with Kilimnik—himself a source of apparent intrigue—and she never follows up, which is downright odd.

Then, when the moment of judgment arrives, she can't be bothered to attend my sentencing. It is as if her piece had already been precooked. It is silly and naive of me to imagine it hadn't been, or that I could help paint a picture for her.

"*We're* not writing this story," she tells me in an irritated tone one day. "I am—try to remember that." I guess the old habits of spinning die hard.

Suddenly, I realize there are more important things in life than a glossy-magazine piece. My sister Eliza calls me with some "hard news." Our mother just had a double brain aneurism back at home in Maine and had my stepfather, Bob, not been there when it happened, she certainly would have died. She's being helicoptered to the big hospital in Portland.

Judge Jackson, who a few months back sent Manafort to jail, allows me to travel to Maine to be with my mother. I appreciate her compassion, and my mother miraculously rebounds after a risky surgery. Outside the ICU, I run into a high school classmate whose stepbrother, a star athlete in our time, had just succumbed to a massive coronary. In that moment, life and death seem so arbitrary, and I'm grateful not to have lost my mom.

When you stand on the brink of losing everything, the only thing you can do is put one foot in front of the other. Some things matter more than others, and a couple of months in prison seems like less of a big deal when faced with the unexpected possibility of losing a parent.

Back at home, Laura and I are dealing with two consecutive IRS audits. When the federal government takes an interest in you, they don't go halfway. It's yet another inquisition, and during one of our sessions with the auditor, Laura breaks down in tears. Will this ever end, or are we simply doomed and fated to be picked apart by birds of prey while chained to the side of a cliff?

Now there's a new delay. The special counsel asserts that Manafort has not been telling them the truth and shreds his cooperation deal. Soon after this, my own sentencing date, which had originally been set for February, is pushed back until April of the coming year.

Until I get this sentencing behind me, there is little else I can do. I've cashed in my retirement savings to pay legal fees and to stay afloat during a period in which no client will touch me with a ten-foot pole. Fortunately, Laura's boss used to work for Arthur Anderson—a company that was destroyed by Andrew Weissmann's heavy-handed prosecution tactics in the wake of the Enron collapse—so he says he has her back. That is one of a handful of points of light that keep us going.

When you are publicly known as a cooperating witness for the FBI, people keep their distance, especially in a city where so many are consumed with secrets. Our social circle shrinks, and if we go out to dinner in a restaurant, others stare and murmur. With the exception of a few brave friends willing to risk association with me, the prospects for paying work are grim.

So I look for places to volunteer and, after bumping into a few closed doors, find a couple of ones I can open tutoring inner-city youth. This takes my mind off my troubles and helps put life into some perspective, just as my mother's close brush with death did. Besides, my own self-worth has long been tied to the concept of being useful. The Mueller probe will not accomplish what its legion of enthusiasts hope. But to the young men and women I tutor in English, I am helpful.

I also learn that in passing its disastrous 1994 "crime bill," Congress cut off the ability of incarcerated persons to receive Pell Grants for education. If men and women leave prison without skills or a degree, they are much more likely to return to crime, so this ban seems not only needlessly punitive but also counterproductive. In lobbying—legally, that is—to lift the ban, I find another volunteer project.

———————

Abdul Saleem left Roland Garris, his old self, behind when he was released from prison four years ago. His twenty-six-year stretch in prison for homicide followed an armed standoff with DC police, who shot him three times in the leg. Despite his massive frame and forbidding appearance, Saleem's shuffling gait is a reminder of the moment when the Man brought him down.

Today Saleem presides over Born Champions, his new domain on Mount Olivet Street in Northeast Washington, where he is often perched on the front steps.

"I'm King Kong around here," he tells me when we meet. The deference passersby and gym patrons pay him confirms this claim. A retired DC police detective named Tony converted this onetime service garage for trucks into a place where inner-city kids could get off the streets, learn to box, and comport themselves with a new-found self-respect.

In preparation for prison, even for a short stretch, it would be wise for me to be ready to defend myself. At least I should have a fighting chance. Moreover, boxing offers a great outlet for letting some of my pent-up anger loose. First I took a class closer to the Capitol, but it was filled with young professionals in spandex, at least some of who were likely Congressional staffers. That felt like a hostile environment to me, but this one seems more relevant to my needs.

Already I've broken the chain that suspended one of the heavy bags from the large metal frame from which it hung. This draws a disappointed look from Saleem, who shakes his head.

"You think you're Jack Dempsey and shit," he scoffs, in reference

264 — SAM PATTEN

to a manual by the legendary prizefighter that I sometimes bring with me. "You got to relax and work that bag slowly, like you're eating pussy."

Good analogy, I think. *Now it makes sense.*

I'm not ready for the ring yet, so I have no reason to memorize the Marquess of Queensbury rules. Instead, I'm just getting into shape and learning how to strike as well as to bob and weave. Most everything in boxing begins with your midsection, and it is from there you throw your punches.

"Never go back," Saleem counsels. "Always be moving forward."

There is a hierarchy here, and Saleem sits atop the mountain. Others, like Coach Bookhard, come and go. Bookhard is the boxing coach in DC Jail, so I figure he's a good man to know. Only once I'm done with Saleem's Extremes—the intensive cardio-workout regimen of running, jumping rope, jumping jacks, squats, planks, and other exercises that are the right of passage to a gym visit—can I move onto the bags. That's where Bookhard comes in with technical tips.

I complain to Saleem about the government slow-rolling my sentencing. They're just watching me, he says, waiting to see if I mess up again. Right now, I need to stay steady and keep my nose clean, he says.

"What about prison?" I ask. "What advice can you offer about surviving that?"

"Be a man. Keep your mouth shut. Go to school. Read books. And exercise your mind and your body."

By school, he's talking about any educational programming that might be available.

Watching Saleem work with young men, it quickly becomes clear he is an ex-con who is now committed to being a constructive member of society. He has found a purpose that redeems him.

"When I came home, I wanted to give back to my community, where I'd wreaked so much havoc in the past. I wanted to pay my retribution and respect in a right, positive way, like a man should and should have done in the beginning," he tells me when I ask him what brought him here.

It's not just boxing I'm learning here; it is also an introduction to restorative justice in a much more tangible sense than one reads about. Though I put on a brave face, the prospect of prison obviously frightens me, and Saleem sees that.

"We got you," he assures me.

In addition to waiting and training, my mission right now is also collecting evidence that I have led a useful life and that the positives in my career outweigh the negative that has landed me in the defendant's dock. God dispenses grace not on the basis of merit but rather simply by his mercy. By contrast, federal judges look for proof that an individual deserves it.

Situations like mine are proving grounds of what, if anything, your life has amounted to up until now. As a key task in my presentencing stage, I am in the process of culling together over twenty-five letters from validators—former colleagues, a childhood babysitter, my ex and current wives, my godfather, my minister, and others who have stepped up and asked how they could help. These support Stuart's memo to the judge, which he will submit in parallel to the prosecutors'. Reading them is both a humbling and a redeeming exercise. I suppose it is a little like being able to listen in to the eulogy and testimonials at one's own funeral.

266 — SAM PATTEN

Every now and then, I commiserate over tea with Rinat who, even though he wasn't charged with anything, has been vilified in the Russiagate spectacle. Born in Russia, he's never lost the accent and sees things through the prism of an outsider. Like Saleem, he offers me words of wisdom: "Right now, you are finding out who your real friends are. They may be less in number than you'd hoped; they count for a whole lot more than everyone else," he tells me sagely, reinforcing what I've already observed. Then he becomes more serious and adds, "The most important thing, though, is that you don't end up becoming roadkill."

Sounds great, I think. *But how do you go about not becoming roadkill?*

Rinat has no quick answer for that. But the more time I spend with Saleem at Born Champions, the more hopeful I become someone won't be scraping me off the sidewalk with a shovel.

Just a few days over a year after the FBI arrived on my doorstep, my moment of judgment comes.

"You are unlike most of the people who pass through this courtroom," Judge Jackson tells me as she prepares to read her decision on my sentence. Maybe she means Roger Stone, on whom she'd placed a gag order after he tweeted an image of her in what appeared to be the scope of a rifle. Maybe she means Manafort, because she then goes on to say, "It's clear to me that you don't simply sell yourself to the highest bidder."

When the judge reads your sentence, you stand before her. Stuart is standing by my side. The fact that she is saying nice things means something less nice is probably coming next.

"I was most troubled, frankly, by your behavior before the Senate," she adds, confirming my intuition. I can feel that Stuart wants to kick me to reinforce his previous advice that I keep my mouth shut. He knows this is a main sore point for me. Even though my transgression was minor, I never challenged my guilt on the FARA charge. But the mere thought of the SSCI breaking its word to me and to my lawyer on the scope of inquiry and then trafficking me to the special counsel as a disposable scalp can make me turn purple with rage. That is not a good look when you're being sentenced.

It isn't just me catching flack in the US District Courtroom that morning though. Weissmann is there, watching, and from the bench Judge Jackson expresses irritation about the special counsel's policy of not making specific sentencing recommendations. In their filing, the Justice Department asked for leniency but left the interpretation of what that means up to the judge.

"Prior to his [criminal conduct], Patten appears to have led a helpful and exemplary professional life," the government stated in its presentencing filing. After a year of being on the receiving end of all kinds of pejorative and unkind statements in the media, in my inbox, and implicitly in the looks from anyone who recognized me, it is a pleasant surprise to hear this, especially from my persecutor.

Even Rachel Maddow is surprised by the government's sentencing recommendation, for what it is. She does a segment the night before sentencing on how the prosecution wrote I wasn't such a bad guy after all in their filing.

Judge Jackson sentences me to three years of probation, five hundred hours of community service, and a $5,000 fine. When I walked into court with Laura and my sister Eliza, I didn't know if I would walk out a free man. Half the country and nearly all the establishment is very angry with Trump, and I could easily have gotten thirty days or even several months in prison as a kind of bread and circus for the frothing elites. So I am relieved, but not jubilant. While it's a little bit at odds with all the contrition I've showed up until this point, I never should have been in this position in the first place.

I am not really a lobbyist. I had no real intention of influencing US policy, which would have taken enormous resources to sway if indeed I had. Ukrainian oligarchs like to show off Washington credentials to one another the way others might show off a Patek Phillipe watch. Essentially the one thing I helped Lyovochkin ask of American elites was to be balanced and fair in how they viewed the evolving situation in his country. Seriously, that's not even something one should have to ask of the US government—in a perfect world, anyway.

But that doesn't matter—what one should or shouldn't have to do. What matters is what is, and I am now a felon. I am not going to ask for a pardon, so I am going to be a felon for the rest of my life. In Russia, Putin's regime is branding dissidents as "foreign agents." Hanging on my wall is the portrait of van Steuben, without whose foreign agency we might still be subjects of the British crown. The US government never formally charged civil rights leader W. E. B. Du Bois with violating FARA, but they threatened him with it for six years. When he finally got his passport back, he moved to Ghana and never returned.

Laura looks relieved. As a former intelligence officer, this is not a role she has relished. She won't have to sit alone in church while

I'm in prison and stare woefully at the Muellers. For the past year and a half, she's been through hell because of me. Our marriage is strong, though, and surely will withstand this. Especially now that this is over.

As we're leaving the courtroom, I see former Obama and Clinton counsel Greg Craig seated with his lawyer in the middle of the room. The day before he'd been indicted for lying to the Justice Department about his involvement in a Manafort-originated public relations campaign, and now he is about to plead not guilty. The charges against him seem flimsy, and his alumni credentials suggest he'll have a good shot with a DC jury. By charging Craig, the prosecutors are trying to make it look like this is not a strictly partisan inquest. Optics don't really mean so much at this stage. His arraignment and my sentencing are the tail end of this whole caper.

Before I can get to the door, Weissmann appears. For the sake of decorum, I shake his hand but don't say anything. What would I say anyway? Maybe "thanks, asshole." But as my grandmother drilled into me at an early age, manners matter.

Before I can leave the courthouse, I have an appointment with my probation officer, who will tell me the dos and don'ts of my new status and set me up on a reporting regimen. It's an important conversation because, according to the Prison Policy Initiative, nearly one in five incarcerated persons in America are behind bars because of a probation violation. I'm not out of the woods yet.

On my way to the federal probation office, a dogged courtroom reporter for CNN asks me if there's anything I'd like to say. I remember how, a year ago, a CNN producer told me they were doing a story on how I was conducting focus groups across America for Vladimir

Putin, gauging how my compatriots would react to his annexation of Eastern Europe. Poorly sourced as that allegation was, CNN never ran with it, but it's hard to forget such an encounter.

"No," I tell her, "I have nothing to say to you."

She follows me to the probation office anyway, hoping to overhear something she can use.

For more than a year, I'd rehearsed in my mind all the things I wanted to say right now. But as the famously reticent Mueller might agree, discretion is the better part of valor.

———————

A couple of weeks before my sentencing, the American Enterprise Institute had advertised a roundtable discussion on "Modernizing FARA." Since it struck me as a useful, if not overdue, cause, I signed up to sit and listen, even though it was scheduled for the Monday after the Friday I would learn my fate. *Were I sent to prison, they could always fill my seat in the audience with an intern.*

One of the panel members is the lawyer Lieutenant General Michael Flynn fired and is somehow considered one of Washington's FARA experts. Another is the Assistant Attorney General for National Security, whose office technically had a hand in prosecuting me, even if their enforcement regime is, in most cases, notoriously lax.

As one might expect, the curated discussion is dull. Then comes question-and-answer time. A professional think-tank event-goer in the front row is the first out of the gate with a question that had to do with the Craig case. Moderator Danielle Pletka, a stately blonde, tells him sternly that the ground rules were that they would not discuss ongoing cases, and while the man grumbled about not having been briefed on this, Pletka is already scanning the audience for a fresh idea.

I oblige and raise my hand to ask, "What if you are a recently adjudicated case? Can you ask a question then?"

The panelists all shoot me mystified looks, so I introduce myself.

Sensitive to Pletka's rule, I make my question to be a hypothetical one. "Let's say," I suggest, "that the country of Ukraine were having an election next week—this is actually happening, in fact. Imagine a DC think tank—not this one, of course—were actively disseminating white papers in support of one of the Ukrainian candidates. One Eurasia-focused outfit has been doing exactly that. Suppose said organization had received generous contributions from backers of that same candidate. Should that think tank have to register under FARA, as the law and this discussion would suggest?"

The room ignites with murmurs, but Pletka smiles because she knows exactly what I'm talking about. The panel hems and haws, with the supposed FARA expert saying it all came down to the question of agency—that is, what was the intentionality of the donor's gift, and how did it relate to the advocacy I'd raised? The assistant attorney general looks irritated and says something about FARA being an "elegant solution" that doesn't square much at all with the ground reality. I guess I wasn't really expecting a truly illuminating answer. Instead, I was trying to highlight the 1938 law's many ambiguities.

Now out on the street, as I'm walking to the subway after the event, Stuart calls me. What have I just done? CNN is running with a story that I'd just challenged the Justice Department only days after sentencing. I guess CNN is not as easy to dodge as I'd hoped. "No," I tell

Stuart, "I hadn't challenged anyone. I just asked a reasonable question."

In Washington, where people will walk a couple of extra blocks to avoid anything awkward, good questions can sometimes get you in trouble.

Noah Shachtman is in town for the White House Correspondents dinner, which the media still attends even if the president doesn't. We have coffee off Dupont Circle, and at one point Noah leans in and asks me quietly, "Did it ever occur to you that you were set up?"

The other thing people in Washington often do is ask questions to which they already know the answer. It helps you look wise.

———————

Weeks later, I am standing in the chapel of the DC Jail giving a talk for incarcerated students in Georgetown University's academic program there. I'd read about this program in the alumni magazine and was intrigued, especially given that the course described in the article was on democracy promotion. From my alma mater to my métier, it seemed like I was destined to be somehow involved with these folks.

Some of the inmates have extraordinarily good questions—far better than I'd ever heard in a university classroom. For instance, one asked whether democratic governance has really improved, on a technical level, since the seventeenth century. I couldn't say that it has. But after my ninety-minute lecture, a devout-looking Muslim asks a question that floors me.

"Listening to you talk about your experience, it's pretty obvious you're a patriot. That being the case, how can you ever forgive what this country has done to you?"

I want to hug the guy asking the question. For the first time in a long while, I feel like I've been heard. But when I look around the room, I see almost everyone is wearing an orange jumpsuit. In maybe half an hour, I will be out of here, but they won't. This is not a place for me to feel sorry for myself. As the saying goes, the one thing everyone in prison has in common with one another is innocence.

With a deep breath and a moment's reflection, I respond, "Thank you for that question; you really moved me with it. But it could have been worse. They could have charged me with treason and then executed me."

This draws a gasp from even this hardened audience. I am just a visitor in prison, and I don't know all the rules about how to say things. But I think we all agree that the Man is more powerful than we are, and it doesn't matter if something is right or wrong. Justice is often just an illusion, or even a fig leaf, to cover some embarrassing or more damning truth.

Georgetown has been teaching academics in a degree program here from which disciplined students are graduating. When they leave prison, they will have degrees. With those, hopefully, a few more options will be open to them, even if they still face an overwhelming array of obstacles.

This encounter gets me thinking on a slightly different track. *What about a nonacademic course?* I wonder. It would be a practical one that teaches how to run political campaigns. The first felon was elected to Congress in 1798. One of the students in that chapel will, two years later, run for an advisory neighborhood council seat from his cell and win.

I design a course to do precisely this, and Georgetown agrees to bring me on in a nonacademic capacity. This could be my first real initiative since my own brush with the law, and I will run it with heart. Notices go out in the prison about the course, and there is an enthusiastic response. But before I can teach my first course, the DC Department of Corrections intervenes. I am still on active probation, they note. As such, I pose a threat to the prisoners—theoretically anyway.

Saddened, I go to Born Champions to pound my frustrations away. I tell Saleem about the episode, and he looks perplexed and a little angry.

"You pose a threat to them? That's fucking crazy. They pose a threat to you!"

Of course, he's right. But I've started to get used to things being upside down. For all practical purposes, it seems to be the new normal.

––––––––––

It is on my first day of freedom that I learn things can get worse. By May 2020, the whole country has learned about lockdowns, thanks to the COVID-19 pandemic. I've been on probation for just over a year—plus the nine months of court supervision before that—and Judge Jackson, seeing that I've completed my five hundred hours of community service in near record time, decides I've had enough. She ends my probation less than two years early "in the interest of justice."

So I celebrate by driving down to Charlottesville for the first time without a court order to see Max, who is buying his first new car from a local dealership. During our visit, Max said he'd like to come up to DC and spend the weekend with his girlfriend, Iris, and us. I love the idea.

Max had been very cautious during the early days of the pandemic, so I wasn't worried he or Iris would infect us. But I didn't ask Laura first, and now she's mad. Once again, I put her interests last.

Instead of just apologizing, I launch into a huffy lecture about the state of human affairs. "There is a dichotomy of survival," I tell my wife, who has been to just as many wars as I have. "We cannot crouch forever. Are we weak, or are we strong? We have to decide," I insist.

"I want a separation," Laura then tells me.

I can see it in her eyes that she's serious. This isn't a feint. I've used the big, bad D as a ruse in arguments before. That was reckless, and it's coming back to bite me hard now. It sounds almost silly to say it, but things between us were changed by Olivia Nuzzi's slash piece on me.

The *New York Magazine* writer not only made fun of Laura's outfit in church but she painted us as a couple out to be shambolic. She'd also highlighted unbecoming things I'd said, in pique, during the nine-month exclusive I'd given her. The day after the piece came out, Sotheby's told Laura they wouldn't offer her a job for which she'd been a finalist. It's hard not to see some causality.

The *NY Mag* piece, like all the Ukraine business, was damage in which I had played a role. I'm supposed to be good at strategic communications, yet I'd invited a vampire into our home and failed to control the story. If Laura's had it with me, it's certainly not without reason.

She's tired of living under siege and has been talking for a while about selling the house and starting over somewhere new. The problem is we have very different visions of where that might be.

I tell her I'll leave in the morning, but first I need a good night's sleep. Devastated, I slink down to the TV room in the basement and spend the night on the trundle bed, feeling immensely sorry for myself. A less self-involved man might leap into action at this moment, try and stabilize things, and beg for a reprieve in which we agree to continue working on our marriage. After all, I'd felt we were making progress in couples therapy. But not enough, apparently, and having become used to being under attack, I retreat to a zone of maximum self-pity, or the terrain of a loser.

Early the next morning, I gather a small duffel bag's capacity of things, climb into the old Mercedes wagon Max has handed back down to us having now bought his own car, and drive north. Maine is the only place I can think to go. There I have two sets of parents, each of whom has two houses in the state, so it is a target-rich environment for couch surfing. And it's an excellent place to think. As children's author E. B. White once mused, "I'd rather have a bad day in Maine than a good day anywhere else."

But it's shock more than reason, or a semi-reliable station wagon, that's driving me right now. I'd taken Laura and her allegiance for granted. Having just completed my sentence, the Sam show is now over. I've been caught flat-footed, too slow to properly react to another major loss.

Pepper is curled up in back, a living testament to the old phrase about a man's best friend.

"You might as well take her," Laura had said. "After all, she's your friend." Thank God—and I suppose Laura too—for that. Our three-year-old niece had once told her parents she thought Pepper and I were married and that Laura just lived with us. It was a keen observation of our codependence.

I'm holding back tears as I keep the wagon between the lines on the road and try to come up with the words to explain to my parents how I've lost yet again. It's been almost twenty years since two friends, both named Josh, helped me move from Portland, Maine, to Washington, DC, in a blinding storm. Now I'm coming home alone—in human terms anyhow—a lonelier, more broken man.

CHAPTER 12
EIGHT POINTS OF DEPARTURE

Tinder almost kills me, but L. L. Bean saves my life. I'm not talking about the comparative wholesomeness of different brands, but rather how I closed out 2020—a year so many wish never happened.

For the last month, I've been doing seasonal work for the legendary Maine outfitter L. L. Bean's flagship store in Freeport. While I'm only earning twelve dollars an hour, before taxes, it is a cool place to work. The job comes with the benefit of 30 percent apparel, which is good because I'm changing my wardrobe from city boy to outdoorsman. Plus L. L. Bean is a destination.

Growing up in Maine, we always knew the flagship store was probably the only place in the state open twenty-four hours a day. The onslaught of COVID-19 has reduced the hours, but it's still one of the best places for people-watching. For Mainers, coming to Beans is a welcome excursion, and for visitors to our state, it's a must.

By now, I've spent five months living in the woods, on an island, and now in a one-bedroom apartment in a building my father owns. It's vacant because he is planning upgrades before another long-term tenant moves in, so I'm essentially place-sitting in the tiny Portland suburb of Falmouth Foreside. As I learned in Moscow, there are benefits to being the poorest resident of a rich community.

It's been very quiet, in part by design. The white Anglo-Saxon Protestant (WASP) male learns from an early age to swallow pain privately and in silence. My friend Josh, who helped me move to Washington nineteen years ago, is probably the only contemporary I've seen since coming home. He's got acres of land behind the house he shares with his longtime girlfriend, Rosie. I take Pepper there to run off leash and practice my aim with my new compound bow that drives arrows at impressive velocity into innocent trees.

If I am to hunt here, I'll need to get proficient with the bow because, as a felon, I can never handle, own, or furnish a firearm in the United States again. Whether that is a commensurate penalty for someone who once didn't fill out a form is a separate question. For me, the name of the game is to adapt.

Working the floor at Beans includes various tasks, from replenishing the shelves to helping customers find things. There's not a whole lot of heavy lifting, but since many of my fellow seasonal workers are retirees, I like to help them out when muscle-intensive projects come up, whether in the storeroom or the shipping bay. Sometimes the tasks are solitary, like sorting the jeans or straightening up the back supplies. Other times they can be chatty, especially in the shoe department.

During my eight-hour shifts, I can get as many as twenty-eight thousand steps in because when you're not standing or squatting, you're constantly moving. Voluntary exercise, like jogging or swimming, I come to learn, is a conceit of the laptop class. Workingmen and women get plenty of it on the job.

The day before my forty-ninth birthday, Laura tells me she wants a divorce. My hope that absence would make the heart grow fonder turns out to have been a hollow one.

I'm not really in a position to argue. From an objective standpoint, I'm no longer much of a catch. While going through hell together sometimes makes your bond stronger, it is not always the case. As I understand, parents who lose a child often experience this. Any tragedy can be devastating, but when they happen in rapid succession of one another, the bobbing and weaving of survival takes over.

Just as our marriage was an exercise in teamwork, so is our divorce. We put the Capitol Hill row house I'd bought a decade earlier on the market and proceed with what folks nowadays call "conscious uncoupling."

We get an acceptable offer on the house. The realtor made us paint the walls in that dreadful gray that millennials for some reason adore and replace a beautiful chandelier I'd hung in the dining room with a Soviet-looking *Sputnik* model.

The young woman who is counsel to the SSCI—the same one who told Michael Bopp they wouldn't ask me about FARA—bought the house two doors down. Before we separated and I left, her constant presence was a depressing reminder of what kind of town this is. Now another young lawyer is buying our house, and who knows, maybe they'll end up friends.

L. L. Bean gives me almost a week off, so I go down to Washington, rent a U-Haul to collect my remaining belongings, and close on the sale. There is some divorce paperwork to finalize as well.

It's going to be a depressing few days, so in the interest of having one good memory of my hometown, I sign up for Tinder to find a date. I've never dated online before, but so many people swear by it. I figure why not try.

On the app, I connect with an appealing woman my age, and we arrange to meet for an early dinner on Thursday, the night before the closing. She chooses the restaurant and mentions more than once that it is near her place, so I am both hopeful and even a little giddy about the encounter. This is going to be my first date sober, and also my first since I met Laura more than seven years ago.

Though I get to the restaurant early and find nearby parking on busy Florida Avenue, my phone lights up with a work prospect. If it gels, it will be a multiyear contract in the Balkans, which is where my foreign adventuring began just after college. I am part of a larger pitch team, but the one who is uniquely able to answer the questions a prospective client is asking. So, eager to forestall any more interruptions during the date, I pound out a memo on my smartphone and hit send.

As I step out of the car and onto the sidewalk, I start scrolling through the emails to find the phone number of the lead man on the pitch team. I want to confirm he got the memo and that all is understood so I can switch off my phone and stop worrying about it. It's a Darwinian error, really. Never surrender situational awareness.

I can hear my assailant approaching from behind but assume he is headed for the 7-11 I'm passing. My assumption has always been if a street person is talking to himself, he is probably harmless and that it is the silent ones you need to watch. There's always an excuse behind every example of surrender.

The first blow lands on top of my skull. He must have jumped up in the air just before to allow it to come down on my head with the force that it does. It is as if the world has stopped and gone silent. Before I can absorb what's happening, he hits my head again with what feels like a rock, and I fall to the sidewalk.

He is right on top of me, now hacking into my upper back with a blade of some kind. It feels like he's stabbed me a thousand times, but in fact it turns out to be only six in the shoulder blades and neck. I'm going to die, right here and now, I assume. But I didn't finish this fucking book, I suddenly remember in that moment when your life is supposed to flash before your eyes.

At first I am embarrassed by my failure to make the most of my last chance on earth, and then I get mad. Why? If I can't even tell my own goddamn story, there has been no point to any of this. Whoever is trying to decapitate me right now is in effect silencing me as well.

Anger can be restorative. I turn up to the left, suddenly seeing the sky again in a flood of blue light. In this moment, I ask my assailant "Why?" Has someone paid him to do this, and if so, who? Or is he just a random psycho? I want to know. I deserve to know. If I'm just an actor in some shitty C-rate movie, I still want to see the scriptwriter and have a word.

Whatever happens next can be attributed to instinct and gravity, or fate. The man looks about my age and has dreadlocks. He says nothing, looks confused or ashamed, or maybe he's just concentrating, and then he swings into my now exposed front. My right arm somehow blocks the blow. It feels almost as though it had been with the palm of my hand where there has long been embedded a cyst. There is also a deep indentation, but no tear, on the outside of my index finger.

Everything stops. I stagger, trying to get up, and look around, but he's gone. I fall back to the sidewalk, feeling very warm on my back and sensing that I'm bleeding a lot. I want to press against the cement to stop from bleeding out.

An irrational thought enters my ruptured head: Can I still make the date if the ambulance manages to patch me up with gauze and tape? No, of course I can't. The sidewalk tile on which I'm crumpled is covered with a large, spreading pool of bright red blood. Just out of my arm's grasp lies my cell phone. Either my assailant was too frazzled to take it, or that was never his goal in the first place.

A few pedestrians coming down Fourteenth Street cut a wide circle around me and keep walking. The clichéd assumption that surely someone will help vanishes. Then I see two teenage-looking girls standing about four or five yards away who appear to be Tik-Toking my writhing about. I am too focused on my own survival in this moment to be outraged, and once I make eye contact with the girls I decide instead to give tangible instructions to each. Chastened, they silently comply.

I tell the one filming me with her phone to call 911. The other one I tell to walk over to the secondary pool of blood across the sidewalk crack from my tile and pick up my cell phone, open the Tinder app, and tell the last person I messaged with what's happened and that I won't be able to make our date. The restaurant is half a block up the street in this somewhat edgy but nonetheless trendy neighborhood.

Then I just lay back and wait for the paramedics. I'm lucky they are very quick. As it turns out, my assailant allegedly stabbed another man fifteen minutes before me, so this block was already on their radar screen. When I later learn the other victim's identity from the police report, I see he looks eerily like me, though without graying streaks in his hair. It's probably just a coincidence.

They take off my *swayzer,* the purple cashmere sweater underneath that I'd bought in Paris with Laura a few years earlier, and then cut my blood-soaked Oxford shirt open. Until a few minutes ago, it was a monogrammed, hand-tailored Turnbull and Asser that Rinat had given me as a wedding present. I suppose other than for the rare date in DC it is of little use to an L. L. Bean stock boy anyway.

Though I'm now naked from the waist up and cold in the November air—even though it's a sunny and temperate DC late afternoon—I sense by the time they lift me into the ambulance that I'm going to live. They count out the eight wounds and radio ahead to the trauma unit about yet another incoming.

Once they're done scanning and sewing and stapling, the sense of urgency passes, and the doctors and med techs move on to fresher, more demanding cases. There is numbness in my right hand, but it's not clear whether that is from blocking what would have been the killer blow or some nerve damage, given that my assailant missed the C5 and C6 vertebrae near the top of my spine by a fraction of a millimeter. I have his poor aim to thank for not being crippled, or dead.

The investigating detective comes by to get my statement. He says he's called Laura and that she is coming to get me. I'd be glad to know that I broke the guy's thumb, he reports with a smile. They have him in custody after following the trail of blood to the alley where he was huddled and quivering.

I ask the detective to call the FBI field office and let them know what happened. When I see him next, months later at the grand jury hearing to indict the assailant, he tells me the FBI never bothered responding to his message. I suppose this is typical. Ex-cooperators are a bit like used condoms, which no one gives much thought to after they've been tossed.

Laura takes me to the Saint Regis on Sixteenth and K because the house we're selling tomorrow is now empty, and both the buyers and our real estate agents want it to stay that way. I tell her not to postpone the closing; I'll be able to make it.

Max drives up from Charlottesville to take care of his old man, relieving Laura of me. He will also drive the U-Haul in my place up to Maine together with my stepfather, Bob, who flies down to join him. My father and his wife, Sydney, are by serendipity near Washington on a tour of the East Coast in a rented Winnebago, which they manage to park outside the Saint Regis for a few minutes before police shoo them away. Back in Maine, my mother is watching Pepper. Even though I am now essentially divorced and technically homeless, I feel my family's embrace more so than any moment since childhood.

God has sent me a powerful message: stay the fuck out of Washington, DC. The city of my birth, where I've now been twice stabbed, is a place where I no longer have any business. A simple note of banishment should have been enough, but as an aunt suggests, with love, I've long been a magnet for drama.

––––––––––

About eight miles up the Kennebec River from its mouth at the Gulf of Maine sits the small city of Bath, a forty-minute drive northeast from Portland. In the 1860s, when American shipbuilding was at its zenith, Bath was Maine's most prosperous center. Today all that is left is the Bath Iron Works, still one of Maine's largest employers, which builds Aegis destroyers for the US Navy. This keeps Bath afloat, or on the map anyway.

I chose to settle here not to build ships but to rebuild my life. It seems as good a place as any. It is far enough away from Portland to get a better value for the dollar on real estate because most people taking Route 1 North just drive by over the Sagadahoc Bridge, headed for the quainter towns that dot the coast. It is also close enough to both sets of parents for me to be useful in a pinch, but just a little too far for unannounced drop-ins.

Back in the day, people named Patten were a big deal here in Bath. The library where I'm writing this book is called the Patten Free Library. Several suitably—but not excessively—grand houses here were built by men named Patten on the street where I live, and still have their names by the doors on plaques made by the local historical society. The library bookstore where I volunteer as a clerk one day a month even sells a book, *The Pattens of Bath, Maine: A Shipbuilding Dynasty*.

I don't know whether the Pattens here bear any relation to the ones in Western Massachusetts my father once considered his paternal kin. It doesn't really matter, because it was Susan Mary Patten's extramarital affair with Duff Cooper, then London's ambassador to Paris, that produced my father. Still, her husband, Bill Patten, probably knew this and passed his name down to my father anyway, who in turn passed it to me. Even if the name is borrowed, or "appropriated," it is done with permission. As far as the Pattens of Bath might be concerned from their crow's nests in heaven, I am a stepson of

288 — SAM PATTEN

sorts. A stepson, that is, of the times.

Soon after moving back to Maine, I started writing a weekly column for three weekly newspapers in Rockland, Camden, and Belfast—towns a little further up the coast from Bath, where I grew up. They include the *Camden Herald*, which my father once owned and where I worked as a reporter straight out of school in the mid-1990s. I call the column "Crossfire Hurricane," in remembrance of the FBI probe that grew out of false reports that Donald Trump paid prostitutes in Moscow to pee on a bed in which the Obamas once slept.

I write about politics because it is a hard habit to kick. In the italicized bio blurb, I call myself a "recovering political consultant," but as an astute nurse I date for several months observes, my "recovery" isn't going so well.

In 2020 I swallow my pride and argue that Susan Collins should be reelected. While I continue to be outraged at how the so-called Senate Intelligence Committee conducted its hack investigation into Russian interference in the 2016 election—and specifically her refusal, as a SSCI member, to even acknowledge my complaints about it—my beef with her is smaller than Maine's need for federal dollars. She is now the ranking Republican on the Senate Appropriations Committee, which puts her in a position to help our relatively low GDP per resident state.

After I'm stabbed on the street in Washington, one of the papers I write for runs a front-page story: "*Herald* columnist attacked!" At the time, it lifts my spirits. After all, I have a role in life. I am a columnist for the same newspaper where I worked a quarter century ago.

In the weeks before the 2022 midterm election, though, I get canceled. The official reason is, I have become "too partisan" in my opinion pieces, which favorably portray several Republican candidates. I don't quit the column though. Instead, I just move it to the only conservative digital news outlet in the state. *The Maine Wire* hires me as a writer, which is like starting all over again.

This also allows me to—sometimes literally—climb up on a soapbox when I see others being wronged or to promote ideas that can help Maine while inveighing against those who hurt us. For instance, we are facing a war on the lobster fishery, which in Maine is iconic. Radical environmentalists and sympathetic bureaucrats in Washington have been trying in recent years to shut down the Maine lobster industry. It was a lobsterman who first taught me to steer a boat and used to give me a ride to sailing lessons when I was a little boy. I can't imagine the Maine coast without them.

Environmentalists are inaccurately claiming the lobster fishery harms the endangered North Atlantic right whale. It doesn't. I empathize with the lobstermen because I have also seen the harm that popular narratives can do if unchecked. That is why I spend half of 2022 pounding out article after article to raise awareness about this injustice. Then, as if it were a Christmas present, the industry wins a six-year reprieve from federal regulations in the 2023 budget bill. If any of my pamphleteering efforts helped achieve this outcome, it's been time well spent.

There will be other crusades, I'm quite certain.

Even if I myself was not born in Maine—a prerequisite for being a real Mainer—my son was. By that association, I call this state home—to "identify" as a Mainer, as it were. It is just like my being a Patten of Bath in name only. I have adopted this identity and am sticking to it.

———————

The one positive, tangible result of all my foreign entanglements is my son, Max. I met his mother in Kazakhstan more than a year before he was born in Bangor, Maine, on the cusp of the new millennium.

When he was a little boy of maybe six or seven, and his mother and I had already separated, we were spending the weekend in Northern Virginia and having lunch at one of the large Asian markets that occupy strip malls on the way to Tysons Corner.

At lunch, I saw a flyer for a meeting of the Thai opposition at a nearby church hall. At the time I was working for soon-to-be-overthrown Thai prime minister Thaksin Shinawatra, so I thought it might make for a useful extracurricular activity to stop by and check it out. While Max is half Asian, I am not. But for the credibility being his escort afforded me, I stood out like a sore thumb. But that didn't stop me from asking people questions. At one booth selling various literature, I pushed my luck, and a middle-aged woman behind the table fired back at me: "Why you ask so many questions? You CIA, man?"

At this, I picked Max up and beat a retreat. Back in the parking lot, I fastened him into his car seat and then hopped in my own to beat it before an angry mob chased us out. Adjusting my rear-view mirror, I caught Max's face, and he was smiling. He repeated the woman's question and laughs.

A few years later, Max and I were strolling through the kiosks of the National Book Fair set up on the National Mall that rolls from the foot of Capitol Hill to the Washington Monument when we ran into the Kazakh ambassador, whom I'd been haranguing from my perch at Freedom House. Personally, we each harbored a little respect for the other. Introducing my son to him and his wife, I told the senior diplomat that Max was the reason I worked in democracy promotion.

The ambassador raised an eyebrow as a way of saying "tell me more," so I shared one of my more aspirational strategies for my son's career development. "When he grows up, I want him to be able to choose whether he's going to be president of my country or yours."

In her letter to my sentencing judge, Max's mother, Aizhan, wrote that I stood out to her when we met back in Almaty in the late 1990s because I treated everyone I met as equals, unlike many of the expatriates who tended to stomp on the terra like Lord Buckley, neocolonialists celebrating another's defeat as their own victory. Reading that made my heart sing, just as it prompted my lawyer to ask why we ever split up.

My greatest regret from all my years of carpetbagging around the globe is the time I didn't spend with Max as he grew up. I've tried to be there for the key moments, but certainly missed a few. The fact that he's had to worry whether I'd be killed in some far-flung land or go to prison in our own weighs on me when I think about it. But as I'm being hard on myself, which is a well-worn habit, another thought creeps into my brain.

Growing up myself, the kids whom I most admired were often the children of diplomats or international businesspeople who traveled the world with their parents. They seemed to share a sense of sophistication and equanimity of which I was often jealous. They'd seen more, understood more, and were less quick to judge. Part of this could have been my imagination.

In fathering a son, I feel I've filled some of those gaps. Through all the ups and downs, he has consistently been the one part of my life that shines with unmitigated pride. He's smarter, kinder, and even more diplomatic than his old man. If in any way my own failings have lit a better road for him, that is all the more of a blessing. Through him, I glimpse hope that there is such a thing as human progress.

———————

I'm sitting in my home office in Bath on a late, mid-March Thursday afternoon in 2022 when my old friend Steven Moore calls me. We've been close friends since we met in Iraq in 2004. Like me, Steve had worked in Ukraine previously on a project for which I'd referred him. When the war broke out in late February, he hightailed it here and set up his own ad hoc relief organization.

Could I drop everything and fly to Minnesota to pick up the radios and then bring them immediately with me to Romania and on to Ukraine?

There wasn't a lot to drop. I did have to cancel one booking from an Airbnb guest, which cost me my Superhost rating, but that seemed a small price to pay to help a country in urgent need that I also happened to care about—despite and perhaps because of everything that happened after my last engagement there.

"Sure," I told Steve. "Why not?"

At zero dark thirty the next morning, I'm racing down an empty highway to Portland to catch my first flight to Minneapolis. On arrival, a good-hearted woman Steve knows from grad school meets me by the ticket counter with two enormous suitcases filled with shortwave radios a former special operator I'd connected with Steve recommended for the combat environment into which Ukraine is now devolving. With her help, I cram the antennae into another bag.

This is my first trip outside the United States in four years. I meet Steve in Bucharest, where I'd run a Romanian presidential campaign in 2009, and visit a few familiar haunts before our drive east. We'll cross into Ukraine just below a mountain range riddled with smugglers' routes. At the border, Steve flirts with an attractive passport control officer who waves us through without delay. The long line is on the other side.

Now we're driving to Chernivtsi, a small city in western Ukraine, where Steve has rented an apartment he's using as a safe house for Ukrainians fleeing the war in the East. What traffic there is drives the speed limit, which strikes me as odd given my past experience on Ukrainian roads. People are cautious, falling into line and playing by the rules. In times of war, society has a way of pulling together.

It is two late afternoons later, a few hours before curfew, when we arrive at the crowded apartment in which a family—several young men; two young women, one of whom later informs me she is a witch, which is a coincidence since I'd been dating a witch in Maine right up until my departure; two dogs; a cat; and a bunny rabbit—are living. Because I am a visitor bearing gifts, I'm given my own mattress on the floor of the large open room in which six of us sleep.

I am so tired from my trip that I sleep through the various air-raid sirens that night. Early the next morning, I rise quietly before everyone else and make myself a coffee before heading out to explore the town. As a rule, Europeans start the day later, and Ukrainians are certainly no exception. The streets are nearly empty because the influx of internally displaced people who fill the hotels, spare apartments, and even some storefronts of this old Carpathian city are still catching a little more sleep. There is no rush to wake up anyway, not when

294 — SAM PATTEN

you're in purgatory.

Several of the parked cars I walk past have the word *children* in Russian taped to the windows and the hood. This was apparently done in the hope that the invaders share some commonsense humanity. In these cases, positive thinking paid off. This is, after all, a fratricidal war. Some Russians will behave like animals—plunder, rape, and kill with abandon. But others will intentionally self-sabotage, the ones who know this is an unjustified war, and Kyiv is not run by a fascist junta.

A pack of stray dogs sunning themselves at the top of the old city's main hill eye me warily. What the fuck am I doing there, they wonder, picking up on the uncertainty with which I myself would answer if actually asked.

When I get back, the safe house is springing to life. Steve is angry the local witch didn't get a Sprinter van for the medicine shipment. Lazily, she'd assumed a couple of sedans could manage it. One volunteer fighter shows up from Kyiv in fatigues with a machine gun. He is supposed to take the nonexistent Sprinter to the front, now just outside the capital. Now delayed a day, tonight he will win—or perhaps earn—the affections of the witch.

I left Pepper with the witch back home so I could come here. I miss my witch intensely—maybe she put a spell on me. And I miss Pepper, too, who carries the same significance for me as the two dogs, the cat, and the rabbit do for the Zamozhny family—all living reminders of a normal life. The Ukrainian witch asked to see a photo of mine, and when I showed her, she nodded and said yes, she's definitely a witch. Years before, Kostya's wife had told me all Ukrainian women are witches, but she was also just angry not to be in Moscow and enjoyed my incredulous reaction.

Being on the brink is not new to Ukraine. There was the Revolution of People's Dignity in 2014 and the Orange Revolution in 2005, both of which led to regime changes. But now the Russians have actually invaded prima facie, and are no longer just working through proxies. It is almost as if previous crises were preparing Ukraine for this moment.

People swing almost naturally into action. Grocery stores cordon off their alcohol stocks to reinforce the fact this is a moment for sobriety—they are also complying with an emergency decree from the president. Everyone, including the grandfathers manning checkpoints with shotguns and young women signing up to fight, is doing his or her part. By invading, Putin has succeeded in unifying Ukraine.

Steven works day and night trying to solve bite-sized problems as he learns about them. Other volunteer militiamen Steven had known in his previous stay in Ukraine come and visit the safe house to pick up supplies he's gathered and bring them to the front outside Kyiv. Some stay and tell stories or share videos of the shelling at night. They are filled with energy, suddenly pulled from their mundane lives as sports trainers or small business owners and consumed with the bigger mission now of defending their homeland. For years, the prospect of this war has lurked like a dark but distant cloud. Now, suddenly, it is here, and still so fresh that people seem amazed yet ready to do their part.

"Does it bother you?" fat Raj, the Senate Select Committee on Intelligence (SSCI) staffer, had asked me during my interrogation now four years ago. Actually, he was probably the most honest of the lot.

Yes, it bothers me that my country used Ukraine as a political football, but until now has done little of practical use to deter Putin's aggression here. It bothers me that through Russiagate we artificially bolstered the former KGB officer's global standing. If Russia could put their man in America's White House, there is nothing they can't do. "We must see the world as it is," Barack Obama declared in accepting his Nobel Peace Prize, "not as we wish it to be."

False narratives are like double-edged blades. Someone obviously told Putin his troops would be welcomed as liberators and have roses thrown in front of their marching boots. Accordingly, the first wave of Russian troops packed few provisions but did bring their parade uniforms.

None of this matters now. All that does is help civilians get to safety and make sure the Ukrainian military and volunteers have what they need to defend their country. There is no doubt as to whether surrender is an option. I only worry how bloody and destructive this is going to get before there can be peace.

It comes time for me to go. As a deliveryman, my job here is done. Pepper is counting on my return as I hope, too, the witch is. I feel the country I once called the land of milk of honey grabbing me by the heart, just as it had done almost every time I left. It is with a good reason. I know I'll be back one day.

My last duty for this trip is to drive a recent émigré's car to where she can retrieve it in Wroclaw, Poland. The route takes me north, alongside the Carpathians, to Lviv and from there a short distance to the Polish border. Here, as I had expected, there is a line. The Red Cross and other NGOs have set up tents where people in need of help can go check in and get a bowl of soup. The air still has a nip to it, and little twirls of steam rise from paper cups.

Altogether it takes four hours to cross, but I had budgeted the time for this. People in this line treat one another with a lot more deference and kindness than say the hurly-burly of Kyiv's Bessarab-siya Market. There seem to be few sharp elbows here, and when an ambulance comes up from behind, cars move over and make way. I finally get to the passport control officer, who is less friendly than the one who greeted me on the Romanian border a few days before.

While I'm waiting for her to check my passport, my phone rings. It's a researcher for ABC News who wants to "brainstorm" about the oligarchs. *Why?* I wonder. *There are no oligarchs here—those that were have long since fled to the French Riviera or Spain.* It's ironic how the media can try to slay a man and then have the nerve to come back to what's left of him for help on other stories once they've discovered their last batch of sources were all spin and lies.

"No," I tell her, "I'd rather not."

The irritated border guard now looks at me with new curios-ity. Perhaps hearing the word *oligarch* she regrets not demanding a bribe. But with my passport back in my vest pocket, it's too late for that now.

This is an in-between zone and, unsurprisingly, the kind of place in which I've spent most of my career: liminal space. Years ago, a border guard checking passports in Kyiv's Boryspil Airport pointed to an old stamp in mine and asked if I knew what that was. I con-fessed I didn't. "It's me," he said. "You don't remember me? See you on your next time through," he told me cheerfully.

On the highway headed due west, Poles seeing the Ukrainian license plate on the car I'm driving honk and give me the thumbs-up when they pass me or vice versa. At the border behind me, Ukraine literally touches the European Union. How tantalizing for those who long for a European future—you can almost grasp it. In front of me, the horizon turns a tawny orange as the sun drops below the earth's curve.

ACKNOWLEDGMENTS

I owe a debt of gratitude to many people along the journey that led to this book, and while I invariably leave some out in this accounting, I would like to express my appreciation in particular to the following people in no particular order:

Reyn Archer, Irakli Alasania, Sam Amsterdam, Patrick Egan, Mark Pfeifle, Melissa Coleman, Tony Marsh, Maya Sloan, Courtnay Smith, Chris Crockett, Chris Burnham, Elizabeth Alsop, Steve LeVine, Bob Perkins, Mike Pajak, Peter Cox, Jason Briggs, Nurlan Ablyazov, Caroline McCabe, Katrina Willey, Eleonora Karamyants, David Satter, Steven Moore, John Mann, Otari Dzidzikashvili, George Whitney, Kyle Parker, Laura Ballman, Lance Copsey, Sean Roberts, Anne Milliken, Marty Youssefini, Tom Wolff, Aram Rostom, Mark Turnbull, Paul Bell, Paula Dobriansky, John Garrett, Susan Mary Alsop, Neil McCabe, Ivo Gabara, Steve Robinson, Rob Morgan, Eric Rubin, Anna Miller, Richard Spooner, Stuart Sears, Dudley Fishburn, Neritan Sejamini, Naren Aryal and the team at Amplify Publishing Group, Dan Muresan, Dinu Patriciu, Lee Busby, Olympia Snowe,

Nick Thompson, Sarah George, Sarah Naim, Josh Sepe, Josh Ellis, Maryna Antonova, Ed Rogers, Merv Wampole, Bruce Kososki, David Sulzberger, Aizhan Patten, Rinat Akhmetshin, Josh Davis, Marshall Comins, Richard Leiby, Willy Jay, Tilar Mazzeo, Eliza Patten, Boris Nemtsov, Salama al Khafaji, Amy Thornberry, Siddique Khan, Sally Brady, Bill Patten, Ken Emerson, Katharine Bacon, and my mother, Katharine Perkins.

ABOUT THE AUTHOR

Absorbed by politics from an early age, Sam Patten dedicated his early career to electoral campaigns at home and abroad. Born into a family oriented around power, Patten considered himself destined for great things. Yet the dangerous company he kept nearly destroyed him.

Like Forrest Gump, Patten appears at pivotal moments in history over the past quarter century: the breakup of the Soviet Union, the millennial election of George W. Bush, America's war in Iraq, Russia's invasions of Georgia and Ukraine, and the investigation of Russian collusion in the 2016 presidential election at home.

The story of Patten's adventures and misadventures reads like fiction. To top it off, at the moment he is exiled from Washington, DC, the city of his birth, Patten is nearly murdered in broad daylight on a busy street in the capital city. But he survived, and this is his eyewitness account of world-shaping events.